AF567123

ADVENTURE BOUND

**From Backpacking in New Zealand
To Bushwhacking in South Africa**

By

Helen A. Wolfe

**Photography by
J. Emerson Wolfe**

ADVENTURE BOUND

Library of Congress—Cataloging
in Publication Data
Published by:
Professional Press
Post Office Box 1384
Mount Dora, Florida 32757
(904) 383-1200

Printed in the United States of America
ISBN: 0-918271-10-X
FIRST EDITION

For Eme

56th Anniversary

Just to clear the books
I want you to know
that beyond sex
and the immutable fire
beyond flare-ups
and the spent stress
as irretrievable as
the unmeant word
there always lingered with me
the devastating idea
that ever since you dropped
breathlessly into my life
you might drop back out.
How young we were
to promise it all,
to lose our first-born
and dare to mirror ourselves
in the other two.
All these years
I've rubbed thin the
medallions you gave me
inscripted with
no cut-off dates
all these unentangled years
rooted in twine.

ACKNOWLEDGEMENTS

Cartography by Diana Clark.

Parts of the Milford Track, N.Z., account in Chapter 1 appeared serially in the *Daily Jeffersonian* newspaper, Cambridge, Ohio. Permission to reprint has kindly been given.

Jacket photograph of author and husband coming down Fire Mountain, Lanzarote, Canary Islands, was taken by Manuel Marcos, a native Lanzarotan.

I am grateful to my son-in-law, Charles L. Porter, and to my granddaughter, Stacy Melissa Wolfe, whose prodding helped make this book a reality.

Warm thanks are due Margaret Davis and Colleen Cope for editorial suggestions and personal encouragement, and to Tom and Mary Lindley for their South African pictorial assistance.

CONTENTS

MAPS

FOREWORD

We didn't wait for retirement, my husband, Eme, and I, in order to discover the pure intrigue of travel. Actually we made the discovery on our honeymoon, despite the fact it was spent in our first tiny apartment — a rented one.

The apartment was a temporary stop, we thought, because Eme had been one of twelve chemists chosen by the research department of B. F. Goodrich Company, Akron, Ohio, to be sent abroad. He was to go to Tokyo as a compounding engineer. I had stopped teaching high school English in Aurora, Illinois, near the end of my second year, because Eme's move was imminent and we were to be married prior to that.

It was at the University of Illinois in 1923 that we met: I, a freshman at seventeen, and he, a sophomore at nineteen. Like strobe lights, the magnetism flashed and never flickered, despite heavy storms on parental fronts. I was too young and he was too young, they agreed. Religion in those days was a horrendous factor too; one of us a Catholic, the other a Protestant. Threats of non-support of our schooling were made. The house mother in my sorority was contacted and told I was forbidden to date J. Emerson Wolfe. So he dated my roommate and I, one of his fraternity brothers, and we swapped partners after leaving the premises. Not until our senior year did our parents concede defeat.

Only by pooling our skimpy allowances (we should be so lucky to have any) were Eme and I able to cut classes an occasional afternoon to take in a killer-diller Pearl White matinee or spend our last half-dollar for Charlestoning until curfew-call at College Hall. But the best things, of course, were free: Benny Goodman played nights on fraternity lawns; the Boneyard ran muddy through the campus but Crystal Lake was clear for swimming off-campus; birdsong en route buttonholed us, and the Illinois Central's whistle nearly broke our resistance. In my sophomore year, at the Scabbard and Blade formal, Eme put his fraternity ring on my left hand and sealed our engagement.

Separation after graduation was excruciating. The distance between Ohio and Illinois not only ate holes in our budget, but also left only patches of hard currency for planning ahead. But we saved on some get-togethers. One Easter Eme landed in my parents' back yard in an open-cockpit plane — courtesy of a friend of his — and one Christmas he hitchhiked his way to Illinois.

The word finally arrived. Goodrich was ready to send their chosen men to foreign places, and we would soon be off. My mother complained (after five years of courtship) of having only two months for wedding preparations!

As a bride, instead of receiving the customary string of pearls as a gift from the groom, I received a set of Elbert Hubbard's *Little Journeys to the Homes of the Great* inscribed in gold letters: "To Helen A. Wolfe as a gift from her husband, J. Emerson Wolfe, May 27, 1929."

Little did I realize what jewels these books were to be. In the following months the Great Depression hit. The twelve men at Goodrich who had been promised jobs abroad were kept in Akron — the voyaging date indefinitely postponed.

Eme's starting salary of $150 a month that was adequate for one, meant belt-tightening for two — especially two who still had education debts to repay. An occasional substitute teaching or tutoring job for me was some help. There were times we turned in a case of empty Coke bottles at five-cents each to get enough for a dance or a round of putt-putt golf. And many times, oatmeal sustained us and our uncompromising budget on the last day of the month.

Long before, we had confided to each other our inner hankering for travel and swapped our prime childhood reading adventures. Eme had spent his early youth inching the blizzardous route to the South Pole with Robert Scott; I spent mine falling down rabbit holes with Alice. But both prepared us for the later rigors of travel and flights of imagination.

During the first months of marriage we never lacked for entertainment because, via the Little Journeys, we clambered up mountains, crisscrossed oceans, raided walled cities, explored castles, cathedrals, winding streets and hidden courtyards, and became intimate with vivid personalities. We took the armchair route for our intensive travels and were hooked.

That winter we picked a variety of treks for in-depth perusal, taking every book the Akron Public Library had on Antarctica and the South Pole. We agonized anew with Scott's heroic and fatal efforts to reach the Pole, with Shackleton, who came so close, with Cherry Garrard, the youngest explorer on that "Worst Journey in the World," with Amundsen who made it, and we cheered Admiral Richard Byrd's airplane expeditions over the Pole. Little by little that year, without leaving home, we absorbed a kinship for travel that has never left us.

We came to realize that whatever our ventures in the future, they would be meaningless unless they offered interior expansion. We didn't want to take to the road just to escape responsibilities but rather to acquire new viewpoints. And in the years that followed, to unlatch as many doors as possible, we introduced our son Tim and our daughter Cynthia to different sections of North America. Like Copernicus discovering the earth is not the center of all things, it often comes as a jolt, especially to children, to learn the United States is not the complete center of the earth.

During the years after Eme left the Goodrich Company to manage several other companies and finally to start his own business, travel was a necessary part of each job. I was lucky enough to be asked to "come along" to Europe, the Mediterranean, Africa, Cyprus, the Middle and the Far East, as well as to a number of remote islands. And since that time we have never tired of challenging ventures.

To keep in shape for traveling we ride our ten-speeds twelve to fifteen miles a day, play tennis, bowl and take long walks. Nights at home that we spend alone are still sacrosanct, with certain hours specifically set aside for reading and vicarious travel.

There are three ingredients in the good life, Christopher Morley said: "learning, earning and yearning". This may not be the exact order in which Eme and I pursued them, but they are all-inclusive and they are open to everyone.

Adventure Bound, an account of the most recent travels in our retirement years, is a continuation of these three components. We'll always be yearning for first-hand experiences in still unvisited places. We'll always be learning from new adventures, and can always be earning the respect of foreigners by meeting them as friendly, interested Americans.

The journeys in *Adventure Bound* were selected from magazine ads, chance notices, repeat yens, and recommendations of friends or former guides. They promised us an excitement in which we could involve ourselves physically as well as mentally, an excitement that would avoid the complacency of merely turning switches.

In contemplating each journey, we think about the notice posted in a hotel lounge in Queensland, Australia: "Thou shalt not expect to find things as thou has at home, for thou hast left home to find things different." We shake hands on that and say, "Adventure Bound!"

Chapter 1

"You've got to have rocks in your head!" everyone said of the trip Eme and I were planning to take: a Questers Nature Tour of New Zealand including the Milford Track and the Society Islands.

An article in the *National Geographic* on the Milford Track only seemed to confirm the consensus. It was not until considerably later, however, that the rattling of granite in our craniums gave us pause. Meanwhile, we cheerily conditioned ourselves for the encounter — Eme by playing a few extra sets of tennis and I by jogging the four miles around Lake Gertrude near our home in Mount Dora on days it didn't rain. Neither of us had ever back-packed before, but the thirty-five miles of walking the boulder-strewn, rugged terrain of the Milford Track sounded like a wonderful challenging lark with rich and limitless scenic rewards.

At a Plastic Pioneers meeting we conceived the idea of this trip when the Miller Sherwoods of Grand Haven, Michigan, asked where we were jaunting that year. I told them we were investigating a tour I'd seen advertised in the *Saturday Review*. They flipped with excitement and wanted to be included. They said it was their cup of tea to be participants in a journey and not just sightseers. We received the tour material and made plans to go together, but when Miller found he had business commitments he couldn't avoid, Eme and I continued alone with our plans.

On Thursday, February 23rd, we flew from Orlando to Los Angeles. The following day we left on UTA French Airlines for Papeete, an eight-hour flight. There we changed planes for the six-hour UTA flight to New Zealand, crossing the International Date Line en route. Arriving in Auckland just before noon and checking in at Travelodge Hotel, we freshened up, came down for lunch and a first meeting with the other members of our party.

It was a small one, only eight of us, including our accompanying

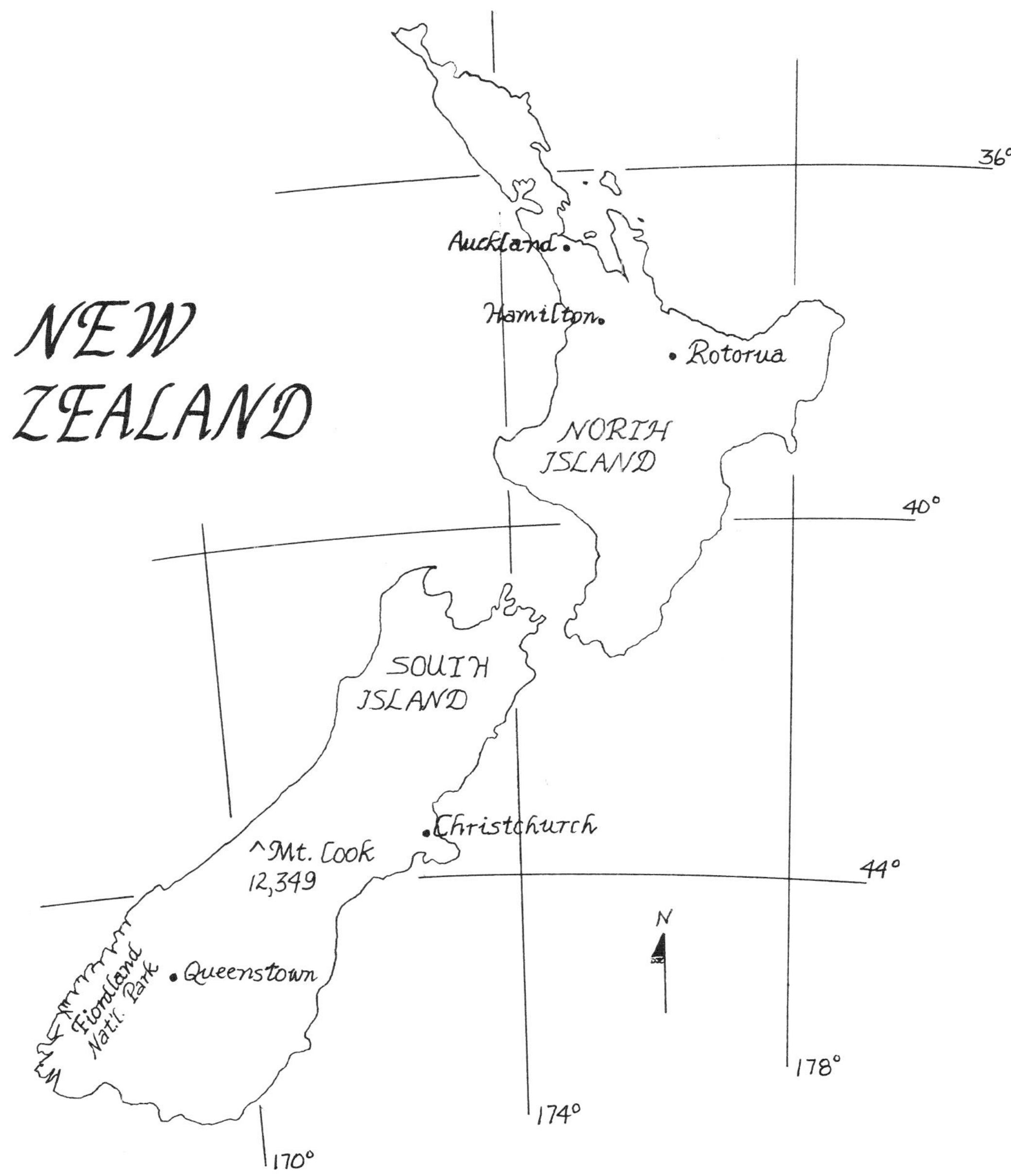
NEW
ZEALAND
Auckland
Hamilton
Rotorua
NORTH
ISLAND
SOUTH
ISLAND
Christchurch
Mt. Cook
12,349
Queenstown
Fiordland
Nat'l. Park
N
36°
40°
44°
170°
174°
178°

naturalist, J. Barry Ferguson of Syosset, New York. Our traveling companions were Charles Sedgwick of McLean, Virginia; Thomas R. Byrd, Honolulu, Hawaii; Iva K. Cunningham, Santa Barbara, California; Miriam J. Free, Bainbridge, Ohio; Sheldon Peck, Newton, Massachusetts.

Charles Sedgwick was a recently retired State Department official formerly in charge of foreign protocol. A Harvard PhD of romance languages, he was a bit reserved but very good company, with a fund of quotable knowledge in history, drama and literature. His fluency in French was of great benefit to us in Tahiti. Of our party, he was the only one who didn't walk the Milford Track. He spent the five days we were gone, snorkeling and swimming, then flew to Milford Sound to meet us.

Thomas R. Byrd, a captain and an M.D. (graduate work at Harvard) with the United States Navy, was stationed in Oahu, Hawaii. About 42, he was lean and limber and had done a good bit of mountain climbing on many of the world's islands. A bit stoic, he was the quietest of our group. When we chartered a twin-engine plane to take us over Mount Cook and could look down on the entire Milford Track where we'd walked, he said he'd been moved by the experience as only two other times in his life.

Iva K. Cunningham was a tall, blond woman in her mid-fifties whose long legs proved a godsend on the Milford Track. Her kindly manner and beatific smile endeared her to us immediately. She and her husband, the purchasing agent for the city of Santa Barbara, have done a good deal of mountain climbing in Yosemite, Nepal, and numerous other places.

Miriam J. Free was a pharmacist and her husband, the bank president in their small Ohio town. About 53, a scout leader and backpacker of note, she seemed at first glance to be a bit officious but as we came to appreciate her true worth we really enjoyed her. Kindly and helpful to everyone, she was game for almost anything. Her son at Ohio State and her daughter, a teacher, sent her lengthy letters filled with rare wit that tickled us all. Miriam had been on three other exciting Questers tours including Africa and Antarctica.

Sheldon Peck, aged 37, was an orthodontist in Boston. He was the clown of our group who often kept us in stitches. Tall and slim, he proved his mountain-climbing prowess in many places but mainly in the Himalayas.

J. Barry Ferguson, our accompanying naturalist, was the ideal guide for this trip, and we were lucky to have him. A man about 42, he was a New Zealander by birth and a botanist, landscape architect, lecturer and television artist. He puts on seasonal floral displays in many New York City parks, culling the flowers from his shop that handles rare plants from all countries. His floral arrangements are featured at Lincoln Center, charity balls and other gala events.

Occasionally he leads travel groups on tours such as this one. He has instantaneous recall of flora and fauna, and a talent for imitating bird calls at will. Before the trip ended, he had made arrangements for New Zealand plants to be shipped to him in New York.

A striking man with prematurely white hair and a short-cropped beard, he had dancing brown eyes, a lithe figure and an infectious smile and manner. On mountain passes he was as agile as a mountain goat, scampering with ease. Having been a drama critic and an actor, with gesticulation and quotation he often waxed poetic on nature's pristine beauty. He has spanned the world many times and is as close to being the embodiment of the free spirit as anyone can be.

He often would say, "I have another surprise for you!" and many of his surprises were meetings with fellow New Zealanders, known, like himself, as "Kiwis". The kiwi is the flightless bird that is the country's national emblem. In both the North and South Islands he knew the topography by heart as well as many of the people.

By virtue of our being such a small group it was possible to do many exceptional things. A tour usually operates with a minimum of ten people and had the Sherwoods been along, we would have met the quota. With eight people, there was the right number to sit together in most hotel dining rooms or fill a small twin-engine plane.

On the day of our arrival we took an afternoon tour of the city of Auckland situated on the North Island. With a population of over 700,000, the city is New Zealand's largest. The Tasman Sea is on its west side; the Pacific Ocean is on its east. The city itself is divided by a harbor, occupying an isthmus. The shopping section is on one side of the city and the suburban area is on the other.

The life of Auckland centers mostly on Queen Street where its major stores and markets are. There are few apartments, since most people own their homes. Everything seems clean and the air is fresh and invigorating. There are three parks within the city and sixteen ex-volcanoes. In the harbor is one of the greatest concentration of sailboats in the world. Auckland's regattas are world-renowned.

In Albert Park a large statue commemorates Queen Victoria. Hibiscus, oleander and bougainvillea bloom in profusion. Banana trees are laden. Frost is almost unknown, the climate is so mild. Here there are Norfolk Island pines and New Zealand's most magnificent Kauri trees, some of them soaring to almost 200 feet. Here also is the Rimu tree, so like a waterfall with its rippling fernery.

At the Eden Garden we stopped to see the beauty wrought in a former rock quarry by an Auckland horticulturist who saw the challenge in turning an eyesore into an exciting garden. Volunteers soon came to help in the project, bringing in the needed soil and water before planting multiple ferns, flowers and trees, then adding pools, fountains, waterfalls and marble sculpture. Speaking of volunteers, civic pride was the greatest here I've seen in any country. Many citizens volunteer as needed on all scenic projects.

There is no poverty in New Zealand and we were constantly aware of how immaculate the country is.

New Zealanders early on absorbed the Maori natives into their national culture. Unlike the Americans who ignored or short-changed the Indians, the New Zealander has been both sympathetic and grateful to the Maoris who settled the country long before the British or Captain Cook arrived. Of dark-skinned Polynesian descent, they originally came, probably, from the Society Islands or Hawaii. Their customs, arts and crafts are an integral part of the culture. We were treated to their songs and dances at a concert and viewed their outstanding and intricate wood carvings. Of the three million people in New Zealand, one-fourth are Maori and they are represented in all fields of agriculture, industry, and the professions, and many are outstanding in sports.

The War Memorial Museum built on a hill in Auckland is a stunning building that houses one of the finest Maori collections in the world. It includes jade weapons, feathered headgear, decorative arts and an extraordinary miniature canoe, carved from native wood, that holds 100 warriors and is named Toki-a-Tapiri. The museum is set in 200 acres of parkland and tropical gardens.

The flax grown in the countryside is long and bladelike with variegated edges, unlike European flax. Out of this is made ropes and fishing lines, garments, mats, canoe sails and baskets.

About sixty million sheep are raised each year in New Zealand. Some two million dairy cows provide much of the frozen cream sent to the USA.

Seeing children on their way home from school we stopped to take pictures of the little boys in Eton suits and caps and the little girls in middy blouses. Children in both the public and parochial schools wear uniforms.

The delightful surprise Barry had for us the first evening was a meeting with his sister, Nancy, her husband, Ted Burrows, and their two great youngsters, Tim, 11, and Nicky, 13, from Caster Bay outside Auckland. They had recently returned from his three-year tour of duty in Singapore with the Royal Navy. Their good friends, Reenie and Joe Wilson, invited us to their home for cocktails. Joe Wilson owns the *Auckland Herald*, the city's newspaper. Their home was elegant and their spacious land a riot of color and beauty — including an English garden of ferns, phlox of all hues, unusual trees, fountains and pools. Rock steps led to their tawny sand beach, and beside the swimming pool was a shower of hibiscus.

When we assembled inside, Reenie invited us into the dining room, up two steps from the living room. On all sides were windows overlooking the beautiful setting. After the first or second drink, we became aware that the scenery outside was not exactly as it had been when we began. Then we learned the dining room was rotating, ev - er so slowly.

After breakfast at the hotel next day, Monday, February 27th, we left for Christchurch, a two-and-a-half-hour flight. Christchurch, a city of 350,000, is the largest on the South Island, and the scenic difference between the two islands is tremendous. Many of nature's wonders of the world are on South Island.

Christchurch is also the takeoff point for New Zealand's and American bases on Antarctica. It was hard believing we were so far below the equator that Antarctica was the next stop and that this was the jumping-off place for Captain Robert Scott's expedition. A statue of Scott, who perished en route home from the South Pole, stands beside the Avon River.

Christchurch was built on the plains by Canterbury pilgrims from England and English names abound. The shallow river Avon meanders and loops through the business, residential and park areas, giving a rural serenity to the busy city. Along its ten-mile course the Avon is spanned by thirty-seven bridges. Gravel woodsy paths let us traverse its banks. Scenic roads also follow the riverbanks which are lushly planted with willows, grass and daffodils. Bicycles are the favored mode of transport and almost everyone rides one.

We drove out to the Sanitarium Health Foods Garden and found its beauty breath-taking. So much color simply dazzles the senses. Every flower known to an English garden is here in great masses. We were told it is the law that all industries must beautify their property with flowers. Private homes vie with them and the result is a photographer's paradise. Mr. Kodak must surely have been happy we came to Christchurch.

One of the lovely trees in the countryside is the Christmas tree, so-called because of its red flowers. The incense bush blooms profusely, filling the air with its heady fragrance. The plume grass is called toi-toi.

Hagley Park within the city has 500 acres of playground and facilities for all kinds of summer and winter sports. It has a beautiful lake and across the river from it are the Botanic Gardens filled with innumerable varieties of roses, a native flora section, azaleas, rhododendrons, water gardens and greenhouses. The coastal and the Sierra redwoods flourish here.

New Zealanders are crazy about racing (horse trotting), yachting, soccer, lawn-bowling and tennis. Small racing courses for horses are incorporated in many people's home grounds.

That night Barry had another surprise for us. He'd invited two close friends for dinner, Hans and Patricia Bohny, who brought their daughter, Heidi. Barry had been Hans' best man. The Bohnys lived at Arthur's Pass, about sixty miles outside Christchurch.

Hans had been a ski instructor in Switzerland before marrying a New Zealand girl and settling down there. In talking to us they reiterated what so many other New Zealanders told us — how eternally grateful they are to the Americans who prevented the Japanese from invading their country in World War Two.

After an excellent meal we returned to Noah's Hotel where I was impressed with the tank above the toilet in our bathroom. On the white porcelain it proclaimed "Royal Doulton"!

After breakfast the next morning we left by Mount Cook Airlines for Queenstown. Our flight took an hour and forty minutes in a small plane equipped with Rolls Royce engines.

Queenstown has a dramatic setting, nestled among the craggy mountains called the Remarkables. On the western heights is strung a cable car. The town crowds the edge of the blue Lake Wakatipu, the longest one on the South Island. It is a shining little resort town and we came to it on a sparkling, sunny day.

After lunch at the Lakeland Lodge, we left again on the Mount Cook Airlines for Te Anau. En route we flew above the snow-fed lakes, set in deep basins scooped out by glaciers and noted for their sport fishing as well as their splendor. The mountains are snow-capped black basalt, striped with shadows. Late summer colors crimsoned the bush and gilded the native flora. Green trees splattered the slopes where mountain ash and rowan trees are rampant. The Maoris call New Zealand "The Land of the Long White Cloud". Against a startling blue sky, it's easily seen what they mean.

Arriving at Te Anau, we checked into the lovely Te Anau Hotel with its detached chalets, heated swimming pool and much-needed laundry room. In a whipstitch we had doffed our clothes and were into our swimsuits for a refreshing dip in the pool.

In the late afternoon Barry took us on a boat ride to the other side of the lake where we hiked a mile and a half through the scrub woods. This was a tiny test run, preparatory for the great trek. For us it was hiking, but to the New Zealanders, it was tramping.

On the morning of March 1st we went to Lake Manapouri, the

deepest in all New Zealand. An unspoiled lake, its shores are draped in the country's commonest big trees, the beeches, that airily bend down to the water's edge. The rock faces on its Cathedral Peaks are a profusion of mosses. In the center of the lake is an island which is the top of a mountain. Our guide mentioned that the snows melt from all but the highest of these South Island Southern Alps, and the run-off fills the lake and helps furnish electric power.

The pampas grass en route looks like fluffy bits of cloud. Red deer abound and are considered a menace because they denude both forest and farms, so hunters are allowed to shoot them in all seasons. Lambs frolic everywhere and our taxi was forced to stop at times to let runaways pass by. As we jounced over bumps in the road, we saw they were marked by signs warning of a "jutter-bar".

Returning to the hotel for lunch we reported at 2:30 p.m. to the Milford Track office. We had repacked our suitcases, removing all that we needed on the Milford Track. We had been issued backpacks and ponchos. Filling our backpacks with our gear, we sent our suitcases by bus to the Milford Sound Hotel where they would await our arrival. At last we were down to the nitty-gritty. At 3:00 p.m. we left Te Anau by coach — headed for Glade House where we'd begin the challenging walk.

Arriving at Te Anau Downs we boarded the launch, Tamera, for the two-hour trip to the head of Lake Te Anau. It was here that Quinton MacKinnon drowned. MacKinnon was a Scot who emigrated to New Zealand at twenty and explored and surveyed it. The pass over the highest section of the Track was named for him after he discovered the surface route from Te Anau to Milford by way of it. In 1892 he set out by boat for the head of the lake to begin another walk to Milford and was never seen again, although his sunken boat was later found. It was he who guided the first parties along the trail.

The Track is open only from November through March and even on some of these days must be closed due to severe weather. It's necessary to book a year ahead for reservations to make this celebrated trek.

The whole of the trail is within Fiordland National Park, which is in the southwest corner of the South Island. Rainfall here is between 200 and 300 inches per year. Only forty people are allowed on the Track on any given day, and they must be equally divided between men and women because the huts are segregated for sleeping, twenty bunks for each sex.

"Some of the most rugged country in the entire world lies in the area of the Milford Track." I had to travel half way around the world to find that statement in a New Zealand magazine. Soon Eme and I would be

Milford Track

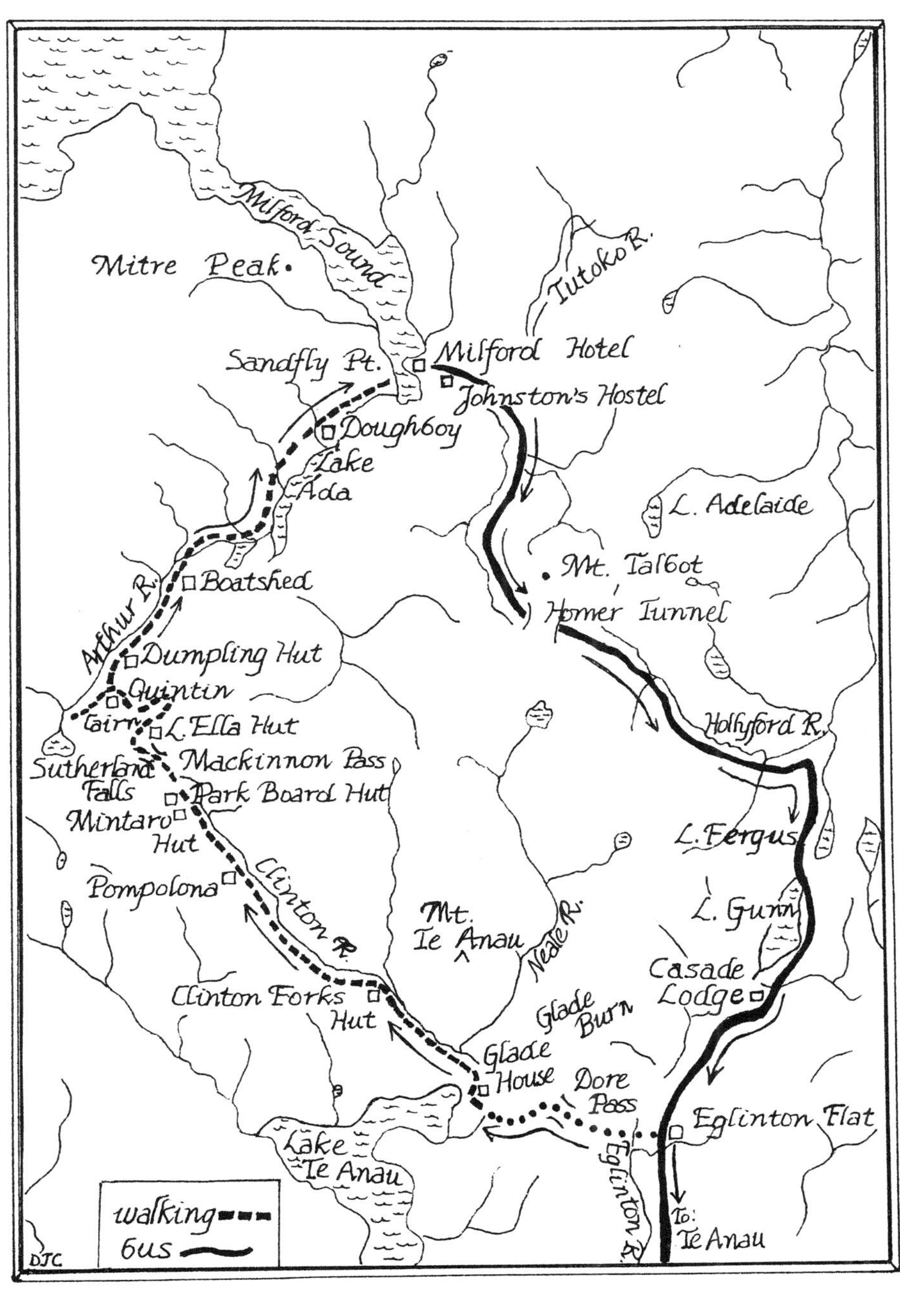

trying it on for size!

I was happy about the shoes I had chosen for the tramp: canvas basketball boots. Eme had opted for heavy tennis shoes. We both had considered wearing heavier leather boots but in the end, changed our minds. Inside my boots I wore lightweight socks with woolen ones over them. Our niece, Marile, had gotten them from a hiking expert and sent them to me. They fit to a T and I was not once bothered by foot problems as were several others in our group, including one woman who suffered with terrible blisters.

From the Lake Te Anau landing it is a half-mile walk to Glade House which sits beside the Clinton River. With knapsacks on our backs, our shoelaces tied tightly, and Cutter's insect repellent (brought from home) smeared generously on us to discourage the sandflies which bite like mosquitos, gaily we started out. This part of the walk was termed in Track lingo, "a piece of cake," nice and easy, two abreast; over not too sharp rocks or tree roots.

At Glade House, our first overnight stop, we were greeted by our pleasant and attractive hut managers, Phil and Betty Turnbull, who served us a hearty meal and briefed us on the trail ahead.

I had my backpack load down to a little more than ten pounds but with the folded poncho and the sheet issued the first night, plus my lunch, I would be carrying about thirteen pounds. Eme's, with his camera and much heavier binoculars, was about fifteen pounds.

The sheet we would sleep on was sewn down the sides like a sleeping bag, but unable to stand the confinement, I lay on top of it and threw the blankets over me. Fortunately, the blankets remained at the huts and we didn't have them to carry too.

After the evening meal, forty of us — eight in our party and thirty-two others — assembled around the hut master and guide in front of a large map on the wall. One at a time we went to the map and placed a pin in the appropriate place of our home town. Counting up we had among us, two from England, two from Ireland, one from Baffin Island, four from Canada, eight from Australia and ten from the USA. The rest were New Zealanders, most of them from the North Island. None of them outside our own party had we met before but at the end of four days we would become not only casual friends but also warm buddies.

The lunches packed for us were not burdensome, consisting of two small sandwiches and an apple. Eme was also carrying a number of Milky Ways which came in mighty handy for energy and a quick pick-up.

With an "all's right with the world" feeling we sallied forth next morning, March 2nd, to walk the ten miles from Glade House to Pompolona Hut on a day that was bright and bonny. At the beginning, the path accommodates two abreast and the climb is minimal. Since you don't have to watch your footing, you can look up through the trees and tussocks to see the mountains, the blue sky and the lush vegetation. "Make your own pace; stop when you choose," we had been told, and the choosing was often that first day for feasting our eyes and taking pictures.

"Lift up thine eyes!" Barry frequently quoted along the path. Stopping to look and ponder, W. H. Davies' words came to me: "A poor life this, if full of care, we have no time to stand and stare."

At each mile marker along the route, signs depict the various birds. On the track in front of us a friendly weka, the scrub hen, came down looking for crumbs from anyone's pockets. Several black robins swooped out of the trees. Their song, which Barry imitated, is almost as clear as the bellbird's which had us all enthralled with its continual rapture. The bellbird is small and olive colored with blue beak and feet and a touch of blue on its tail. A dozen riflemen, New Zealand's smallest birds, flittered in the branches. They are like wrens but have green backs, yellow rumps and a high-pitched call. With scarcely any predators and no snakes, New Zealand's birds can be both bold and friendly.

"How would you ever describe all this?" I quizzed Barry at one stop.

"Well, start with a million ferns," he said blithely.

That *is* a good start; they are the stalwarts of this rain forest. There are 150 species of them, Barry told us, ranging from the majestically plumy tree ferns to the tiniest of fronds. Some bitsy ferns nestle among the carpets of moss covering the tree trunks.

We tried translating the "various languages" nature speaks at every step of the trail. The Clinton Valley passes through a primeval forest of inscrutable density. Moss clings everywhere — on the Track, along the banks, among the ferns, on the tree trunks and in all the rock crevices. Some mosses on the forest floor conceal roots of delicate little green and white orchids. The mosses display many colors and the fleecy clouds overhead are gorgeously hued. It's impossible to encompass the beauty and magnitude of it all with canvas, brush or pen, so stupefying is its grandeur. White and yellow buttercups pop up unexpectedly in barren rocks or brown tussocks. One's spirit seems to expand trying to absorb it all.

We climbed imperceptibly those first several hours but toward noon the path steepened and narrowed. No longer could we walk two abreast and the tug on our lungs was greater. Small gushers, long and feathery waterfalls and white cascades striped the mountainsides. The forests are full of black beech. Barry pointed out the mountain bog pines, the cabbage trees with huge leaves, the colorful scarlet rata tree and the supple jacks which often entangle the forest.

When we reached the Six-mile Hut we were noticeably tired. We heated water for instant tea, coffee or chocolate to drink with our sandwiches. We took off our parkas and made use of the outside two-holer, a real convenience and much preferable to the bush.

On our way again the climbing became yet more rugged. We rested oftener, not just to ponder but to stop our panting. Moss was festooning the trees, some of it a russet shade. Varicolored lichens clung to bark of trunks and parasitic air plants softly trellised the giant limbs.

Trout are abundant in the Clinton River and from some of the bridges we could see them and long eels swimming below. The whistling blue ducks love these waters. Runnels seam the canyon walls. Barry, busy with minute flora he was explaining, called back, "The world is too much with us," leaving the rest of the quotation for anyone to finish.

Most of the New Zealanders and many others had long since passed us on the Track. In fact, Eme and I were among the last ones still slogging along. Of our group, Sheldon Peck was way ahead. At the end, where the rocky climb stiffens and steepens, we were really trailing, so that when we arrived at Pompolona Hut at 5:30, we found we were the last to arrive. There to congratulate us on getting that far were the host and hostess of the Hut, Buster and Madge Martin. A hot shower felt wonderful and limbered us up considerably.

I asked Sheldon Peck how we were going to be able to get up on time next morning. "That's simple," he said. "A gong rings at 5:00 a.m., your bed collapses like a Venus flytrap, the ceiling opens, the rain pours in — and there you have it!"

No doubt his words were prompted by the ominous sign of rain in the offing. That night in my bunk I thought of his words as the water plinked on the corrugated roof of Pompolona.

We ate dinner seated at long tables. The meal, dished up in the kitchen and handed us through a wide opening, consisted of beef, dry mashed potatoes, three canned vegetables and lots of bread and jellies. For dessert it was a choice of pudding or cake with a beverage. After dinner, some played games, read or wrote. We listened to the trail guide explain what lay ahead for tomorrow — expected to be the toughest day on the trail.

At each hut were large, well heated drying rooms. When we had taken off our track outfits and boots, we hung them there until morning to dry, along with any other wet things we had.

After lacing our boots on next morning, eating our porridge and breakfast and picking up our lunches, we were off, our cameras and food stuffed into plastic bags, our ponchos covering all. What we had dreaded had happened. The rain had not ceased and although it was a light one, it could change at any moment. Too, it had turned much colder and a wind had risen. We packed our binoculars but Eme kept his camera out, hoping that in spite of the rain he could catch some of the magic.

Clutching hold of a narrow swinging bridge, we looked down on the Clinton River, still keeping us company. The clouds were getting grayer and heavier, the drizzle picking up. Gloom was in the air but it had a silver lining. Had it not rained, we would not have witnessed the forest in all its glistening fairylike shimmer, nor seen the cascades marbleizing the mountainside. Although the rain silenced many of the birds, it set to roaring the waterfalls and the rumbling of torrential creekbeds.

We were to zigzag up to the rocky summits of the MacKinnon Pass, the awesome divide, the saddle hung between the shoulders of Mount Hart and Mount Balloon. We had to bend and watch our footing on the slippery and jagged rocks, over logs fording bulging streams, watching out for upjutting tree roots, sloshy stones and slippery mud. Water thundered down the sheer rock walls as multiple new gushers opened in the granite troughs. The exertion of jumping and wading ankle deep through rushing streams took its toll.

Many of our forty members stopped to chat a few moments before splashing on. But one who kept behind us, carefully studying all the flora, was the interesting young chap, Bob Nicholle from Adelaide. He and his father, in business together, are the largest propagaters of orchids in the world. One who stopped was Hildegarde Corbet of Christchurch — she who was so kind to me in sharing necessities in the dormitory. Hildegarde is a practicing psychiatrist in a large hospital. Also passing us were our new and special friends, Norman and Rosa Wreford of Timaru, who own a large sheep ranch in the North Island and who wanted our whole group to visit them for a day and an overnight stay. Unfortunately, time didn't permit. We were forever eyeing Norman's beautiful sweaters that Rosa spun the wool for and knitted.

Finally, we could dally no longer. The wind had picked up; it was starting to hail, and light snow was coming down even though it was March and summer had not quite ended. The climbing was sheer and steep, stretching our muscles at every move. We had ten miles before we would reach the MacKinnon Pass, the most treacherous stretch of all. Out of the forest, we were in open high country, above the timberline, facing the Pass and shelf of the Jervois Glacier.

The cold was numbing and I was moving like a robot. Wherever I looked waterfalls were exploding. The path was puddled and water was leaping down the great spoutings of the peaks. I shivered not only from the increased chill but from the rising tumult of the scene. We buckled down to making better time, climbing, climbing, and climbing. The wind gained such velocity toward the top, it almost buffeted me off the Track. As we passed the cairn erected in memory of Quentin MacKinnon, Eme stopped long enough to take a picture — hoping it would come out — and quickly got his camera back under cover. With my teeth chattering, I turned my head away from the wind and stumbled on.

We made it to the mid-way stop for lunch. About a half-mile from the Hut, Norman Wreford came to meet us, asking if he could carry my pack. "Bless your heart," I told him, "I'll make it." Behind us, Miriam Free, troubled by blisters, was struggling, and he went on to help her.

This was how we found all the New Zealanders: willing to go out of their way to help any newcomers to their land.

The early arrivals were waiting at the door, clapping for our arrival, offering us hot tea and blankets. Tears hovered on the lids of my eyes. We ate our sandwiches in the shelter, drank our tea and pressed on. We had all the going down yet to do before we would reach Quintin Hut.

We'd heard the going down was almost worse than the steep climbing because the drops are so great they threaten to dislocate your hips. I found them much easier and hopped, straddled and slithered along at a rapid clip, despite some thudding jolts onto outsized rocks. Eme, however, found it much worse than the precarious ascent.

Iva Cunningham and Barry passed us. Iva, an avid bird-seeker and Audubon member, had just seen a tui, a biggish bird with white throat feathers and white stripes on its wings when in flight. It has an extensive repertoire but is quiet in the rain. Goggling at it, Iva had slipped and gouged her leg in five places. Afterwards she displayed the cuts proudly, claiming them as mementos of the Track.

There were scarcely any trees on the Track at that elevation, but thousands of white water flumes streaked the gray mountains. You would need circlevision to take them all in.

We straggled into Quintin Hut after five, scarcely ahead of the last ones, and pulled in to a warm welcome and a rousting cheer — the customary greeting to those who'd made it. Sheldon Peck stood in the doorway and I told him a good stiff drink would be great to keep our teeth from chattering.

"That's right," he said. "Candy's dandy, but liquor's quicker!" Anyway, such products were not available.

A long, luxurious hot shower helped greatly though, and our appetites were whetted for almost anything. Anything was soup, lamb stew, two canned vegetables, potatoes not very well done, and the inevitable bread and fruit or cake for dessert. We ate all of it and drank plenty of Sanka.

We were to spend a day resting at Quintin Hut before the final day and the last thirteen-mile trek. On our day of freedom we went to Sutherland Falls, the third highest in the world and only a mile and a half distant. The rain persisted through the night and the next day so we had to be content just to look at the falls in their three giant cascades spilling down from Lake Quill to the Arthur River in bursting billows of water. It's doubtful anyone's pictures turned out.

One thing we did get done was to wash some clothes and have time to dry them. I was happy to get a lower bunk since the bathroom was quite a jaunt away. And all the New Zealanders offered me their extra blankets because I was having such a hard time keeping warm.

Quintin Hut held many surprises. First of all, there was a piano. Mr. Anderson, whom we met there, a gentleman of eighty-six, had been associated with the Track for many years and spent summers working at Quintin. His book, *Milford Trails*, describes his involvement with the Track and, helped by his wife, Dorothy, he has kept it up-to-date. We bought two of his books and both he and his wife autographed them. He told us that years before, when his first wife was living and they had charge of Quintin Hut, she had yearned for a piano. For several years they planned how they might inch one up. And with the help of countless others, they did just that — moving it about a mile and a half a day.

What a boon the piano was to our group of hikers! One in our party, Barney Thorne, was a wizard at the keyboard, able to play anything anyone suggested. With carefree abandon we sang everything from "Home on the Range" to the New Zealand national anthem, plus "Jingle Bells," "There's a Long, Long Trail Awinding," " Sweet Rosie O'Grady," "Show Me the Way to Go Home," and many others.

On our second day at the Hut, we went outside to watch and feed the keas who flocked around and are perfect clowns. They are big, strutting, noisy birds — mountain parrots with colorful, large wings, especially the underside when outspread.

Breakfasts in all the Huts started with oatmeal porridge (real soupy) sprinkled with brown sugar, bacon far too fat to be edible and scrambled eggs that were awful, but the toast and marmalade were good. We filled up on that as well as the fruits, which are excellent, especially the fat, juicy plums.

On the night of our day of freedom, we received our certificates of award for accomplishing the walking of the Milford Track, signed by our good hosts, Beryl and Ray White. The reason for receiving the certificates the night before we finished was that Quintin is the point of no return: you either make that next thirteen miles or else! More singing followed, then we hustled to get arranged in our bunks, toiletries over, before the generator and lights went off at 10:30.

Up early, toast and porridge swallowed, Eme and I were among the first to set off, determined that on this last lap we were going to be among the first ones in.

"On your own but stay close!" Barry yelled as he and Tom Byrd buckled into their gear.

Our ponchos covered our packs, and my extra sweater was tightly buttoned under my jacket, as we went striding out. I was stretching my legs for taking longer steps and covering ground faster. We had to make the launch at Milford Sound by 4:00 p.m. Down into the valley of the Arthur River we trudged, crossing the river at one place on a huge watersoaked log with small bits of chicken wire placed here and there to give some kind of foothold. The Track is constantly crossed by side creeks in the thickening forest. We finally climbed above Lake Ada and then descended again to the river. Above us the splatter of rain was louder than the roar of the river. Ahead and on our right, we faced the Mackay Falls, not as imposing or hypnotic as Sutherland, but beautiful nonetheless.

Eme and I knew we were way out in front and going strong, despite the mud oozing into our shoes and the streams we had to ford becoming deeper and deeper. There were innumerable swinging rustic bridges to cross and in some places, wire strung on trees helped us maneuver around curves and bypass the impassable. In places, the only way I could jump to the next boulder was by hanging on to the heavy ferns along the bank, using them for leverage to swing. Eme was keeping an ever-faster pace and I was his shadow, trying to keep up. On the first day I had outclimbed him but he was really outstriding and outslogging me on the final day.

Unfortunately we couldn't linger too long in any scenic area. The rain had increased and we raised our eyes to the mountains only when we dared. Torrents of streams cascaded, walls of water erupted. We wanted to look up at the thousands of opened up cataracts deluging the sierras around us but we had to discipline our feet to this inhospitable terrain. A voracious wind continued. We'd been told that this discipline was character building, although someone suggested it might be a bit late for that.

We passed the ten-mile marker — only three more to go. Just a "wee way", the New Zealanders would say. We had learned to take that word "wee" with a huge grain of salt. Still, no one had passed us!

The wilderness was supreme. Yellow-green moss hung from treetops. We swished by several of the unique Rimu trees. There was a mountain fuchsia, its head beaten down. We forded a rushing rocky creek and sank suckingly into raw mud, leadening our feet.

Eme, ahead of me, jumped down a lengthy step and went striding on. With my pack gaining weight on my back, I looked down, knowing I couldn't drop to one knee and make it. So I clutched a huge fern (the ferns had been my boon and my strength en route) and swung from it. Midway it broke. My left foot hit the slippery rock and my right slid lurchingly sidewise across another slick flat boulder. And with that, my feet parted the ferns on the embankment and I shot through. I took one sickening look at the raging Arthur River below and the 300-foot steep gorge. Casting about frenetically for anything to grab hold of I let out a terrible scream. "I'm going, Eme! I'm going!"

How, with a fifteen-pound pack on his back, his camera around his neck and wearing a poncho, he was able to catch my disappearing shoulders, I'll never know. But he did, and dragged me inch by grudging inch onto the slippery rocks.

"Lie still!" he shouted, and I did, petrified and shaking, for a good five minutes.

To get me to my feet, backpack and all, was a herculean task, but he finally accomplished it and we lumbered on, sobered and slowed down.

Almost the first to arrive at Sandfly Point and twenty minutes before the launch would leave for Milford Sound, we knew one thing for sure. In weather like that we should never, not ever, have left the others behind. Later Barry told us they tried to catch up with us and kept wondering where we could possibly be.

A little New Zealand government bulletin warns: "Do not ever undertake the Milford Track lightly. The Milford Track is not just a scenic adventure; it is a total experience." I buy that! Eme does too!

Most of us stayed on the launch's deck to view Bowen Falls close by and the famous and spectacular Milford Sound, not looking its shimmering best in the spitting rain, but still the grandest inlets of Fiordland National Park. Mountain walls rise almost perpendicular from the water's edge and Mitre Peak, its top smoking faintly, casts its reflection in the waters of the Sound. Waterfalls are backdrops of the scene.

We checked in at the Milford Sound Hotel — a lovely and luxurious one — tired, dirty and spent, yet completely exhilarated over our completion of "The Finest Walk in The World", the Milford Track. The suitcases we'd left behind were in our rooms.

In the new wing of the hotel where we were housed, all bedrooms face the Sound with a splendid view of Mitre Peak. In the main lounge a landscape window frames the peak.

That night at dinner there was much celebration. In the attractive Lobster Pot Restaurant, we chose al a carte from all the choice seafood and goodies, and sealed our success with wine and good spirits.

After sleeping late the following morning of March 6th, we took a launch excursion around Milford Sound. Porpoises and fur seals came right up to the boat, flipping and showing off, keeping us entertained. The scenery held our eyes glued to the view of Mitre Peak, Bowen Falls and the Glacier of Mount Pembroke. The Milford Hotel is at the base of Sheerdown Mountain at the head of Milford Sound where the valley opens up to an unforgettable panorama of forest and ice and cliffs that go straight down to the sea.

The hotel favored us with fine food and good service. Interestingly, tipping is forbidden in New Zealand and turned down if offered.

Next morning at eight we left on the Road Services Coach for Te Anau after breakfasting with Norman and Rosa Wreford. The government permitting, Norman promised to send us a Red Admiral butterfly, the country's most spectacular one, for the fabulous and very scientific collection of our grand-nephew Brent, a dental school student in Iowa.

Steadily climbing, our bus headed toward Homer Tunnel, completed in 1952, while the coach captain explained points of interest along the way and Barry ticked off various flora as seen from his window. The road goes through three valleys and the tunnel. On either side are high, snow-swathed mountains and a good view of one of the mightiest peaks in Fiordland, Mount Tutko. About half way along are the Mirror Lakes that reflect the snow-capped peaks.

Only twenty-five minutes of traffic in one direction is allowed through the Homer Tunnel to minimize the effect of motor exhaust fumes.

The mountains are dazzling, ice-capped and shining. Up the precipitous side of the glacial valley the road crosses the divide where nearby spread a whole plantation of flowering ribbonwood trees. Gradually we descended to Cascade Creek and a stop at the lodge for a cup of tea and a chance to stretch our legs. Barry found us an edelweiss flower.

Back in the bus again, we passed through beech forests, crossing creeks and following the Eglinton River with its towering mountains on either side. After the road leaves the forest there is a striking view of the north fiord of Lake Te Anau after which the traveler is flanked by the middle and the south fiords.

One of the many gardens in Christchurch, New Zealand — a truly picturesque city.

Our leader, J. Barry Ferguson, who, on the Milford Track has reached MacKinnon Pass en route to the Sound.

Moaris in one of their ritual dances in Rotorura, New Zealand.

In moss-covered Fiordland National Park along the Milford Track.

Our leader, J. Barry Ferguson, contemplating Mt. Cook.

Kea birds in Te Anau that came to our door for nightly feedings.

Milford Track as seen from an airplane — showing the Arthur River at the bottom.

Mt. Cook — as seen from an airplane.

Mt. Cook range.

The author on the final day on the Milford Track.

A sunset in Tahiti.

After lunch at Te Anau Hotel our taxi driver, Marge Small, took us to Mount Cook Airlines, giving us a running commentary of points of interest on the way.

Our flight to Mount Cook lasted a little less than two hours, and on arrival we were taken to the Hermitage for a three-day stay. The Hermitage, which is government-run, is an award-winning architectural showplace. Our ground floor rooms in this delightful hotel allowed us to walk out on individual porches to bask in the blessed sunshine and suck in our breath over the awesome scenery facing us.

From here we looked up at the highest peak in New Zealand's Southern Alps, Mount Cook, 12,349 feet high. Clouds of the warm Northwester were fluffy white in a French blue sky and around the white funnel at the tip of Mount Cook spiraled broad white smoke rings. The Maoris call this mountain "Aorang", meaning cloud piercer. On the snow and ice of the mountains are seals, but at the Hermitage, countless rabbits romped in the front yard.

Charles Sedgwick rejoined our group at Milford for the next day's scheduled trip, a cinerama flight over Tasman Glacier in a small four-seater ski plane. Because of snow conditions it was not possible to land on the glacier.

The first four of us took off while the other four waited for the next plane which should have taken off in twenty minutes. But the weather didn't cooperate and fog settled in, so although the first plane was gone the scheduled two hours and had no problems landing on its return, visibility was too poor for the second plane to take off. Instead, our foursome sun-bathed and took walks up the labeled trails — something of an anti-climax after our Milford Track experience.

The following morning was sunny so the four of us who had been left behind the previous day chartered a twin-engine plane to fly not only over the glacier but for an extended three-and-a-half hour flight over the Milford Track. Several who had taken the shorter trip opted to join us. When the shiny twin-engine Islander took off at 2:30 p.m., it carried Barry, Sheldon, Tom Byrd, Miriam Free, Eme and me, and two pilots.

What a super thrill ride it was! As we gained altitude it seemed like the plane brushed the very sides of the mountains. The expert pilots were marvelous, swooping in and out for looks at everything.

Tasman Glacier, covered with ice, is about twenty miles long. The mountains look bleak underneath. Marenos graze on the tussocks of some of these peaks where there are pockets of snow between small lakes, rivers and streams. The country is craggy and rugged. Shading in the sky resembles a rainbow. Flying at 10,000 feet we went over thick beech forest and looped over Mount Tasman, the second highest in these

Alps. The sea looked like corrugated pewter in spots but was clear green toward the shores. The Red Hills Range shimmered copper-colored. Barry pointed out Mount Aspiring as the men sat literally spellbound and Miriam and I, enthralled. It was this trip Tom Byrd said he'd been touched by as only twice before in his life.

As we approached Te Anau Lake and our take-off point for THE walk, Barry described it piecemeal and our eyes were riveted on the scene below. Could we really have hiked this murderous trail? The thrill welled-up anew and the sense of adventure persisted. "Hi and good-by again Sandfly Point!"

As we settled down gently into Milford Sound, Barry invited the pilots to join us for tea. We walked into the Milford Sound Hotel to hear a voice chanting, "Barry! Barry Ferguson!" Standing in the lobby were Eleanor Gordon and her husband, Horace, from New York. They had seen Barry there three weeks before and now were meeting him again as they arrived in New Zealand!

Barry asked me to take over pouring the tea and the hotel served us crumpets and cookies as we passed a pleasant half hour with the Gordons, particularly Eleanor, who is a world authority on china, porcelains and antiques.

Back in the plane we battled the elements. We looked down on the deep fissures in the glaciers. Wafting white clouds licked the sleek snow on the mountaintops with crevasses stippling their sides. We were lost in meditation as the pilots were weaving us in circles around the peaks of Mount Cook. The coloring of evening set in a little after six o'clock, a mixture of mauve, purple, deep blue, green and pink.

That night the kea birds paid us a farewell visit at the Hermitage and we treated them to leftovers of another festive dinner.

Next day it was on to Rotorura on a Mount Cook Airlines flight leaving at 4:50 p.m. that lasted slightly more than two hours. We arrived at the Shaw Savill Caravel Hotel — another outstanding one — in time for dinner, also a happy occasion since one of the tour benefits was a la carte meals that allowed us our choice.

After dinner we took advantage of the hotel's laundry room and at ten o'clock Eme and I went for a swim in the thermal waters of the huge heated outdoor pool. How lovely and relaxing it was! We slept like logs. Also, there was mail for us and that's a real booster in a foreign country — to hear from home and loved ones.

Rotorura is a city of about 40,000 and New Zealand's number one tourist drawing card. Some seasoned travelers say this is the most spectacular thermal region in the world. Although tourism has played a big part in the city's past, newer industries of farming and forestry now outstrip it.

On our first sightseeing trip our driver, Mike Scott, took us to visit the famous Whakarewarewa Thermal Reserve with its geysers, hot pools, springs and boiling mud pools in fascinating variety. Our Maori guide was a vivacious young woman, Rihi.

Next, Mike took us to the Maori Arts and Crafts Center where an attractive and talented young Maori guide showed us through and explained all. The Center houses separate arts and crafts sections for men and women as well as separate carving schools.

To qualify as a master carver a man must have completed seven houses. The carvings are very spiritual and the philosophy is not unlike the Navajo's. In Maorian human representations the head is the most prominent — the eyes representing all-seeing eyes. From fifty-two varieties of flax and tanico the women weave piupiu skirts, first rolling the flax leaves into tubes, and do basket-weaving and mat-making.

Our next visit was to the Rainbow Trout Springs and the Kiwi House. Trout is mentioned almost with reverence among New Zealanders. Rainbow Springs is a park with a cool, green abundance of trees and ferns for which Barry gave us the botanical history. The size and condition of the rainbow trout is legendary, and native birds and other wildlife are also displayed in a natural setting.

Our walk began at the Rainbow Pool into which flows a million gallons of water daily from several springs. Underwater mirrors allow visitors to view the undersides of the trout which average ten pounds each. Young rainbows are reared separately in the Fry Pool, then promoted to the Yearling Pool, also closed to adult trout. The spawning age ranges from two to three years so the two-year-old trout are transferred to the Holiday Pool from which they may swim downstream whenever they are ready.

In the park proper are lacy specimen of the silver ferns, New Zealand's national emblem. The ferns have a silver layer on the underside of the fronds. Unusual fungi sprout on the forest floor and here we saw the brilliant yellow flowers of the kawhai tree, its nectar enticing to many birds. Paradise ducks swim in the streams; they are intermediates between ducks and geese. The native forests of New Zealand are unusual in that almost all trees are evergreen — replacing their leaves as fast as they fall — but few are coniferous.

At last, the Kiwi House! We had all been anxious to see this nocturnal bird which gets its name from the "kee-wee" cry of the males. The birdhouse is kept dark but the opaque glass permitted us to see inside without the birds being able to see out.

The kiwi has no real feathers but is covered with what resembles hair, and it has neither wings nor tail. Whereas other birds have keen sight, the kiwi's is poor, but it makes up for it with a keen sense of smell which most birds lack. Its nostrils are at the end of its long bill. Among the oldest bird-form known, the kiwi has affinity with the extinct moa.

Speaking of moas, in the March 2nd edition of an Auckland newspaper, a bold-print box ad appeared, featuring a picture of a large, stalking moa (which resembles a big ostrich). The ad stated: "Japanese Film Team Requires New Information About The Last Sighting Of The Live Moa. Write to NVT Film Unit, 22 Chelverton Terrace, Red Beach, Orewa, by March 15th." There was a great stir while we were there because an actual sighting of one had been claimed.

At the Agrodome we stopped to watch a sheep shearing in a pavilion where trained rams are led onto a tiered stage. The demonstration was put on by Ivan Bowen, the world's leading sheep shearer who presented a similar show at the 1970 Exposition in Japan. After describing the nineteen breeds of sheep in New Zealand, he demonstrated his skill — after which each shorn animal shook itself and paddled off the stage. The sheep were so loveable that you wanted to cuddle one in your arms. Afterward, he showed us how the sheep are worked and herded by trained dogs. Directed only by Ivan's whistles, the dogs showed how they can bring in sheep anywhere, even between Ivan's legs.

Shearing 457 sheep in a day, Ivan broke the world's record in 1953. He reminded us that sheep are the only animals which both feed and clothe us. Sheldon Peck, our orthodontist, was interested to learn that sheep have no top row of teeth.

Barry had yet another surprise for us. He had Mike stop a little outside of Rotorura at a friend's house. Barry's friend, Herbert Howe, is a horticulturist and is part Maori. He treated us to sherry and the view of a beautiful lake in front of his well-tended and glamorous gardens.

Incidentally, Mike originally met us at the Rotorura Airport and was our constant driver and guide after that. We settled back comfortably in his ten-passenger curtained limousine!

Because it was a bright, shimmery, clear day, Mike suggested we take a floatplane ride around Lake Rotorura to get a closer look at the active volcano, the many geysers, the crater, and pastoral scenes, as well as the scope of the redwood pine forests. Afterward we trollied by foot to the home of Mike's friend, Reggie Turner. The Turner house, perched high on a hill, has a sublime view overlooking Lake Taramera, a Maori name meaning "long house on a far water". Reggie and his wife, Liz, a school teacher, served us tea and delicious freshly made scones.

That night Barry brought other friends to have dinner with us. They were Beverly and Murray Gow who lived about forty miles distant.

Murray is both a farmer and an artist and Beverly is a coloratura soprano.

Later in the evening some of us attended a traditional concert at the Maori Cultural Theatre. The program, in song and dance, is called the Migration of the Maori. Costuming was boldly colorful and the singing, fervent. The Maori war dance staged by the men is a posturing and grimacing one. The graceful poi dance of the women is performed with flax fiber balls on the end of cords swung and twirled with a rhythm like that of paddling a canoe.

Afterwards we had a late night swim in the hotel's thermal pool before turning in.

Mike was back for us at 8:15 the next morning, Sunday, March 12th, and after loading our suitcases into the limo, we were ready to begin our last day in New Zealand.

Over the heavily forested Manaku Hills we traveled, through rolling and fertile green farmlands, and past meadows mottled with sheep. The whole country has a vivid greenness—free of smog or pollution.

Outcrops of limestone showed this to be cave country, including Waitoma Cave, New Zealand's most popular attraction with its world famous phenomenon, Glow Worm Grotto.

The tour takes some forty-five minutes and cameras are not allowed, we were forewarned before starting the deep descent of 200 steps, clutching the handrails. Down we went into a vast, high-roofed cavern where flatboats awaited, each able to carry twenty passengers.

Absolute silence must be maintained, we were told, because the glow worms stop glowing if there is light or noise. We glided silently ahead into solid blackness along the underground river, the Waitoma Stream. Neither rowed nor poled, the boat was pulled along by the guides grasping an overhead wire. We looked above, breathless, at the thousands of tiny, starry lights stippling the ceiling, eerily jeweling the dark with their reflection twinkling in the water. It was like something out of another world.

The insect that provides this magic scene in the grotto is the larva of a gnat that looks rather like a small daddy longlegs. The glow is to attract its prey — the glow worm's only predators being other glow worms. A larva hatches from an egg laid by the mother on the grotto ceiling. It exudes a hammock of silk much as a spider does, fastening it with mucus. Living in this about eight months until the larva is about an inch and a half long, it feeds from its silky web, lowering it to catch any midge attracted by the light. The larva worm then draws up the midge, eats it and drops another line. According to the guide, after the larva changes to the pupal stage, it hangs vertically by a single thread for weeks but this is the non-feeding stage since adults do not have mouths. Then the gnat-type fly emerges from its casing and begins procreating. The males are waiting to mate with females which then lay about 100 eggs and die in three days; the males die in four days.

Often the parent insects are then eaten by the larvae.

The glow worm's light is at its excretory end and the amount of light depends on the amount of its excretion. Glow worms of Europe and America differ from New Zealand's since the former are either female beetles or fireflies which light up to attract the males, and in the case of the firefly, the light is not constant but flashing.

After lunch at the Waitoma Hotel we drove on toward Auckland but in the late afternoon, Barry had a final surprise for us. In Hamilton, a thriving city of 80,000, we met his older sister, Patricia, who had invited us for tea. Barry's sister and her husband, Ian McMullen, were gracious hosts and their daughters, Angela and Gabrielle, winsome. Their home stretches out on a hill overlooking the Waikato River that divides the city and their yard and garden had the expert touch of loving care. Patricia made the most feathery scones I've ever eaten, passing them hot from the oven, and thirteen-year-old Gabrielle played the piano for us. Patricia was happy to see her brother, Barry, for the first time in two years but the reunion was short-lived because we had to resume the last lap of our limousine journey.

We drove into the Auckland Airport about 7:00 p.m., had dinner and went outside for a last look at the Southern Cross sparkling in the clear sky and for a silent good-by to this peaceful land, these friendly people.

At 10:15 we left on the UTA French Airlines for Tahiti and arrived at 6:15 a.m. to be taken to the Hotel Maeva in Papeete, the capital city. The rest of the day we caught up on our sleep and lolled in the sun and water, renewing our strength for our week-long stay in the islands.

Next day we took a complete tour of Tahiti, picnicking for lunch at a tropical open-air restaurant. Tahiti is the largest island of French Polynesia. It is dominated by two towering peaks, Orohena and Aorai. Originally, we were scheduled to climb Aorai and camp near its peak but Barry had learned this was a feat for professionals and that let most of us out. In the heat and humidity, none had the breath for climbing.

Papeete, with about 30,000 people, is the main settlement and one of the most romantic and legendary ports of call in the South Pacific. The harbor front is busy with copra schooners, ocean liners and yachts. Away from the harbor are green lawns and foothills tufted with coconut palms while around the island there are both black and white sand beaches.

On our first night we were guests of the hotel at an appetizing barbecue served on long tables filled with Polynesian delicacies. For dessert we tried poi, the sweet made of banana and papaya. And while we finished our wine and coffee, Polynesian dancers entertained.

The grass skirts slithered, the hips rolled and swayed to the music's beat as young, barefoot Tahitian men and women performed. Then the stage was cleared, leaving eight girls who came into the audience to choose partners. The girl we had been umming and aahing over came to our table and we all cheered as she tapped Eme's shoulder and led him to the stage.

"Follow me," she said, placing her hands behind her head and swaying to the music. Eme did as she asked and the rest of the dance was so hilarious we were in tears.

Eme and I have had a continuing love affair with islands, sampling them much of our married life. We were late coming to those in the South Pacific although they were among the first we'd longed to see. We don't appreciate the overcommercialized ones but the natural, out of the way ones excite us. So, left to our choice, we made an unscheduled trip to Bora-Bora. James Michener, in his book *Tales of the South Pacific*, described it as the most beautiful island in the world. We had to see it! And Charles elected to go with us.

Arriving at Bora-Bora, Charles left us to go snorkeling while Eme and I toured the island. Famous Films was remaking "Hurricane" at the time, and most of the houses we saw were on stilts.

Our guide was the host of the hotel where we had lunch, the OaOa. Originally from Germany, his name was Hans Flesch. He took us to see the luxurious Bora-Bora Hotel, the best occupied one in the tropics, surrounded by a lagoon and enticing beaches.

Bora-Bora is sometimes called "the Pearl of the Pacific". Its population is around 2,650 and over thirty percent of the people are non-Tahitian. It is just an hour away from Tahiti by air and it looks like a black jewel ringed in the waters of the lagoon. Of volcanic origin, it has steep cliffs and a barrier reef that surrounds it. The lagoon is well stocked with fish and changes color according to its depth, going through all shades of blue and green. Charles told us later the snorkeling was the best he'd ever experienced.

During the second World War, Bora-Bora was an important base for the U. S. Marines.

The island is poor in fresh water and excessive measures are taken to ease the shortage. In the 1970s the problem was particularly pressing because of a dry year and increased tourism. The municipality acquired spring water by drilling into the island's base. New hotels will doubtless have to depend on desalinization of sea water.

Nonetheless, Bora-Bora is a luxuriant green island. Everywhere we looked there was wild, spontaneous beauty. But one thing that struck me was that green is the only color — from the heights of viridian mountains to the emerald of the sea. Only small amounts of colored flora have been introduced here to relieve the monotone. Coconut trees abound, and their fruit are stacked like fences along some routes. After this lovely, contemplative day, we flew back to Papeete, looking down to the white beaches and grassy slopes.

The next day, March 17th, we flew to Moorea. Why, I wonder, did Michener pick Bora-Bora over such a bea-u-tiful island as Moorea? We were guests of the Bali-Hai Hotel for the day and here we met Margaret and Per Benterude again, having met them for the first time in Bora-Bora. They were from Oslo and Per had been importing plants from Honolulu.

Whimsical in design, the mountains of Moorea are full of color. Some look like towering castles under the puffy white clouds and the gold of the sun. Color is everywhere. The alamanda, like morning glories, are a burst of yellow. Other rainbow-hued flora variegate the landscape. There are coconut palms, the tiara plant (used in making leis) and gardenias. Pandanas plants grow abundantly. Pineapples, oranges and mandarins are cultivated, as well as bananas.

With only about 4500 inhabitants, Moorea is a closely knit community and its charming houses are flower-strewn and picture perfect.

A coral atoll formed by a volcano, the island is shaped like a large basin and surrounded by two bays. White sandy beaches stretch for miles. The barrier reef encircles the coast and the lagoon is a fascination of color, from azure to the deepest emerald. Along the coast are many kinds of houses: some on stilts with coconut palm roofs and woven bamboo sides, some square houses with pandanus roofs, and some of painted wood with iron roofs.

The Bali-Hai Hotel is especially plush and commodious, its beach superb. The main fear for this beautiful island is that, because of its proximity to Papeete (only seven minutes by air) it may lose its original and radiant flavor and be taken in by the city as a suburb.

After lunch we went to Cook's Bay in the village of PaoPao where during World War II, many American submarines were hidden. Lying in a hammock with a huge array of nets strung up was a young Polynesian with a CB radio. He was waiting for a report from the other side of the bay as to when the mackeral would come in from the ocean. At the signal he got into action with his nets, scooping up large quantities of mackeral and keeping them alive in a nearby pool. Daily he sold as many as he could to the markets.

It had been a lingering, refreshing day, but at 6:00 p.m. it was time to return to Papeete, enjoy our farewell dinner, then pack our suitcases for the next day's takeoff at 7:45 a.m.

Arriving in Los Angeles Airport from half a world away, Eme and I said "au revoir" to our ebullient leader and our intrepid friends, hoping we would all meet again someday.

Chapter 2

In *Voyage of the Beagle* Charles Darwin wrote: "But there is growing pleasure in comparing the scenery in different countries, which to a certain degree is distinct from merely admiring its beauty. It depends chiefly on an acquaintance with the individual part of each view."

It is this acquaintance with ancient South American cities and Darwin's specific islands — the Galapagos — that Eme and I, along with our good friends, the Sherwoods — were anticipating.

But on the morning of February 22nd we did everything but throw ourselves under the wheels to stall Braniff Flight 911 from leaving the Miami Airport without the Sherwoods aboard. We were to take off for Quito, Ecuador, at 3:00 a.m. At 11:00 p.m. Miller and Barb had called to say they were delayed in Chicago because their Delta flight was over two hours late. We pleaded in vain with Braniff and even though the Sherwoods arrived twenty-five minutes before departure time and Delta rushed them to the Braniff plane, Braniff had closed its international gates. And that was that. The Sherwoods' luggage was aboard but they had to spend another day in Miami! Quite a few choice words were later addressed to Braniff about that.

The rest of us were met in Quito the next morning by our tour director, Whitney Nichols, a native Vermonter. His assistant, Daniel (Woody) Hartman from Bethel, Maine, had met us at the Miami Airport.

We were a group of twenty-one besides the two directors. With us were a doctor and his wife from St. Louis; another doctor and his wife from New Hampshire; a charming woman gynecologist from Portland, Oregon; two administrative teachers from Northfield, Illinois, on a year's sabbatical; two from the U. S. Department of Agriculture in Alexandria, Virginia; a professor of psychiatry and his wife from State College, Pennsylvania; a young woman judge from Washington, D.C.; a semi-professional photographer also from D.C.; two former teachers and three manufacturers and their wives from Wisconsin, Michigan (the

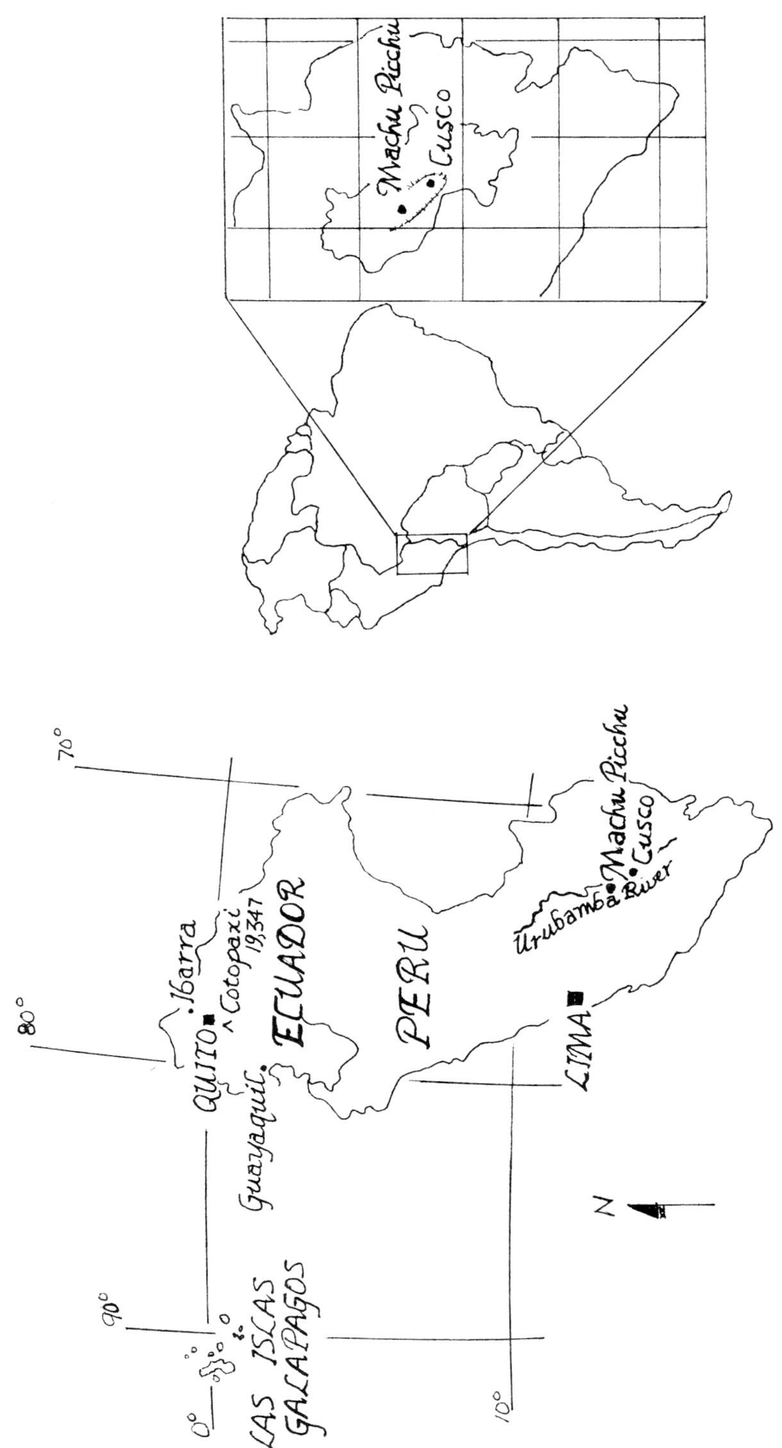

Machu Picchu
Cusco
70°
80°
90°
0°
10°
Ibarra
QUITO
Cotopaxi
19,347
Guayaquil
ECUADOR
PERU
LIMA
Urubamba River
Machu Picchu
Cusco
LAS ISLAS
GALAPAGOS
N

Sherwoods) and Florida (us).

Arriving in Quito we got our first look at the Andes towering grandly above the valley city and shimmering in the forenoon sun. So close to the equator, we were at the center of the world. From the airport to the hotel, the tabebuia trees (known as silver trumpets in Florida) spun a golden trail.

Spread at the foot of a volcano, Quito is the oldest capital city in South America. At 9200-foot altitude we were breathing a little faster and had been warned to take it easy — at least temporarily. After unloading our luggage and having a light meal at the hotel, we changed some of our money to sucres — worth twenty-seven to the U. S. dollar.

For five months this teeming city of 600,000 had been suffering from a drought. There was dusty dryness everywhere and electricity was rationed.

We threaded our way through the old intriguing section of the city which looks like areas of Spain or San Francisco with its narrow, steep, cobbled streets, its grillwork and flowerpots, its air of intimacy. White houses have wood balconies painted blue, a tradition honoring San Francisco de Quito, the patron saint of this archbishopric (founded by the Roman Catholic Church) which flies its banner of white and blue. Days are warm and sunny here, Sebastian told us. Nights are cool in a perfect springtime weather.

Ecuador's birthrate is one of the highest in the world. We guessed almost every female over twelve to be pregnant. Poverty is rife and misery rampant. They had a military dictatorship but our guide assured us they were having a democratic election: the choice to be among an admiral of the navy, a general of the army or a general of the air force.

A Metropolitan Tour bus wheeled up outside to take us to the museum and on a tour of the city. Our guide for our stay was Sebastian Cornejo, a well-groomed, smiling, vivacious and knowledgeable man who spoke English well. A law student lacking only his thesis for a degree, he spent two and a half years in the U.S. on an Exxon scholarship, studying first in Chicago, then at the Colorado School of Mines. For six months he traveled the U.S. from coast to coast in a small car he bought. He vied with our leader, Whitney, in naming and pointing out the flora and fauna of the countryside.

During the afternoon we saw the sparkling violetear of the hummingbird family, swallows, swifts, and the rufus-collared sparrow. As we followed the Guayllamba River, Whitney identified the giant hummingbird, as well as black phoebes, for us. Scotch broom and century plants were in bloom and we stopped to take pictures at the stone pylon which is the official marker of the equator line. We drove on to Lake Cuicocha to have our picnic lunch.

This lake is in a stunning setting at almost 11,000 feet elevation and spread on the slopes of snow-capped Mount Cotacachi, ringed by other treeless peaks. We took boats to one of the two islands in the center of the lake and finding a good rock for a ground lean-to, we opened our picnic lunches and drank in the delightful scenery. There was a dwarf forest swept with bromeliads, passion flowers and buttercups. A buzzard eagle circled overhead, waterfowl tested the lake, and a soft wind blew. En route to the hotel we passed pre-Inca burial mounds.

In Ibarra we checked in at the Chorlavi Hotel which has an attractive courtyard and flower gardens bordering the paths to the cottage-type rooms.

In an excellently displayed Central Bank Museum, Sebastian traced for us Ecuadorian history and culture from its earliest beginnings through the times of the Chimus, the Quitos and other pre-Incas, and through the Inca civilization. This is one of the greatest art and archaeological collections in the Americas, displaying some 23,000 pieces, some dating back 10,000 years to man's beginning in the western hemisphere.

After dinner, we watched, at a theatre nearby, the colorful folkloric performance of Ecuadorian Indian dancers in their gala, brilliant costumes.

On our second morning the bus was waiting at the Quito Airport for the arrival of the Sherwoods. The fates smiled; Braniff was on time and our weary wayfarers joined us as we set off for the countryside and travel north along the Pan-American Highway.

At Caldion we stopped at a factory that makes decorative artifacts of very hard dough. Fortunately, for Miller and Barb Sherwood, this was their second time around this country and the Galapagos Islands. Along the route they pointed excitedly to a friend's ranch where, in 1971 they had ridden horseback over much of the rugged terrain. Looking up we could see the volcano, Sum Cayambel. At 19,300 feet it is snow-covered year round.

We were looking forward to the famous weekly market at Otavalo. The Otavalo Indians are a pre-Inca people, artisans with great color and design creativity. En route, Sebastian filled us in on many Indian customs, such as throwing stones at one another to begin a courtship!

Although converted to Catholicism many retain their pagan beliefs, we were told. The Indian men, always seen in ponchos, wear their hair long and braided. The women, also long-haired, adorn themselves with many gold-colored beads and necklaces. The Indians have strong family ties, do not intermarry with other ethnic groups, and seldom divorce.

They are well educated, clever, clean and productive, and maintain their customs and their costumes.

At the marketplace it was color, color, color — as far as the eye could see — and blocks and blocks of animals and throngs of humanity. The farmers and artisans had been up before dawn to get here and spread their wares for this choicest of Indian fairs. The sale of squealing pigs first riveted our attention but the weavers soon gained it with their wares. Displayed on wires, hangers, in mounds, or on tables, their dashing and beautifully made sweaters, caps, scarves, ponchos, mittens, rugs and wall hangings deserved our attention. Some weavers artfully placed stacks of the brilliantly colored skeins of wool beside their finished work. As one entrepreneur hung a large wall tapestry (much like a Navajo's) he was singing the "Battle Hymn of the Republic" in Spanish.

Astute tradesmen, they bargained with us, but only to a point.

As well as the outdoor market there are indoor stores offering woven goods, leathers, wood carvings of cedar, and silver and other wrought metal objects. One entire block displays foods of all kinds. We have fun looking and purchasing and once back on the bus, hold a style show and display of our woven goods, leather bargains, and innumerable trinkets.

Returning the twenty-four miles to our hotel, we enjoy a sumptuous barbecue in the gardens among the hibiscus, daisies and avocado trees—topping it off with good sour-sop sherbet for dessert.

En route back to Quito in the afternoon we crossed the two main ranges of the Andes. Eucalyptus trees shimmered blue in the sunlight. Washings were spread out by the streams. Vegetation is lush in this high country where they get light rains and all the hillsides were terraced and planted. We passed the deep canyons of the Chicho River where cactus clings spiderlike to the walls and from the oceanic highway we could see llamas in the open fields. Just outside Quito are spectacular homes pinnacling the mountains that tower over the city.

On the Sabbath our bus took off with the same good driver, Rolando, at the wheel, and Sebastian at the microphone, as we drove south from Quito. Carnivals, Sebastian told us, precede all holy days. The monetary unit of Ecuador, the sucre, is named for Marshal Sucre, the leader of their independence movement. Ecuador produces and runs through the highest pipelines in the world, 250,000 barrels of oil a day, exporting 120,000 barrels which represents thirty-eight percent of the economy. Sixty percent is based on agriculture — primarily wheat, barley and corn. The average per capita income is $800 a year.

W. J. Turner's poem, "Romance," seemed to me as a child, the ultimate; I loved rolling and tripping my tongue over its words, wondering all the while where in the world the places mentioned could be. The poem begins:

When I was but thirteen or so
I went into a golden land;
Chimborazo, Cotopaxi
Took me by the hand . . .

I need no longer wonder. I was seeing in the distance, Cotopaxi—all 19,700 feet to its snow-swirled summit. What a glorious early-morning sight to see the variegated shadows playing on its slopes! No wonder it has been called the ideal volcano; its symmetry is so perfect. Further south sits one of the highest peaks in the Andes — Chimborazo, reaching 20,702 feet.

Over dusty roads after leaving the Pan-Am Highway, we headed for Cotopaxi National Park. Five million small pine trees have been planted along its approach and wild mountain daisies, yellow and white, speckle the lane. Whitney spotted for us a sparrow hawk and a long black-tailed trainbearer. The thousands of red fox and deer that once roamed the park are now extinct.

In the museum we saw a stuffed Andean condor, a magnificent bird threatened with extinction. The condor is Ecuador's national emblem. Whitney offered a free dinner and drinks to any of us who spotted a condor. A pretty safe bet!

In the museum we found restrooms but no water, which we'd find in many places to be almost as rare as the condor.

On the flank of Cotopaxi, the world's highest active volcano, we stopped for lunch beside a tiny lake at 14,500 feet. It was cold, but not as cold as we'd expected. However, a soft rain quickly turned to hail, and snow began covering the mountainside. We fled to the bus for shelter. Some campers were trying to dig in under huge rocks they were using as caves while bracing their small tents against the wind. Whole areas here reminded me of Switzerland. As for us, we were soon on our way back to Quito, to our very comfortable and inviting Hotel Colon for hot showers and dinner.

In the heart of Quito we visited LaCompania Church, undoubtedly one of the most baroque and lavish with its exquisite gold-leaf ornamentation. The entire interior glitters and its high altar (roped off) is solid gold. Ninety percent of the population is Catholic, we were told, but only forty percent are active communicants.

From the top of Panecillo Hill we looked down on the sparkling picture of Quito set in the shallow valley and framed by the imposing Andean peaks.

After lunch we drove down the western slopes en route to Santo

Colorful costumes of the Peruvian Indians.

Pisac Market of Peru, near Cusco.

Cotopaxi — 19,700 feet — Ecuador.

Blue-footed boobies, Fernandina Island, Galapagos.

Sea lion, much larger than the fur seals, Santa Cruz Island, Galapagos.

The Hiram Bingham Road winding up to our tiny hotel on Machu Picchu, Peru.

Machu Picchu, as seen from our helicopter.

Only 100 pair of these oyster catchers are left in the Galapagos, on Hood Island.

The diesel-powered pong boats on which we ferried from the Buccaneer to various islands in the Galapagos.

Marine iguana of Hood Island. The only one with red coloring on its body.

Galapagos tortoises.

LaCompania Church in Quito, Ecuador. Baroque and lavishly ornamented with gold leaf; its high altar, roped off, is solid gold.

Domingo de Los Colorados. In the highlands is the thunderous, stupendous scenery where misty clouds hover above the gorges and cascades spurt and spill down the slopes to reach the Toachee River in the lowlands.

In this temperate zone, blue lupins nodded along the way and the flowers, Sebastian said, are edible. Orchids grow wild here and the everchanging vegetation is luxuriant. Cattle and horses browse the green fields. Silver maples shimmer in the sunlight.

Descending 7,000 feet from the highland zone to a semi-tropical one, we found the landscape drastically changed. Our destination was the province of Santo Domingo where we would spend two days and nights at the Hotel Tinlandia, run by a White Russian countess who escaped the revolution, and her second husband. The accommodations were miserable, offset only by the fantastic natural beauty and idyllic grounds surrounding the place.

Some cabins — one of which we got — were dank and foreboding, providing sagging mattresses and no hot water. The food, served on an open porch or inside the dining room with unscreened windows, was but partly edible and eagerly shared by innumerable flies. Several cats joined us for meals, both on top and underneath our table. We loaded up on pills, added halazone tablets to the water, crossed our fingers and hoped for the best.

But outside, what a different story! What a shining, cheery, exotic fairyland with flowers bursting from spathe and bough amidst the canticle of birds that feather an alluring trail through seven and a half acres of grounds. Our field trip took us past balsam trees, green orange trees, bamboo groves, and over ground sprinkled with wild flowers where bright orange butterflies dallied.

Miller followed a rufus fly-catcher, and Whitney and Woodie pointed out a laughing falcon among the many tropical birds. But it was here that Woodie came into his own, pointing out the trails of the leaf-cutter ants close to where he stood. For fifteen minutes we were enthralled as he detailed the lore of these job-assigned, marvelously-organized, hardworking, tiny creatures.

With an afternoon at leisure, we found an enticing flowered patio with good white wicker chairs, and a table just right for a game of bridge with the Sherwoods. Miller proposed a great drink to help us play that called for vodka (which he'd brought from Quito), soda, green oranges, and Compari. We had everything but the last ingredient. It was the Russian countess who provided it, bringing us what remained of her own bottle. And where did we get the green oranges? We simply reached up into an overhanging tree to pluck them. We set up a picking and squeezing relay and we were in business. The fact that Eme and I won the opening game, of course, was due neither to the vodka nor the cards but to our fine playing.

Whitney was a punster, beginning each day by greeting us with a play on words. But it was Dr. Strayer who best retaliated, telling Whitney, "you're not just a bird watcher, you're also a word botcher!"

Along the coast road to Guayaquil are numerous plantations: cocoa, coffee, castor bean, fibers, and bananas. Here grow the tropical lipstick trees — source of color for foods — and the flowering African tulips. Buzzards are everywhere and snowy egrets wing the rice fields.

There are police stops in every city en route. According to Sebastian, the speed limit is the same as ours, but nobody observes it.

On the main street of a wayside village we parked to eat our box lunches, but we left the bus on reluctant feet. Beggars, kids, filth and flies greeted us as we gingerly sat on open-air stools to picnic. Eme's photos do more justice to the scene than my words but they can't convey the 100-degree sultriness that added to the ghastliness. So much poverty, everywhere, was overwhelmingly depressing.

At last we reached Guayaquil where the enormous monument to Jesus Christ dominates the hill. One million people live here in Ecuador's largest and least attractive seaport city.

At five in the afternoon we boarded the Buccaneer, our ship and home for the next eight days. All of us looked for our cabins and hoped for the best since the ship's accommodations for ninety people were booked full.

The Buccaneer is used exclusively in the Galapagos Islands, named by the Spaniards as the Enchanted Islands. It has a swimming pool, library, small boutique, television and radio, a bar, and a separate hall called the Duke and Duchess Lecture Room. It has central air-conditioning inside and sundecks outside. And we had nothing to worry about in the way of cabins. All in our group were given outside rooms with private baths and Eme and I shared a cabin with side-by-side beds separated by a table.

Cruising was done at night to allow the daylight hours for field trips on the various islands. We were accompanied by four top-qualified, well-versed young naturalists — three men and a woman — all multi lingual. On board they lectured, led discussions, and showed films to prepare us.

Following an early breakfast, we attended a geology lecture by Jack Grove, a personable marine biologist and expert on the Galapagos. There are thirteen major islands located in the Pacific Ocean 650 miles off the coast of Ecuador and astride the equator. Except for the two northern ones, the islands rise from a shallow submarine platform. All

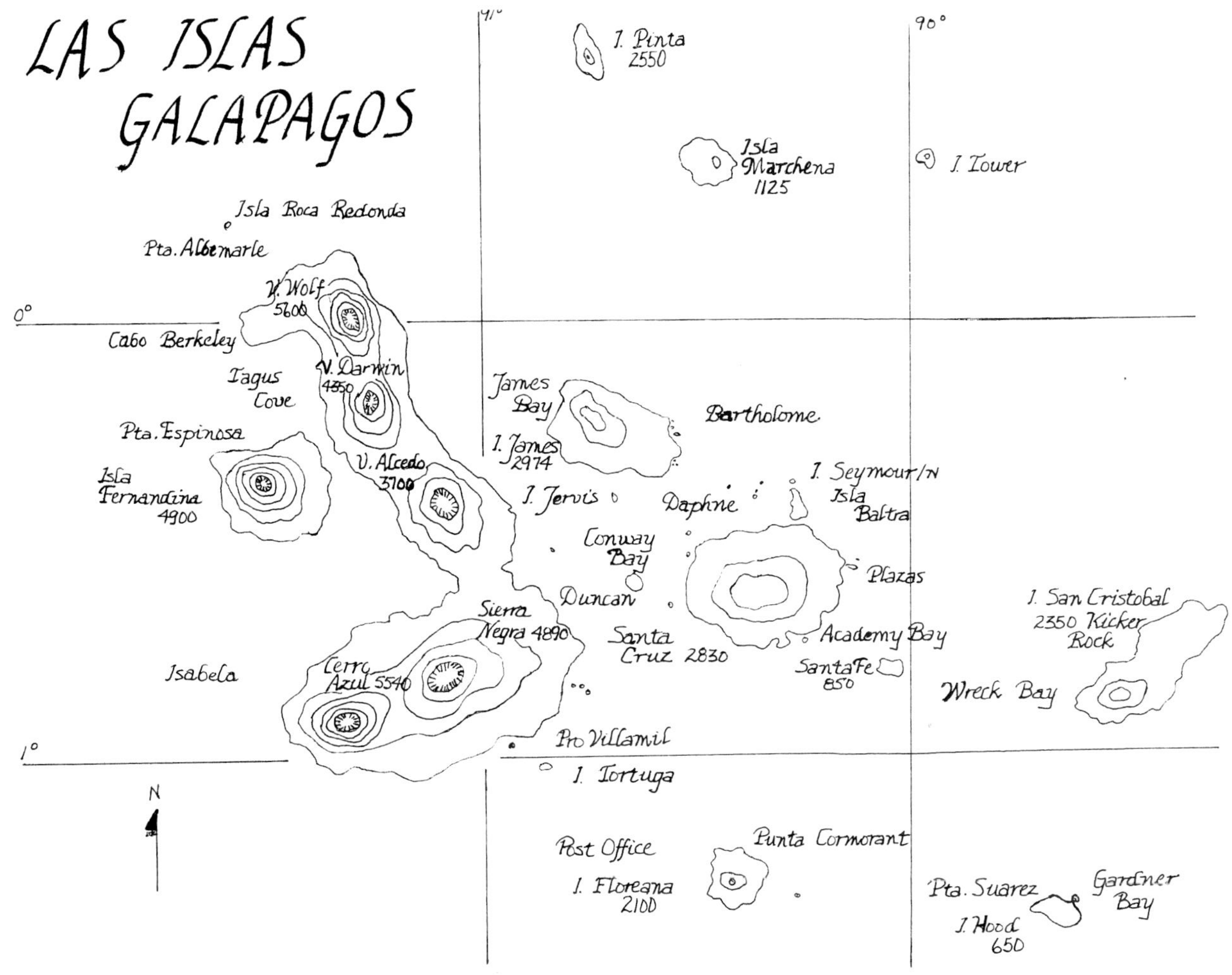
LAS ISLAS GALAPAGOS
91°
90°
0°
1°
I. Pinta 2550
Isla Marchena 1125
I. Tower
Isla Roca Redonda
Pta. Albemarle
V. Wolf 5600
Cabo Berkeley
V. Darwin 4350
Tagus Cove
Pta. Espinosa
Isla Fernandina 4900
V. Alcedo 3700
James Bay
I. James 2974
Bartholome
I. Seymour/N
Isla Baltra
I. Jervis
Daphne
Conway Bay
Plazas
Duncan
I. San Cristobal 2350
Kicker Rock
Sierra Negra 4890
Santa Cruz 2830
Academy Bay
Santa Fe 850
Isabela
Cerro Azul 5540
Wreck Bay
Pto Villamil
I. Tortuga
N
Post Office
Punta Cormorant
I. Floreana 2100
Pta. Suarez
Gardner Bay
I. Hood 650

are created of basaltic lava. The rocks are estimated to be some five million years old, and each island is a volcano. Because the tectonic plates are separating, earthquakes and volcanic eruptions occur more frequently here than anywhere else on earth.

After an ample meal, featuring some Ecuadorian specialties, we lolled in the brilliant sunshine until four o'clock when Dave Kiehn, an extremely tall and handsome biologist, gave us a fascinating account of the islands' evolution and biology. He told us the tiny spores and lichens were first brought here by winds, jet streams and sea birds carrying seeds. The Humboldt Current brought logs by vegetation rafts. Neither amphibians nor salamanders could make it across 650 miles of ocean, but reptiles could and did, as did plants able to utilize sea water. And thus began the process of natural selection and creation of the gene pool which permits interbreeding. The adaptive radiation from original species has emerged with many variations so that here you find in one location: tortoises that grow to gigantic size, cormorants that have lost the ability to fly, lizards feeding on seaweed under the ocean's surface, and sunflowers that have evolved into trees. All this was contemplated by Darwin more than 100 years ago.

That night it was pisco sours on the house and a gala dinner to meet the crew, the naturalists and the captain.

After dinner it was back to the lecture hall for a talk by Lynn Fowler, a vivacious naturalist, on the history and physical description of the islands. The Galapagos were officially discovered by Fray Thomas, Bishop of Panama, in 1535 when his ship was becalmed and carried 500 miles off course. Later, freebooters used the islands as a base and reportedly buried treasure here.

The islands were first charted by the navigator, Ambrose Cowley, who named them Galapagos while sailing with Captain Cook. The first permanent inhabitant was an Irishman, Patrick Watkins, who lived on Floreana Island from 1807 until 1809. Not a scientist, he must have been fleeing something to have remained where eventually a penal settlement was established.

Santa Cruz is the largest of the four inhabited islands.

The species introduced in these islands include dogs, cats, horses, donkeys, pigs, cattle, rats, mice, and goats that obtain water by eating cacti. During the last two centuries man has introduced species that are causing vast upheaval and disturbances of the islands' natural wildlife. In the 1950s it was finally realized that the natural species and the environment were endangered. In 1959 the Charles Darwin Foundation for the Galapagos Islands was founded under the auspices of UNESCO and the International Conservation Union. At the same time, the

Ecuadorian government set aside the islands as a wildlife preserve and established the Galapagos National Park.

The Buccaneer dropped anchor off Hood Island to give us a closeup look at this uninhabited place, an uplifted block of submarine lavas. Because the island's ecology is in very delicate balance only a limited number of outsiders is allowed to visit each year, and the size of vessels cruising the waters is also restricted. We got into broad-beamed diesel-powered boats called pongas, lowered from the Buccaneer, to take us to the island for a wet landing — which meant wading in knee-high water the last few meters to shore.

As much as I'd read about these islands I could not have predicted my first impressions. I share Herman Melville's feelings which he described in one of his *Piazza Tales*. He wrote, "Take five-and-twenty heaps of cinders dumped here and there in an outside city lot; imagine some of them magnified into mountains, and the vacant lot the sea; and you will have a fit idea of the general aspect of these 'Enchanted Islands.' A group rather of extinct volcanoes than of isles, looking much as the world at large might after a penal conflagration, it is to be doubted whether any spot on earth can, in desolateness, furnish a parallel to this group . . ."

This verdict, pronounced in 1841, is just as true today.

It was on Hood Island that Darwin first set foot on the Galapagos. He came as a young naturalist aboard the British survey ship, the HMS Beagle, in 1835. But he didn't publish his findings until twenty-five years later in the *Origin of Species*, the work that began a revolution in human thought. During his brief six-week stay on the islands, he noted the plant and animal life were markedly different from any other place in the world and they also differed markedly from island to island, adapting to the necessities of each. He identified fourteen varieties of finches alone and theorized that the strong winds and Humboldt Current had carried these and other species to these barren volcanic outposts.

Hood hosts a dazzling variety of animal and bird life. There are bright orange and red marine iguanas along the coast, lava lizards, snakes, finches, tortoises, and the great frigate birds. Feral goats have heavily damaged the vegetation so that only a few cactus plants and many thorny acacia trees, are left. The ever-playful sea lions are resident mammals, nursing their young for two years. But I wouldn't want a standoff with the big bull ones — some were touchy enough to chase a few of us. Iguanas bask in large herds on the guano-whitened rocks.

Although famous for its albatross, we saw none. Yet, nowhere in the world are they known to breed except on this island. They need enormous runways for taking off because of their large, webbed feet.

There are many blow-holes through which trapped water explodes, gushing fifty feet into the air.

The Sally Lightfoot crabs redden the rocks and the almost tame blue-footed boobies are the most common seabirds. It's interesting to note that of these fearless groundnesters (my favorites) the male whistles and the female honks. Doves, mockingbirds, and Darwin's finches sing and forage, and overhead hawks circle. Behind Point Suarez, both the blue-footed and the masked boobies nest.

Back to the Buccaneer for lunch and we were off in the small boats for Floreana Island, forty-six miles from Hood. On this island is the famous Post Office Bay where letters are mailed in a wooden barrel and, God willing, finally picked up by passing boats and sent on to their destination.

The hills, densely studded with volcanic cones, go up to 2,000 feet but as we climbed, we saw some green vegetation. Whitney pointed out shearwaters and ruddy turnstones in the mangroves and going on to Punta Cormorant, we spotted shy flamingos in the lagoon. On the western coast was a black sand beach where we swam before returning to the Buccaneer for refreshing showers, dinner, and a slide lecture of the next day's tour of Santa Cruz.

Up at six on a Sunday morning we got into the pongas for the voyage to Santa Cruz, the second most populous island and one with diversified flora, fauna, and terrain. Eight of Darwin's finches breed here as well as most other species of Galapagos birds. At the Darwin Research Station we saw young tortoises hatching and, after a short walk, the enormous giant-size adults. Although there are a number of tortoises on the islands, they're not easily seen because they seek isolation. We chanced to be there during the mating season and while we felt we were intruding into the privacy of one couple, the scientists among us displayed unabashed delight.

The males weigh as much as 550 pounds. The female, after mating, makes a long trek to seek a nesting site in a low, dry location, and with the use of her hind legs, digs a nest. She lays her eggs and covers them with moistened mud. Four to eight months later, the young hatch and dig their way out.

The Station has also created nature trails through the wildlife sites, well marked to avoid breaking off the lava or destroying any endemic flora. Salt bush and sunflower trees are prevalent.

Hard to believe but we had a bus ride on this island and saw houses, boutiques, a naval base and hospital, as well as ships harbored in an inlet.

Most flowers on the island are not native but have been introduced.

Blossoms of a same species grew bigger as we reached the better soil of the highlands. Heavy jet-black lichen hangs in the trees. A brilliant yellow butterfly — the only one on the Galapagos — is the main pollinator. Wild cucumber and elephant grass are staples. We saw a darkbilled cuckoo winging through the feathery bamboo trees. Fern grass, sedges, the quinine bush, avocado and sunflower trees abound.

After a final stop to purchase glasses of a tasty, thirst quencher called naranquilla, we started back to the boats—only to have our bus break down. But luck sent along a small truck with two farmers and three grinning youngsters in it, and we were mighty grateful for a lift as we jostled in its rickety rear until rescued by the arrival of another bus.

In the afternoon we visited the eastern coast of Santa Cruz where a sandy cove gave haven to wall-to-wall sea lions, hordes of land iguanas, and tropical birds. The sea lions have no fear of humans and delighted in joining the swimmers and snorkelers. The iguanas, plagued by small ticks in their leathery folds, consider the finches that feed on these insects their pals.

After dinner on board the Buccaneer, our lecturer was another able young naturalist, Robert Dale, who prepared us for the next day's trip to Bartolome.

This is a stark, cindery, volcanic island, rugged to climb, but with a beautiful view from the top of the peaks looking toward Santiago. The swimming area on one side of Sullivan Bay has white shell sand beaches separated by a mangrove forest.

The afternoon was spent at Buccaneer Bay off Bartolome. From the strata of volcanic material, weird shapes predominate; one exotic form looks like a huge green goddess. Here Whitney kept track of the oyster catcher as it swooped to the water's edge and we caught sight of the elusive wide-winged, red-billed tropic bird high overhead.

Once aboard ship with the Sherwoods, we caught up on cool drinks and a little bridge before dinner. Afterwards, Lynn prepared us for the next day's trip to Isabella and Fernandina.

We anchored in Tagus Cove off Isabella, the longest island in the archipelago and one with six volcanic craters. One named Wolf, at 5,600 feet, is the highest point in the Galapagos. In the northern part of the cove is a circular saltwater lake and the cove itself is the remains of an ancient crater. We spent time watching the penguins, and cormorants found only here.

Fernandina is one of the world's most active volcanoes. The caldera is an awesome pit but fur seals consider it a haven.

After dinner that night, Dave presented an entracing color slide show synchronized with music — the pictures all taken by him. Later,

Lynn took us on deck for a brief but instructive astronomy lesson, starting with the Southern Cross.

Five dolphins and two whales were playing around the prow of the Buccaneer the next morning as we left for Tagus Bay on Isabella, the largest of the islands.

On Isabella we sighted penguins of a much smaller variety than the Antarctic ones, tattlers, and knotty terns. Frigate birds whiffled the water and floated.

On the open sea there were more whales and spinner dolphins that are usually wary of boats, but these rode the wave of the bow. Excitement was high as we spotted a lone albatross floating in the water. He was "alone, alone, all all alone, alone on a wide, wide sea," and we shot him — not as the Ancient Mariner had, but with our cameras.

More bridge with the Sherwoods before dinner, putting us one game and $2.00 ahead. After an elaborate meal we were entertained by our peppy and attractive young naturalists who donned pirates' costumes to present a clever skit. Then we received colored certificates attesting to the fact we had plied the waters of the Galapagos and learned its mysteries.

Next morning, some of us are off on a short visit to Seymore Island before leaving for Baltra which has an airstrip to accommodate Galapagos visitors. It is from these two relatively barren islands we bid farewell to the archipelago Roger Tory Peterson called "a harsh Eden".

Our bags were ready and waiting on deck when word came that the plane was three hours late, so it was back to the bridge table and this time the Sherwoods came out on top, leaving us owing $2.00 as the sum total of the trip.

After an unplanned lunch aboard the Buccaneer we took the short boat ride to Baltra, a bus to the airport, and had another long wait before boarding the plane. Back in Quito, Sebastian's happy face greeted us. He transferred us to the Hotel Colon for the farewell dinner with our friends and leaders. Next day they would be flying back to Miami but Eme and I were headed for Lima, Peru.

Arriving in Lima at noon we were met by our tour guide, George, who collected our luggage and whistled us into a waiting car to go to the Lima Sheraton, a beautiful ultra-modern hotel with blooming flowers and splashing fountains in the airy lobby. My first great mission was to get my hair washed of the accumulated salt, sand, sun and sundries. At a delightful candlelight dinner, three strolling violins serenaded me and I'm not yet sure whether or not Eme planned it.

Lima is a rather bland metropolis of 2.5 million people. Few traces remain of the era in which Pizarro made it the seat of Spanish sovereignty, the wealthiest and most famous city of the New World. Today it is a busy city, trying to cope with rampant inflation and heavy pockets of poverty. Subject to earthquakes, Lima is situated in an arid zone that gets scarcely any rain and the environs look like a desert. Fortunately, the nights are cool when the Humboldt Current brings its breeze.

In the main commercial district elegant shops rub elbows with the street vendors backed against their doors. What most bothered me was the little children, their faces turned to the walls as if in utter resignation while their mothers attempted to sell food or trinkets. When grimy little hands stretched up for a handout Eme had to stop me from opening my purse to one of them unless I meant to treat each of the hundreds alike. The terrible entreaty of the eyes haunted me, almost suffocating me. I never saw any parent abuse a child with slaps or kicks but a guide told us that many sick or deformed children are sometimes neglected.

The Museum of Anthropology and Archeology in Lima is rich with samples of pre-Inca textiles, pottery, and tools artistically displayed.

The money exchange in Peru was 170 soles to the U. S. dollar. Gasoline, which was sixteen cents a gallon in Ecuador, was seventy-five cents a gallon in Peru because it must be imported. From the moment of our arrival we heeded the warning: "Watch your pocketbooks and wallets!"

George came for us at nine the next morning and we were on the Pan-American Highway, south of Lima, headed for the Inca ruins of Pachacamac on the Pacific coast. Only two other couples rode with us in the small, comfortable bus. One was an interesting couple from South Africa, the other, from Germany.

Pachacamac, the most renowned and typical of the Inca genius, is close to the city. The blockwork walls and fences remain but they are, a small sample of what was to be seen the next day at Cusco.

We arrived at Cusco at 11:00 a.m. to be met by a Receptour guide and taken to an utterly charming hotel, the Libertador — an old mansion of 160 rooms modernized but with the original Spanish flavor intact. The walls are decorated with handsome tiles. The restaurant overlooks a garden giddy with color. Delphiniums graced the dining tables and vases of gladiola were everywhere. The courtyard with its fountains and Moorish archways is almost a replica of the Alhambra.

In the lobby we were served coca tea, made from the coca leaves from which cocaine is obtained. The slight narcotic helps one adjust to the altitude of this Andean city, well over two miles high. En route we'd had a glimpse of the flowered boulevards, the city sloping down the mountainside, and trees and lakes and the bursting greenness of it all. We could hardly wait to absorb it, but not too soon. We were advised that no matter how wonderful we thought we felt, we must take it easy the first several hours. So we had a short nap and a leisurely lunch before being picked up for sightseeing at 2:00 p.m.

What warmth you feel toward this city almost immediately. It has its own distinctive allure with Spanish grillwork on the windows and red-tiled roofs. Everywhere are terraced gardens, flowering trees, vines and shoots springing from the rocks. Stone steps wind down narrow Inca streets flanked by hewn-stone walls — walkways on raised platforms abutting the walls.

Cusco, once the Inca capital of the greatest empire ever to exist in South America, today is the capital of thirteen provinces, a city of 140,000 people. The mixture of two cultures, the Incas, and their final Iberian conquerors, can be seen in the blending of Moorish-Spanish balconies, sunlit patios, and Inca blocks of stone so exquisitely fit that not a knife blade can be wedged between them. At least three-quarters of this city is built on Inca walls and foundations.

It was summer and the orchids, daisies, iris, glads and mint were in colorful evidence. I picked wild forget-me-nots and have pressed them.

On a steep, winding street behind St. Blas Church, llamas padded leisurely along, bringing their bulging burdens of farm produce down to the market. Beautiful white alpacas, shepherded in the fields by Indian girls, are cherished for their silky fleece. The vicuna, llama, guanaco, and alpaca are all found in this country and all are members of one family.

A guide told us of a recent dig near here where a great quantity of lima beans have been unearthed, all intact with signs and symbols on them. Hope was running high that these might be the long sought "Rosetta Stone" to decode the Inca language.

On Sunday we made an early excursion to the Pisac market. Our guide was an interesting Swiss economist who is a professor of economics at both Lima and Cusco Universities, dividing his time between the two. No more than eight people were to take the bus tours and we often felt we were being personally conducted by the Receptour.

Eucalyptus trees lined the route. It never snows here, we were told, so they are able to plant three crops a year, mainly barley and alfalfa.

Sixty-five percent of the Peruvians are Indians who eke out a living, unable to contribute anything to the economy. The inflation rate is thirty-eight percent. We passed vendors and farmers, thirty miles from the city, walking to the market. In the fields, we saw both oxen-drawn and foot plows.

Pisac huddles in the gorge of the Urubamba River where terraced gardens crease the hillsides. At the market both Indian men and women wear paint-pot costumes and multi-colored hats with bright red broad-brimmed ones predominating. But, in my opinion, the market could not begin to compare with that of the Otavalos in Ecuador. The wares are neither as cleverly nor as cleanly displayed and the market lacks the excitement and overall eye appeal.

For lunch we went to the nearby Rio Grande restaurant, a converted home. We ate a delicious buffet served outside where an old, gnarled Ceibo (flaming tree) graced the yard.

Midway back to Cusco we stopped in the mountains at the Pisac Observatory. Leaving the bus, we made a very steep climb up innumerable rock staircases to the highest peak for a spectacular view from this old Inca fortress, once a royal retreat.

Returning to the hotel we packed our large suitcases to be left during the two days we would be gone to Machu Picchu. Putting nightwear and a clean shirt in our hand luggage we were all set for *manana*. "Must be ready at 6:30 a.m.," our guide advised us. Ready? That was the understatement of the trip.

On a bright clear morning we traveled by narrow-gauge railway, a three-and-a-half-hour ascent to 12,000 feet. Outside Cusco we passed by red-roofed houses with assorted decorations on top: bottles of holy water, painted good-luck pigs, crosses, statues of the virgin, and vases of artificial flowers. Our Japanese-built train made four switchbacks in a zigzag pattern to reach the top before beginning its snaking descent past the snow-topped Andean peaks above and the rock-strewn streams rushing pell-mell into the sacred river of the Incas, the Urubamba, below. The annual rainfall in this area is thirty-six inches and scotch broom, yellow and white daisies, and blue lupin emblazon the route. We chugged along past the tropical forests, primitive villages, and towering slopes.

At the Machu Picchu railway station nine buses with expert drivers carried the train passengers up dizzying, hairpin curves to the sixteen-room Machu Picchu Hotel. Eme and I were pinching ourselves in reassurance of our good fortune. We were to stay overnight and another day, too, instead of the few hours other passengers had before returning. For nine months we'd had our application in for a room, then just one week before leaving, the cablegram arrived telling us we had a reservation!

This plain little hotel has magnificent views from most rooms. Its veranda, where we lunched, overlooks the 2500-foot drop to the river and train station below. And from this height we could look down on the entire circuitous route we'd traveled — the Hiram Bingham Highway.

The highway was named in 1948 to honor the American archaeologist who discovered the mysterious lost city in the clouds on July 24, 1911. What a treat it was knowing we didn't have to rush through our exploration but could savor, through both sunset and sunrise, the contemplation of it all!

When the crowds thinned, we started out on a narrow path leading through a gate near which two alpacas wandered. Then we continued, our guidebook in hand, past a rock outcropping. Spread out before us on the sloping spur of the Andes we caught our first dazzling glimpse of this renowned citadel, this spectacular, inaccessible city built entirely of white granite and set in a hideaway geographical position second to none. No wonder the Spaniards or anyone else could not find it for over 400 years.

Surrounded by a wall sixteen feet high and six feet thick, its many terraces connect by narrow flights of steps cut into the huge rocks. The sentries' observation tower is at the very top of the mountain of Machu Picchu (Old Peak) which rises loftily above nearby Huayna Picchu (New Peak) and where the precipice overhangs the Urubamba Canyon and the city below. The horseshoe-shaped building clings to a perpendicular wall.

This is an awesome sight, not only for its panoramic view but in its marvelous state of preservation, and in its organization and design is revealed the prodigious achievements of the Incas.

It was Dr. Bingham who, in four scientific expeditions for Yale University and the National Geographic Society, diagrammed the city and catalogued its buildings. In the city were homes, houses for caretakers, palaces, temples, granaries, tombs, jails, a cemetery, an industrial district, schools, and observatories, as well as subterranean passages and bridges.

The Incas planted their crops on mountain terraces and worshiped the water and sun as gods. Water was brought great distances by precision-built aqueducts. Roofs are generally made of straw, preserving the authenticity of ancient times, are sharply gabled and built on wooden beams. Clay mortar binds the rock walls. The doors are of special interest with stone devices for locking them. We ran our hands reflectively over the smooth stones and considered the round and square stone pegs in them, the neat niches. The quarries are still open.

This was the flowering season and daisies, poppies, orchids, lantanas and begonias brightened the landscape.

At 5:30, lost in our maze of wandering and wondering, we heard the loud clanging of a bell. Up the steps came the caretaker. "¿Que hay?" I asked in my fractured Spanish.

I had to slow him down to translate his reply to my "What's up?". We had to be out by sundown, he said.

There were only five of us still roaming around. One Britisher confided that he planned to maneuver his way back in that night to view the ruins by the light of a full moon.

"In the variety of its charms and the power of its spell, I know of no place in the world that can compare with it," Dr. Bingham once said.

After dinner at the hotel we tested the crisp air outside and looked up at the full moon and the proliferate stars that seemed nudgingly close. The two alpacas kept us company until we turned in for an early rising the next morning.

The dawning sun first tinges the misty clouds a seashell pink and the light reddens the mountains. We had Machu Picchu almost to ourselves so early in the morning and could amble at will. We crisscrossed the two sectors of the city and clambered its walls. Not until hours later did we hear the distant train whistle and know the buses would soon be unloading scores of sightseers.

Lunching at the hotel, Eme eyed a notice that a helicopter could be hired in Cusco to circle all of Machu Picchu and then return you to Cusco. "Let's do it for the thrill of a lifetime," he suggested.

The hotel summoned the 'copter by radio and it arrived at 3:00 p.m., landing near the rail station. The pilot kept the blades rotating while we climbed aboard.

My adrenalin was racing as we effortlessly soared, dipped, and circled. Whenever Eme wanted a better view for a picture the pilot obligingly recircled. It seemed as if I could reach out and touch the tips of the Andes. Talk about being in the clouds! This was it. Finally we headed for Cusco, gently setting down there twenty-five minutes later. The cloud dust lingers; we'll never forget this highlight.

The following day we stood in a long line at the airport waiting for the plane from Cusco to Lima. No Hollywood mob scene could compare to the violence! We waited at Gate One for ninety minutes because no seats were assigned in advance; seating was on a first come, first served basis. Suddenly Gate Two opened and nonchalantly the gatekeeper announced "Lima!"

The sequence of events that followed was such a hugger-mugger chaos it's hard to piece it all together. Eme said to me, "I'll take the hand luggage plus the big sack (with all the last-minute gifts in it) and you go ahead and get us a seat." Jabbed, grabbed, wedged, tripped, and spun, I was all but suffocated in the crush. A woman's large fishnet totebag broke, spewing its contents in front of us. She knelt to retrieve her belongings and I, being pushed, fell on top of her. Extricating myself and attempting to run at that altitude took some doing but I finally huffed out to Fawcett Flight 901 and puffed up the plane's steps. Frantically I searched for a vacant seat, pushing my way past others also looking for seats and who should I see calmly sitting center stage with two seats "reserved", but Eme. Don't ask how he did it; that's a whole other story.

Arriving back in Lima, we headed for lunch at the Sheraton. In the afternoon a charming guide, Ursula Brinkman, showed us through the cathedral and the remarkable Gold Museum and took us to an industrial outlet factory to see handcrafts being made. At midnight, we left for Miami and connecting flights for home.

Chapter 3

The start of a trip is always a good time to reassess one's expectations. The part of Asia to which we were going — India, in particular — we had back-shelved for many years, beckoned, instead, in other directions. We'd been captivated by trips to India's neighbors — Turkey, Bangkok, and Iran — but hadn't before ventured into the subcontinent.

From the time we were cradled on *The Jungle Stories* and cut our teeth on the "Just So" stories, we'd wandered intermittently through a part of Kipling's India from his birthplace in Bombay to the outer margins of the Himalayas. Too, we'd romanticized the country long ago with Haliburton and Pearl Buck, empathized with Ghandi, exulted with Hillary on Everest and Herzog on Annapurna, and in contemplative moods, been touched by the exquisite writings of the Upanishads. But, frankly, what had always repelled us was the Hindu caste system — especially in its modern, abortive form.

The purpose originally, as proposed in the Hindu religion, was to assure a system that would eliminate economic competition from life and ensure everyone a due place and vocation in society. Neither the Untouchables, as such, nor the current mockery of the system was envisioned. Add to this the travesty of torturous poverty and utter despair, plus the deification of cattle that are allowed top food and billing while the populace starves, and the answer for our dragging feet is given. But it shouldn't be. Not when one considers that there is found the earliest known cultures, the earliest written religions, the mightiest mountains on the face of the globe, the greatest memorial on earth to view, and countless other marvels to encounter. These many years we'd doubtless been coddling stereotypes; now we hoped to defigmentize them. Questers Worldwide Nature Tour helped us make up our minds when it offered a three-week indepth journey through Sri Lanka, formerly known as Ceylon.

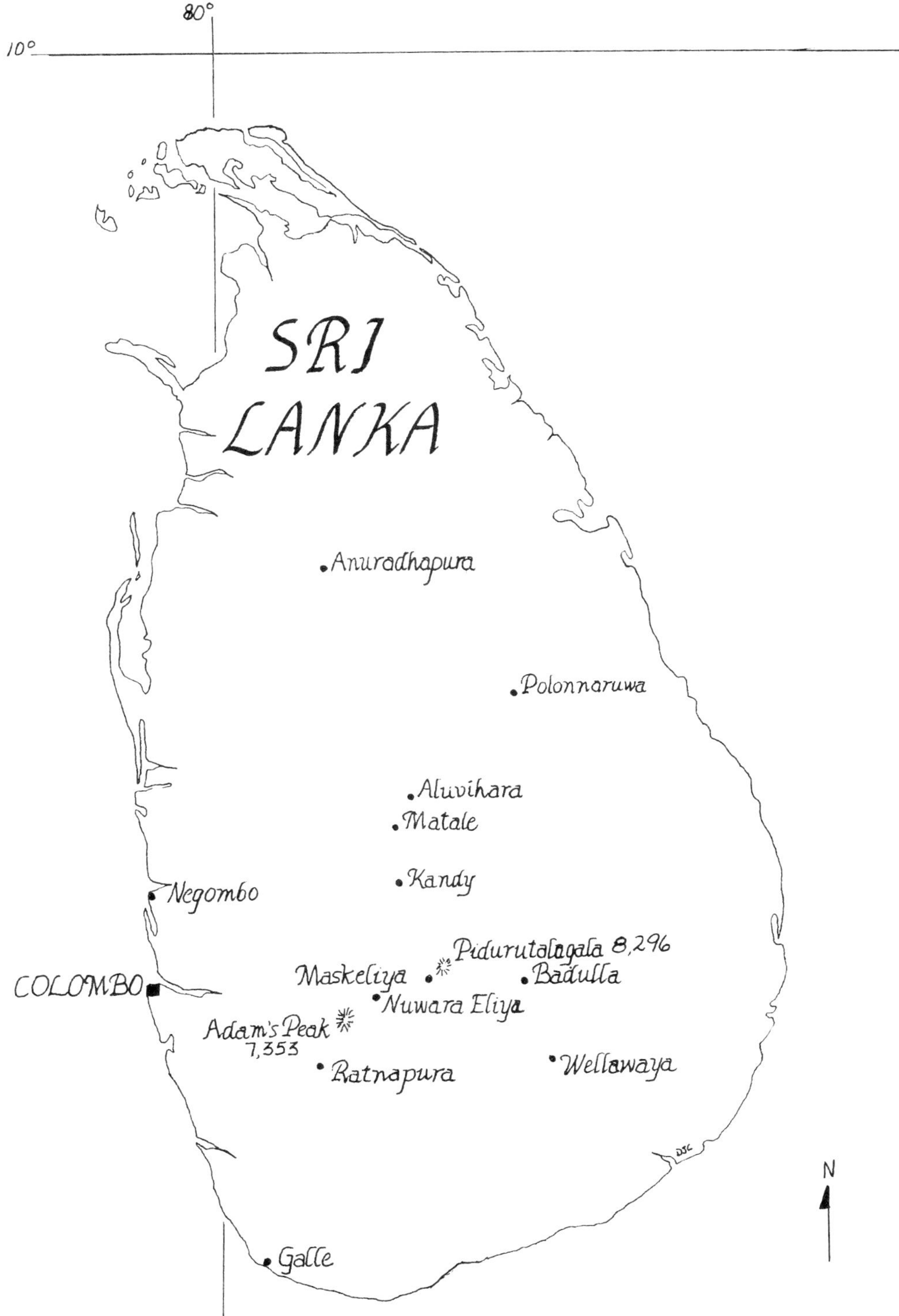
80°
10°
SRI
LANKA
Anuradhapura
Polonnaruwa
Aluvihara
Matale
Kandy
Negombo
Pidurutalagala 8,296
Maskeliya
Badulla
COLOMBO
Nuwara Eliya
Adam's Peak
7,353
Ratnapura
Wellawaya
N
Galle

Leaving Orlando at 1:00 p.m. Thursday, February 21st, on TWA's nonstop flight to New York, we'd been ground flying, literally, in an attempt to get good seats together on it. We'd had plush ones a month in advance only to find out, at the airport, that TWA's computer was on the blink and there would be "Open Seating." The definition of that is: dash like crazy to beat your fellow passengers to the plane steps. Eme, carrying our bulky underseat bags, used me to run interference and to nail down the seats.

TWA had assured us that our baggage would be transferred in New York to British Airways so that, in London, we could check it through to the end of the trip. Our baggage should have been sent straight through to Sri Lanka, we later learned. When, in London, no bags of ours appeared on the carrousel, we stood in our crumpled outfits wondering how long we'd be living in them.

By some phenomenal fancy footwork, British personnel located our two bags just as they were being put on the flight to Calcutta. Since this was nowhere near our destination we'd have done a lot of traveling not smelling like roses.

After this two-and-a-half-hour delay we checked into day rooms at the nearby Excelsior Hotel to freshen up and wait for the two missing members of our tour groups — a doctor and his wife from California who were due at 2:00 p.m. to join us in London.

Hot showers and four hours sleep completely revived us. All eight tour members were to meet at 5:00 p.m. and leave at 7:00p.m. on British Airways Flight 33 to Sri Lanka.

En route we stopped at Dubai where deplaning passengers were alerted over the loudspeaker to take their malaria pills and a ground search was made of the plane. After a royal Elizabethan dinner on board, we cruised in darkness and passing over Saudi Arabia and Kuwait, could see the gas flame of myriad oil wells far below.

Photography is not allowed at Indian airports and later we understood why. The final approach to Bombay, for example, is made through a mess of moldering houses and piles of undeodorized garbage! Then, facing a layover of several hours, we were instantly and completely surrounded by the pull of woebegone eyes and the pressure of hands "palms outward".

Our tour director, Frank Oatman Jr. of Craftsbury, Vermont, boarded in Bombay. Two tour members had been with him on other Questers trips. Our group included Jean and Harold Jones of Murphysburg, Pennsylvania; Dr. Harry Ryan and his wife, Jane, from Altadena, California; a widow, Isabelle Barbee, from Jacksonville, Florida; a single woman, Helen Stewart, from Pawling, New York; and

Eme and me. To distinguish the two Helens I was called Ellie on the trip.

Before the tour ended, Jean Jones turned out to be Frank's most apt pupil in cataloguing the flora and fauna of the island. Harry Ryan, Eme and I learned, got both his undergraduate and medical degrees from the University of Illinois, so we exchanged many campus reminiscences with him along the way. Isabelle was game for almost anything, and Helen was our constant source of laughter. A woman fiftyish, almost everything she said in her rather high-pitched voice seemed funny. The brunt of incessant kidding and jokes, she never lost her good humor or sportsmanship.

Shortly after takeoff from Bombay, Isabelle brought Frank to the back of the 747, where Eme and I were sitting, to introduce us. When he'd returned to the front, a young British Airways secretary sitting beside us summed up Frank in just one word: "Wow!" she exclaimed, rolling her eyes.

A cleancut six-footer, fresh-looking in a short-sleeved safari suit, he had honey-colored hair, a healthy tan, velvet brown eyes and an infectious smile. We liked him instantly.

He was the tour's Staff Naturalist and had an impressive background: a BS degree, cum laude in zoology, Phi Beta Kappa, a master's degree in English, and a soon-to-be-awarded MS in ornithology. Speaking three languages fluently, he spent four years in Europe conducting natural history tours. In the U.S. he had been an editor and author and conducted a Naturalist and Conservancy series on educational TV. A story teller with a flair for drama, his depiction of characters was hilarious. More recently, he had been teaching literature and creative writing at Goddard College. His home in Vermont was a farmhouse he was restoring in stages. His vitality and enthusiasm, throughout the entire three weeks in Sri Lanka, never diminished.

Arriving in Columbo, the capital of Sri Lanka, we were driven to the Blue Lagoon Hotel in Negombo. At dinner, Frank introduced Teka, a native guide, who would be with us during our stay in his country.

Teka's full name was Teekshana Wijesinghe. A personable and knowledgeable young man, he had previously worked with the entomological survey group for the Smithsonian on several projects. He went out of his way to be helpful, intent on seeing that we thoroughly enjoyed and appreciated his native land.

After breakfast we began our rolling travels in an almost-new tourist coach with Narida, our expert driver, and Perez, our gracious handy boy whose duties included guarding the bus while we went exploring. Starting at the south of the island we were to work our way north up the west coast and return down the east and central sections to our starting point.

We headed first to Kala Oya. En route, Teka told us there are 13,400,000 Sri Lankans who speak Sinhalese but learn English in school as a compulsory second language. Along the way we were seeing the madra de cocoa trees with bright pink blossoms and the copperpod trees with yellow blooms. Frangipani perfumes the countryside. It's called the temple flower because the Buddhists use it as their floral offering at their many shrines. Hibiscus is everywhere! The island is blessed with bright red soil that grows almost anything and yields two and three crops a year.

We spotted many birds as we traveled, such as the black-winged kite, the pheasant-tailed jacana, and the red-wattled lapwing.

Friendliness lighted the faces we saw; everyone was smiling; men, women and children waved. Frank told us the "peoplescape" here was one of the most fascinating anywhere. Marco Polo thought this the fairest island in the world. Its name means "the resplendent one" and was adopted officially in 1972, replacing Ceylon, which the British and Portuguese had called it. Its recorded history dates back 2,500 years and many original monuments are still in evidence. Early commercial trade was in elephants and minted coins. Some 10,000 artificial lakes already existed. Later, when conquest fever was high, Europeans sailed here because of its strategic position in the Indian Ocean, and some stayed: the Portuguese first, next the Dutch, and then the English — each for well over a century.

Three-fourths of the easygoing population are Sinhalese and Buddhist. The largest minority group are the Tamils who come from southern India, speak their own language and are Hindu. The literacy rate, eighty-six percent, is among the highest in Asia, yet about one-fifth of the people are unemployed.

The Buddhist doctrine of peace, tolerance, and compassion is much in evidence, and there is complete religious freedom.

"Dear me, it is beautiful, and most sumptuously tropical," Mark Twain said of this island, but Arthur C. Clarke went further, saying: "And always it is the same: the slender palm trees leaning over the white sand, the warm sun sparkling on the waves as they break on the inshore reef . . . This alone is real; the rest is but a dream from which I shall presently awake." And he should know; he stopped here twenty years ago but couldn't break away. He has stayed on in Columbo to write more than fifty science-fiction and nonfiction books.

In the rural districts men wrap themselves in colorful sarongs, and women, in two types of vivid saris; the fancier one, known as the Kandy type, runs a slanted ruffle around the rear.

Shadows fingered the trees in cool coconut plantations, but rice paddies were suffering from the dry season. We stopped long enough for the excitement of binocular-tabbing some whiskered terns, blackwinged stilts and the pond heron's flash of white. A Moslem minaretted mosque loomed on the horizon and the silhouette of Kelaniya Temple enhanced the skyline.

More and more huge coconut plantations came into view and Teka gave us some statistics: A coconut tree takes five years to bear; well-cared for ones produce every two months. From the tree comes the fiber for ropes, brushes, mats and car seats, thatching for ceilings and roofs, filling in mattresses, and the stuff of many drinks. Toddy, the native drink we sampled, is made from the milky liquid tapped from the flowers of the coconut palm. This is also distilled into arrack, a brandy-like liquor that contains, it is said, pure fire, and can light up more than you bargained for.

The fig trees and sacred Bo trees spread broad-brimmed shade. The golden rain trees grace the countryside along with the thorny black bark of the Indian coral tree. Chicken houses are strung high in the trees to escape poisonous ground snakes. Of the eighty-seven kinds of snakes in Sri Lanka — including the sea snakes — nine are poisonous. Most deadly is the cobra, but it is sacred and people don't kill it.

The free family-planning clinics are supposedly a success. Either that's too much to believe or it's too new a project to show results yet because there are youngsters by the zillions in school uniforms and swarms of tinier ones tagging their elders. I can still hear laughter and see their eager, shining faces as, hands out, they caught up with some of us heading for the bus. At times they chased behind for at least a half-mile.

What pictures we focused in our glasses: an Indian roller on a telephone pole, turquoise of wing and red at the base of his blue-capped head, and beneath him, a white-breasted kingfisher. The yellow heart-shaped leaves of the tree-hibiscus turn red and when the lagoon goes out to sea, the lotus flowers and tamarisk trees are in bloom.

Both the old and the young men and women are slender. The life expectancy is seventy despite widespread malnutrition.

We saw a native teenager wearing a T-shirt that said: "Swing south to Alabama" and knew another American had passed this way. Surprisingly, we met only one American here. The bulk of the tourists seemed to be Germans, French, and Danish.

The teak plantations have a soft, feathery look. On one tree we tabbed a jacana with a great long yellow tail outlined in red, an Indian shag and several cormorants that look like snakebirds. Macaque monkeys ran wild and we watched a star tortoise in transit on the road.

After an early breakfast at the Wilpattu Hotel followed by an early field trip around the environs, we left for Wilpattu National Park, transferring at the park entrance from our coach to a jeep. White-breasted water hens and pintailed snipes followed us. The crescent serpent-eagle skimmed overhead. On top of rice stacks, piled like hay, ten or twelve parakeets were vying for food. School girls in white uniforms and wearing red ribbons in their hair were on an outing.

"Hari-hari," Teka told us, means "Go ahead." After a stop for picture taking or "glass viewing" we would climb back into the bus and it was "hari-hari" again.

Dense forests, soft green terrain, and blue fresh-water lakes form the park. Teka predicted, and Frank agreed, that we could see a leopard. We didn't, but we did see the Ceylon jungle fowl — which is only found there — fishing eagles, a herd of huge elephants swishing through the jungle-like interior, water buffalo immersed in a lake, spotted deer and sambhurs.

Two trees were filled with painted storks and winging past was a green bee-eater, a pied-crested cuckoo. We saw land-monitor lizards by the dozen and crocodiles slithering into the water. Two jackals combed the bushes near the ebony and cumbuck trees — the latter found only in Sri Lanka.

It's not often you are magically cloaked in pure white butterflies; we were as our jeep suddenly plunged into thousands of fluttering wings swirling in the air like snowflakes. Not once but several times this happened. One gorgeous Morwan butterfly floated right into the jeep with us. Since a butterfly walks on its feet, grasps and tastes with them as well, I wondered what of consequence he found among us.

Helen had answers to most important things. When we couldn't see beyond a tree to a special bird we wanted to catch in our binoculars, she helpfully suggested, "Just cut down the tree!"

Coming upon a sun-dew, a small bog plant, orange-green in color, is a unique experience. Frank explained its cunning ways. With sticky hairs it snares insects into its open frilly frond and silently salts them away.

A great day this was, and back at the park bungalows where we spent the night, the fresh fish dinner was surely the icing on the cake! Eme and I didn't drop the mosquito netting hanging from the ceiling over our beds because the paddle fan dispatched the insects.

In the morning we enjoyed an open-air breakfast to the trumpet of bird song and remonstrance of monkeys. Then it was off to Anuradhapura for our first sight of oxen working in the fields.

Sri Lanka's jungle and treasure-topped city of antiquity dating back to 437 B.C. is Anuradhapura. Its towering shrines, some as high as the pyramids, are visited by innumerable pilgrims. The brick dagobas house relics of the Buddha in sealed-off, bell-shaped structures. Monks once thronged the city to take their daily portions of rice from stone troughs, some of which still exist. Buddhism first came to Sri Lanka in this city and now the saffron robes of monks and the Buddhist roadsigns are a part of its daily life.

An overpowering thrill for me was contemplating under the sacred Bo tree. This grew from a branch brought to Anuradhapura in the third century B.C. from northern India and is the same one under which Buddha found enlightenment in Buddhaganya, India. Awe-inspiring, it is the oldest documented tree in the world.

At Nuwarawewa we ate a delectable curry and wine lunch at outdoor tables. The "popadons" they served were big and crackly, similar in taste but not size to our potato chips. The monotony of curry and rice and all the attendant side dishes for both lunch and dinner was a little much. It was a neat panoply of food, but usually far too hot for our taste.

Tootling along the road again we were entranced by the scarecrows in the rice fields to ward off the evil eye. Many are highly imaginative.

In the mountainous country of the north were lots of cattle. Some herders wear the G-string as total garb!

A man is allowed fifty acres of land free and his descendants can buy another fifty at a later time, Teka told us. To qualify for a government house, one must be poor and it helps if "you know somebody", he added. It is possible, he said, to rent a home first and buy it later.

In Polonnarawa the man-made lakes called "tanks" were dug by the powerful Sinhalese kings. It was Parkrama Bahu the Great who, in the twelfth century, fortified the city of Polonnarawa, built the royal palace and pleasure gardens, and ordered the carving of the forty-four-foot reclining Buddha. With his arm under his head and pillow under his arm he seems stretched out in the sunlight of pure nirvana. We also viewed nearby, a standing Buddha and a seated one meditating.

At the hotel that night we ate wild boar for dinner. It tasted like pork, as of course it would, but, thanks to expert preparation, the gamey taste was eliminated.

On the route to Sigiriya we saw both the lacewing and the common butterfly flutter by our open windows and the common Immigrant butterfly that commutes back and forth to India. All along this road was stacked firewood to be used for cooking meals, in the open, by people making religious pilgrimages. Canned sardines have it roomier than the people we saw pressed into some of the big buses on their way to work or to festivals. There looked to be as many clinging to the outside as there were inside.

The government has planted eucalyptus trees and the fragrance of these mingled with the frangipani is heady.

In the center of the great central forest is the fortress of Sighariya. In the fifth century King Kasyapa built the city but due to violent quarrels with his brother, it was inhabited for only eighteen years. On the walls of the approach to the king's palace are some beautifully preserved rock paintings. Eme did some great camera work on these sensuous Sinhalese masterpieces. Only twenty-one of the 500 original frescoes are intact and the colors in them are extraordinary.

Twelve miles from Sighariya is Dambulla, a temple built of mountain rock. Each of its five cave temples we entered contained an enormous reclining Buddha as well as dozens of seated and standing Buddhas around the walls. The somewhat crumbing ceilings are covered with murals.

It was a glorious drive to Kandy, past oleander and frangipani that brighten the landscape, past rubber and coconut plantations, past teak forests that require fifty to eighty years to mature, past the hum of the working lumber mills and past the egrets wheeling around the mountains and flitting in the shadows.

We stopped at the Spice Gardens where pungent herbs of all sorts are grown. Black pepper vines wound around a huge kapok tree and dry coconut husks mulched the bases of shrubs and bushes. We drank a complimentary iced tea, savoring its delicate flavor, and drove on.

We looked out on green terraced rice paddies, and tea plantations stretched for miles ahead until we arrived at Kandy and the Queen's Hotel where we would stay the night.

Houses lined the hillside surrounding this picturesque city on the banks of a beautiful, artificial lake.

Against a wooded slope stands the famous Temple of the Tooth. Legend has it that about 1500 years ago, Buddha's tooth was hidden in an Indian princess's hair and smuggled out of India. Long the object of theft, the tooth changed hands many times but now lies secure on a lotus flower of solid gold inside a citadel within the temple. Seven jeweled gold caskets contain it but only the outer casket is visible. The caskets are protected by bullet-proof glass, a gift from Japan. Sri Lankans flock here by the thousands to venerate the symbol that can't be seen — only believed.

We visited the Royal Botanical Gardens, famed for their giant bamboo trees and shaded avenue of palms. In the afternoon we made a field trip to the Udawattakalle Rain Forest that lies above Kandy Lake. In Kandy, we browsed through the stores to buy batiks and, in the evening, watched the gyrations of the Kandian dancers to the accompaniment of many drums.

As we drove out of the city the next morning, some of Kandy's working elephants plodded along the road transporting branches and logs. The two-lane road throbbed with conglomerate bustle and our driver was a genius in avoiding the cattle, skittering monkeys, bullock carts, bicycles, motorcycles, speeding cars, wedding parties or funeral corteges on foot, waving school children, and parasol-sheltered strollers. I loved the vivid rainbow-hued parasols of Sri Lanka and took pictures of bridesmaids in their confetti-colored saris. But each time we stopped for pictures, road vendors and scores of children gathered around the bus and it took a lot of puffing to get back inside.

Harold Jones recommended jokingly that all drivers here be given a course in horn-blowing before applying for their driving licenses. Nothing seemed to miss our bus by more than a split whisker.

On we went, past breadfruit, papaya, mangrove and avocado trees while above them we could see the houses perched like eagles' nests in the mountains.

Melfort and Rothchild are names reminiscent of Britain's domination of the tea industry here and these names still label the large tea estates. In the fields, we watched the women picking tea. Using large oval baskets, worn like backpacks, they lean down to pick from each tea bush only the two newest leaves and adjacent bud, and throw these over their shoulders into the baskets. Tea plants produce from forty to fifty years and the white flowers of the bush belong to the camellia family. Govillia, the lacy oak, is used to shelter the growing plants.

The Tamil people were brought from southern India to help pick Sri Lanka's tea.

At the Melfort tea factory we filmed 105-year-old living roots of the bushes, then went through the factory to have the whole process shown and explained, to drink some tea and be told how to brew it. Begin with a hot pot, said the experts, but never one with moisture in it. Of the nine grades of tea Melfort blends, the lowest grade is exported to the U.S. — to be used in tea bags!

Waterfalls could be seen spurting in light cascades as we started up hairpin curves, to climb to an altitude of 5,200 feet. Huge blue morning glories hugged the road together with amaryllis, wild calla lilies and Gerber daisies. Every few miles another tea factory cropped up. Vegetable gardens and cabbage fields were profuse. All the old-fashioned flowers were here: nasturtiums, pansies, snapdragons, roses, rhododendron and purple sage. We spotted the scimitar babbler and the Ceylon blue magpie. Of the 400 species of birds on this island, we identified 172 of them. I use the term "we" very loosely; my compatriots and leaders did!

This was the day I believed I'd made history by sighting an absolutely new bird for Sri Lanka. Cautiously I called out and Frank came to study it through field glasses. Teka studied it, but neither could supply its name. It flew and Frank ran through the woods after it, recording all its markings. Tabbing it together, Frank and Teka agreed they hadn't seen its variety before. They gave me a pat on the back and said they'd have to research it. They did, and my elation was deflated. What I had discovered was a warbler that by some mischance had lost its tail.

You can feel the pulse of colonial Britain at the Hill Club where we checked in for a two-night stay. The Victorian atmosphere prevails. An open wood fireplace glows in the dining room; another in the library. Stag heads are mounted on walls. Books are sheathed in glass cases. Our elegant multicourse dinner, served by candlelight only, was brought by waiters in starched white uniforms, wearing white gloves, padding silently on bare feet.

Toting packed lunches we drove, next day, to Horton Plains by jeep, a distance of forty-six miles. This is Sri Lanka's highest plateau — 7,000 feet in the air. The drive was rough but rewarding. We saw the purple-faced monkeys and added new birds to our list. We hiked five miles through intricate forest trails to a roadside sign: "World's End". Standing on the very edge of the plateau, we stared in wonder at the incredibly beautiful valley spread out below as far as the distant sea.

Leaving the hill country after an early morning bird walk and breakfast, we began our descent to the coast, stopping at the half-way mark at Ella, wedged between the high ridges, for a superb view of the low country. Magenta bougainvillea emblazoned the wayside, among candle bush, cashia, and scarlet tulip trees.

Helen answered a tough geology question that Frank posed and no one else could answer. After being applauded, she was prepared to elucidate until Frank stopped her, saying, "Now, Helen, retain image by keeping mouth shut."

At Ella we ate lunch in a flower-strewn pastoral spot facing the mountains, terraced rice paddies and woods, then took pictures through Ella's Gap, a tiny opening that frames the scene. From a grubby small and smiling boy, Eme and I bought some mica and quartz for Cynthia's rock collection, as other children streamed down the road on their way home from school, lugging their books. Through the valley roamed the water buffalo and the wind blew the butterflies past the tulip trees.

Another special jeep tour took us through Rhunu National Park with a stop to pick up park guides. We were not allowed out of the jeeps to wander in this jungle. In the distance we heard the loud trumpeting of Ceylon elephants, then watched them stampede toward the lagoon, riddling a few trees en route, and encircling a baby elephant protectively.

This seemed to be the day we'd been waiting for. There was so much to focus on: wild boar, spotted deer, scads of bright-winged water and land birds, purple-faced monkeys, sambhurs, monitor lizards and two kinds of mongoose — the gray and the rufous. Finally surfeited with pleasurable pictures and sensations, we were ready to return to the hotel when, at dusk and right before our eyes, slinking out of the bushes was what we had given up hope of seeing: a leopard! His spots were darker than I'd pictured them. Warily, he took his time and the measure of the terrain as he crossed the road, giving all cameras on-the-ready a shot of him. Eme got a beauty before the leopard disappeared into the dense undergrowth.

That night a mongoose visited Frank and Teka's room, racing under the beds before they could invite it to leave.

Next morning, with packed lunches in hand, we were off to Kalametiye and Tangalla in magnolia-scented air. We stopped to watch outrigger fishing boats and paused by a tree where fruit bats with faces like foxes hung upside down. Rice stalks were stacked in bundles along the road, awaiting delivery to the rice paper factory. We stopped for sweetmeats made of molasses and coconut (Frank's treat), and beside the ocean for a swim and to watch the men picking coconuts. With ankles hobbled they frog-stretched up the enormous trees, first clearing out the fronds, then dropping the coconuts.

En route again, we took time to inspect the slender rubber trees being tapped for the milky white liquid.

Reaching Dondra we were at Sri Lanka's southernmost point. We lunched at the Coral Gardens Hotel and took a glass-bottom boat excursion over the coral formations.

In Bentota, where we spent the night, we swam both in the fresh water pool and the Indian Ocean and lolled on the sandy beach.

The next day at Matura, a sizeable city, we visited a monastery to view the country's largest Buddha and to watch the stilt fishing.

The gasoline we stopped to get sold for almost $2.00 a gallon. It was here that Helen, who of necessity was haunting restrooms, announced, "If you don't know where I am, you'll know where I am."

Much of the southern coast is rocky and some of the ports are treacherous, as is Galle, the Sinhalese word for rock. This old city with its grass-covered wall retains its Portuguese-Dutch influence. The

70°
80°
90°
30°
20°
10°
NEPAL
Delhi
NEW DELHI
Mount Everest
29,028
Kathmandu
Agra
Darjeeling
INDIA
Calcutta
Bombay
N
Madras

Portuguese landed here in 1505; the Dutch in 1658. Their dominance was about equal for 140 years until the British took over in 1796.

At Ratanapura, a major center for mining sapphires, rubies, moonstones, and garnets, we visited the gravel pits to observe the gems being dug up and panned like gold before being cut and polished. In the Gem Museum, our eyes were boggled with the dazzling collection. Eme and I succumbed to a ruby with an exquisite clear-cut sparkle.

That night we said good-by to our group and our able leaders. Eme and I were leaving early next day for Colombo where we would have to buy new luggage. Our bags had all but disintegrated in the airline shuffle. I hated to bid farewell to my easy-to-pack-and-handle case of long years' standing, but with its bottom ready to fall out there was no alternative. Also, Eme's light meter in his Leica had defaulted and he'd depended on shutterbugs in our group for light readings. Without their help, he needed a new meter for the rest of our journey.

Colombo is a relic of colonial days, an interesting port on the Indian Ocean, said to be the cheapest place in the world to live. It was here we left this island of "serendipity", a word coined by the English author, Horace Walpole, in gratitude to Sri Lanka's unexcelled delights.

Our extended independent tour began with an Indian Airlines flight to Madras and Delhi at 3:40 p.m. At the Madras Airport we were met by a travel representative who assisted us through customs and immigration before making our connection for Delhi. Before this trip ended we would have inwardly blessed this travel service many times for its courteous, prompt and efficient service. Leaving Madras at 7:00 p.m., we arrived in Delhi at 10:30 where we were met and taken to the almost new Taj Mahal Hotel, an absolutely glamorous place where glowing jewel tones are juxtaposed with pristine white marble. In the lobby is a unique shop — the first to feature a complete selection of India's arts and crafts — a shop in which one can buy anything from a Kashmir carpet to a potted plant.

In the morning we left for Agra in a private car with Mr. Sing, our driver for the next three days. Extremely tall, Mr. Sing wore a crisp white tunic and knife-creased trousers. A Sikh originally from East Punjab, his native language was Punjabi. Unlike the other seven religious groups, of which the Hindus constitute ninety-four percent, Sikhs do not speak the language of the regions they inhabit, he told us.

From New Delhi we traveled a four-lane highway with a boulevard and bicycle path in the center. As on every other road we encountered in India, the idea of driving was to accelerate freely, blow the horn without let-up, miss everything by an "almost" and pray. Pedaled and pulled rickshaws weave in and out of the tooting traffic and gasoline and diesel fumes are in the air, but the condition of the road is excellent.

The houses along the way looked smaller than some dog kennels and not so modern as stables.

Mr. Sing left us at the Moghul Sheraton in Agra at lunchtime to return for us in the early afternoon. The hotel is built like a brick fortress outside and a palace inside, but what captured my fancy was the big crystal chandelier in the lobby, shaped like a twinkling bell.

A short ride, and, at long last we had come to the Taj Mahal! At the entrance gate under the towering arch ornamented with mosaics and inlaid with inscriptions from the Koran, we stepped out of the car for our first broad view of the Taj. Its pure white marble shimmers in the setting of a spacious garden of dark cypress trees, green turf, and reflecting waters. We stared without moving.

Only later did we admit to each other our disturbing thoughts prior to going there. So many marvels of the past have been overrated, overstated, or suffered from the incursions of time. The Taj Mahal is a living exception.

The Taj was built by Shah Jahan, grandson of Akbar the Great who ruled India from 1627 to 1658. His favorite wife was Mum-taz Mahal who died suddenly while pregnant and accompanying him, as she always did, on a long journey.

"It is not that I am lonely for you . . . I am mutilated, for you were a part of me." These words were not said by the shah but he might well have borrowed them from the author, the poet Robinson Jeffers, who wrote them while mourning the loss of his wife.

To make Mum-taz Mahal's name unforgettable and erect a fitting tribute to his beloved, the shah consulted with hundreds of famous architects. "It must bespeak my love," he told them. "It must transcend all the barriers of caste, creed and religion."

Possibly no building in the world is more often photographed, drawn or described, yet it's impossible to impart to those who haven't seen it, its dreamlike aura, its utter delicacy, and complexity of design.

Why I try to describe it, I don't know, but the details both outside and inside are so much greater than I realized, I shall put down a few of my impressions. We first saw it in afternoon by full sun, then by a quarter moon at night (would that it could have been a full moon), and then came at dawn to record it on film and heart and eye. At the first break of light the birds were singing and winging but few people were stirring.

Some 20,000 Hindu architects and artisans labored twenty-two years to erect, in the Persian style, this building of such wondrous beauty. Constructed entirely of white marble and set on a white marble terrace, the eight-sided building soars almost 200 feet, topped by a huge towering dome.

On two sides are two slender minarets, four in all, slanting eight inches outward so that in the event of a hurricane or an earthquake, they will fall away from the tomb rather than onto it. At the back of the building some jutting prongs remain in place from the time when the British camouflaged the entire structure for fear of air raids during the last war.

Boys waited to cover our shoes in sock-booties before we went inside. There, under the great dome, are cenotaphs of Shah Jehan and his empress. Of white marble, they are studded with jeweled flowers and Koran script. The sunlight filters through marble trellises as delicate as lace. The interior walls are dextrously inlaid in Persian floral designs of onyx, jasper and other semi-precious stones. Quotations from the Koran are ornately carved in Arabic calligraphy. The actual tombs rest side by side in a room underneath the cenotaphs.

So keen are the acoustics under the dome that when a guard called out, the echo lasted fourteen seconds.

Outside crowds thronged the four wide walkways flanking the gardens and pool, but it didn't seem crowded. All were in their gala best dress and spoke with modulated voices. One million foreigners and four million natives visit the Taj Mahal each year, our guide told us.

Bayard Taylor said, "If there was nothing else in India, this alone would repay the journey." That, for our money, is surely true.

As an example of India's screaming contrasts: On the close outskirts of the matchless beauty of the Taj, it's necessary to wade through the degradation of humanity in a quagmire of filth, misery, and despair.

Immaculate in fresh tunic and headgear, Mr. Sing greeted us the second morning for our trip to Fatehpur Sikri. But first, Eme and I took a short jog on a camel that had been tethered outside the hotel.

In the car we took in the passing scene: Eagles, ravens and kingfishers were vying for airspace with minah birds and bright green parrots; uniformed children wended their way to school and women balanced ewers of water on their heads. The women were returning from the River Jamuna, preparing to mix the sacred dried cattle dung and smooth it into uniform round cakes to be sundried for fuel. Five kilos of dung sell for one rupee, about eight cents. We passed by innumerable gypsy huts, ramshackle in appearance, putrid in stench and buzzing with insects. Of the 750,000 inhabitants of Agra, a small percentage are gypsies and they are the ones who charm the snakes, lead the monkeys, and train bears to stand and dance.

Fatehpur Sikri is twenty-three miles from the Taj Mahal. Akbar the Great planned it to be the capital of the Mogul empire and built it in gratitude for the birth of his only son. He adorned it with magnificent palaces, temples and courtyards and a great mosque stretching over a two-mile area. Abandoned for lack of water, the city is now empty except for caretakers and archaeologists' bungalows.

At 9:00 the following morning Mr. Sing had us at the airport for our flight to Varanasi and Katmandu in Nepal. Outside the airport entrance we were stopped at the gate to clear Arab security and given a metal tab to be presented inside. The stewardesses, waiting to see us on board our India Airlines flight, nodded and smiled, extending their hands up, palms together, in the Hindu attitude of supplication.

As we winged over the drought-stricken landscape we recalled reading in the *Hindustanti Times* that one-third of the globe is being ravaged by drought.

Jagged crests of mountains passed beneath us, the Nepalese villages clinging to the steep slopes amid stairways carpeted pale green with rice plants, and pink or red huts scattered like random polka dots. The great peaks of the Himalayas with their mighty masses of rock and snow are the steadfast sentinels of the country.

As our plane approached the flat expanse of the Valley of Katmandu, I could see the box-type houses with their tiled roofs.

Our guide during our stay was Indira Rizal who had a university degree in economics but with no job in her field available, had taken one as director of the English-speaking tourists for Yeti Travels. Her paisley and muted-color silken saris were so elegant that I cringed as these long swishing skirts swept the dust, narrowly missing the excrement-laden pavements.

Katmandu and three smaller cities in the valley comprise a population of one million. This is the capital of the landlocked country of Nepal which is about the size of Florida, and its extreme temperatures range from sub-zero to tropical. Until 1951 it was a forbidden kingdom. Only a handful of outsiders were permitted to enter because feudal rulers kept Nepal as their private domain and no contact was allowed with the outside world. After the British left India in 1947, Nepalese exiles conducted a coup to restore power to the king, ending Nepal's long isolation. Adjustment to the jet age continues and other countries have offered the nation much technical and financial help to bridge the gap.

Though made up of many races, tribes and languages, the country is predominately Hindu. Yet all are Nepalese and revere and respect their present ruler, King Bierendra, Indira told us. Cultural and religious discrimination are now unknown and even the caste system brought here from India has mellowed, blending in with the tolerant traditions of

Buddhism.

For over 2,000 years the Newars have spread their art in this valley from the humblest peasant cottages to the gilt-roofed and copper-towered pagodas and steepled shrines. Houses and temples have delicate decorations of gods, animals, or imaginative beings carved in dark wood often above pink bricks. Doorknobs, locks, shutters and windows are equally adorned. Thousands of stone Buddhas, Hindu gods, and shrines line bridges, roads and bypaths. Architects have meticulously designed the structures and goldsmiths have richly embellished the pagodas. The Newars, descendants of the first settlers in the valley, originally lived in Lhasa and the cities of ancient China and India.

Katmandu is situated at an altitude of 4,400 feet. It has new buildings and hotels such as the Soaltee Oberoi where we stayed, but most of the city is traversed by narrow lanes and alleys crowded with pagodas, temples, idols, monuments, stupas or Buddhist shrines, and people. The heart of the city is Durbar Square where you catch the whole flavor of the place in its vegetable markets, outdoor barber shops, Hindu religious ceremonies with gongs and cymbals, holy men, and people carrying loads of firewood and pottery. Hindu women in their splendid saris, with the red Tika mark on their foreheads, mingle with Tibetans in fur caps and high boots. Pedicycles go everywhere and sacred cows have the right-of-way at all times. The exotic smell of curries at open-air restaurants mingles with the fetid fumes of burning dung.

Patan, three miles from Katmandu, is considered the artistic capital of Nepal. Its history goes back 2,000 years. A virtual museum of artistry, it is also known for its phallic and erotic carvings that appear on Hindu pagodas and shrines. Indira explained that these symbols represent potency and the creative aspect of God.

Children in the street play chess. Bazaars are numerous. The public bathhouses are thronged, and the temples are used not just for worship but the many aspects of daily life. American hippies are not as much in evidence as they once were, Indira mentioned. Wandering minstrels play and tiny beggars badger. A real salesman, about seven years old, through persistence and bargaining from thirty rupees down to two, managed to sell Eme a tiny brass medal.

Brahmans, the priestly and supposedly learned caste, wear a halo of sanctity regardless of their personal characters. The men have the title of maharaj or prince; the women have diva or goddess preceding their names, and both enjoy the cast supremacy in this social and religious system. But the domination of the Brahmans, who claim to be the

Puppet dolls of Nepal.

Entrance to a dagoba in Patan, Nepal.

Above the entrance to a building in Patan, Nepal.

Children playing chess on a street in Patan, Nepal.

Taj Mahal, Agra, India. Taken at dawn.

Seldom pictured interior of the Taj Mahal — enclosure of cenotaph.

Dagoba, Sigiriya, Sri Lanka.

Sinhalese trescoes on walls of fortress of Sigiriya, (built in 5th century), Sri Lanka.

Dagoba, Anuadhapura, Sri Lanka.

Figure on a Hindu Shrine, Katmandu, Nepal.

Buddhist Temple in Nepal.

Buddhist Shrine, Bhatgoan, Nepal.

Mount Everest.

Band playing for wedding, Katmandu, Nepal.

Wedding at Kandy, Sri Lanka.

Govilla, the lacy oaks used to shelter tea leaves — Sri Lanka.

Buddhist prayer flags in Sigiriya, Sri Lanka.

Coconut plantation near Columbo, Sri Lanka.

Pole fishing on Indian Ocean at Matura, Sri Lanka.

intermediaries between God and man, is being challenged.

The caste system purportedly guards morality and acts as the trade union for a common occupation. It is said to be sanctioned by scripture. Reformers can't break its shackles but the stigma of the Untouchables was, through the efforts of the late Indira Ghandi, outlawed by the state. Caste concepts permeate all of Indian society: Hindu, Muslim, Christian and Sikh.

"Today the vast majority of Hindus believe in a variety of gods and goddesses - human, animal, floral, and phenomenal," wrote Khushwant Singh, author and editor of one Indian newspaper.

Pilgrimages and holy-river bathing are essential to devout Hindus. With reverence for the Brahmans on the decline, the religious teacher and yoga are much in vogue. Horoscopy and astrology are still ultra-important. There are many religious ceremonies and thousands of festivals for the devout to observe.

Hinduism has no clear definition; it has no prophet or messiah and no one sacred book, such as the Bible, the Torah, or Koran. Remarkably, 3,000 years ago it speculated about a creator, birth and death in Rig Veda and Upanishads. The Upanishads, almost 200 in number, are like Platonic dialogues between teacher and pupil and exhort adherents to search for Reality. They and the Vedas are believed by Hindus to have been revealed by God. The Bhagavad-Gita, a religious epic poem with hundreds of verses, was written around 500 B.C. The God-philosopher in it is Krishna, the most popular character of Indian literature, the supreme God influencing literature, music and painting. Krishna gives the essentials of yoga (meditation). Bhagavad-Gita's emphasis is on renunciation, especially of rewards, but despite its lofty ethics it relegates the Untouchables to a status outside the pale of human society.

After independence in India, terrible massacres occurred between Moslems (who look on Hindus as heathen) and the Hindus. It was the bloodiest slaughter in all Asian history. In Calcutta alone, 10,000 died in street riots.

At dusk in Calcutta the sights and smells are hazily gruesome; in daylight they are shattering. Calcutta is a revolting city. A sprawling, giant industrial port on the murky, muddy waters of the Hoogley River, almost everything about it is repulsive, including its climate which is so pollutedly steamy. Only the most expensively kept buildings avoid the look of decay and delapidation. The smog could be sliced with a knife. It includes factory smoke, diesel and gasoline fumes, smoke from coal braziers used for cooking on sidewalks, from countless dung fires and from the long fat cords of smoldering hemp dangling from buildings or posts to light cigarettes or pipes of hashish by people walking by.

Riding in a motor vehicle here is a hair-raising, sweat-soaking experience. All traffic, large and small, human and animal, powered or pedestrian, misses by no more than the peel of one's skin. With foot on the accelerator and hand on horn, you weave through the most preposterous assortment of locomotion, disbelieving that each successive target has, somehow been missed. We were happy to be leaving for Bhatgaon, although later we would return.

Bhatgaon is the valley city known for its sculptures, fine wood carvings and colossal pagodas. The Golden Gate, a dazzling spectacle, is exuberantly decorated. Circular prayer wheels spin above the shrines and prayer flags flap in the wind above houses, on roadways, in niches or in children's hands. Mostly they are triangular in shape and multiple in design, fluttering in chains like a series of tiny kites. Of various colors and materials, they're hoisted daily in appeal to Buddha for prosperity, health, or healing.

The man who initiated the tourist business in Nepal is a colorful spirited personality named Boris Lissanevitch, known to all as Boris. A White Russian, he fled his native land in 1924, danced in ballets across continents, and in 1952 was invited to set up a hotel here in what was formerly a palace. This was Nepal's first hotel and because of its kingly quarters, he named it the Royal Hotel. Every piece of equipment had to be imported - either specially made and flown in or carried in on the backs of porters from India. A friend of the present king's grandfather, Boris had a monopoly on Nepal's hotel business for ten years. When the Royal closed its doors in the late 1960s, Boris opened a gourmet restaurant, personally supervising the cooking. We lunched here one day with Indira and thoroughly enjoyed the food and the decor. While we were at lunch, tables were being spread for twenty-one U.S. Embassy officials who were to have dinner there that night.

Hippies pick the hashish (illegal) that grows wild here, but use of the betel (both leaf and nut are chewed) which stains the teeth and often drools down chins, is not as widespread as in India.

The commonest trees are the Sal and the teak. The Sal has broad shiny leaves that are used as small plates when serving crowds at festivals and weddings.

A red letter day! At the hotel we had a chocolate soda!

On a much-anticipated day despite the threat of inclement weather, we flew on a Royal Nepal Airlines plane for a view of the eastern Himalayan range from only fourteen miles away. After reaching cruising altitude of 20,000 feet, the captain invited the fourteen passengers, individually, into the cockpit for better views and picture-taking. Eme was able to get pictures of Mount Everest, of Annapurna and Kanchenjunga. What a superb thrill was this trip on a just-right day! When we deplaned we were given small silver charms and certificates saying that this day Mount Everest had had the privilege of greeting us.

"Wanoste" means good morning or good-by in Nepalese, the official language derived from Sanskrit and spoken by most. The Sherpas who live in northeast Nepal speak Tibetan. Many of the Nepalese people also learn English. Nepal sets its clocks ten minutes ahead of Indian time and, all in all, its dignified mountaineers are perhaps ten leaps ahead of their neighbors.

There was a queue-up at stores one morning because of a sugar shortage created by exporting much of it to India. At a nearby temple we watched young Buddhist boys with shaved heads and wearing saffron robes, learning to dance with swords. Monks in a corridor were spinning prayer wheels and chanting, " Om mani padme hoom," the mystic formula and devotional prayer of the Hindus.

In the afternoon we went to a Tibetan camp on the outskirts of Katmandu where the government and Swiss Red Cross sponsor 1,000 refugees. We watched the adults weaving heavy wool rugs and plying their crafts while, in nearby rooms, their children were cared for in nurseries. They are a rugged and hard-working people.

Disease, especially tuberculosis, typhoid, malaria and cholera, takes a dreadful toll among the inhabitants of Nepal.

En route to the airport we were struck by the neat brick-lattice work boxing in the cherry and poplar trees lining the roadway. Our driver saw us through customs and immigration, and we were airborne once more for Calcutta.

There are nine million people in Calcutta, and, as in all India, more than eighty percent are Hindus. There could be no greater mistake than to generalize about Hinduism because there is scarcely a general rule that has no exception, but the caste system is a blight. Tagore, the Hindu philosopher, called it a gigantic system of cold-blooded repression.

Over miles of sordid landscape in the suburbs rise the dirt, dust, misery and wretchedness of the multitudes. Narrow streets are lined with gutters flowing with sewage. Wherever roofs overhang, the prostrate and the squatters line the walls. Bulls, cows, goats and sheep wander at will. Inert skeletal beings sit or lie anywhere. Nude and ragged children play amid the offal. Beggars in tatters turn palms out. Mile after terrible mile, degraded humanity reel in misery in the reeking stench. Yet, the country establishes homes for its aged sacred cows so that in their senility and uselessness they can be pampered with food and comfort!

In the center of the city is the Maidan, a park in which stands a fort, originally a British settlement. Near the river is the Victoria Memorial, Calcutta's finest building, dedicated to the long reigning queen. It adds a baroque touch and houses a British museum. Near the Maidan is Calcutta's main business district, Chowringhee, a two-mile stretch of clubs, shops, and hotels, including ours, the Oberoi Grand.

A beautiful old country house contains the National Library. The Jain Temple with its intricate mosaics is interesting as are the botanical and zoological gardens with its nine white tigers.

The race track is reportedly among the finest in the world. Three stadiums encircle it and thousands come to watch the running of imported, thoroughbred horses. The headquarters of the Mission founded by Swami Vivekanada, who exported Hinduism to the United States, is here.

Behind the race track are the grandiose residences of Alipore where rajahs and maharajahs and the super-rich live surrounded by spacious gardens, high walls and armed guards. The contrast between these homes and the shanties and sheds only a block or two away, produces a shock that is almost traumatic. Statues and memorials and straying cattle litter the city. Uniformed children in high white socks, white shirts — the boys in short khaki pants and the girls in colored skirts — add life to the drab scene although the outfits are, for the most part, grimy and threadbare.

The trams are trolleyed and so loaded that dozens hang from the outside. Over 20,000 human-drawn rickshaws carry people and cargo. The ragged runners with bare feet on scalding pavements get $1.00 to $1.50 per day and pay half to the rickshaw owner. A subway was under construction at the time we were there, designed to connect the north and south ends of the city.

The bridge over the Hoogley River is the only land exit and entrance to the city. A million people cross the bridge each day. Eight lanes wide, it accommodates trams, trucks, cars, pulled and pedaled rickshaws, bicycles, motorcycles, bullock carts and assorted scrawny animals. The pedestrian lanes flanking the roadway handle some twenty-five people abreast - many of them leading animals.

Calcutta is the world's jute manufacturing center and also has foundries, paper and oil mills, and tanneries, our driver told us.

The Oberoi Grand Hotel is five-star resplendent, its grandeur executed in silver, crystal and gold. One of its many dining rooms is inlaid with marble and features Oriental carpets and sunken seats with velvet pillows. The hotel averages some ten uniformed, turbaned (and shod) servants for each guest. Intelligent, attractive, soft-spoken girls in exquisitely decorated saris assist at the reception desk. But as you exit its air-conditioned luxury, the bejeweled doorman opens the door and you walk into the arms of pathetic beggars and sidestep water-filled potholes in the pavement. There are half-nude sleepers under the storefront overhangs and, across the street, under the leaden atmosphere of soot and stink are piles of rubble, pitched tents and flowing gutters. Only within a few feet of space surrounding the Grand does garbage and trash not accumulate. Two blocks away, tiny children scavenge in it.

Nehru called Calcutta the nightmare city. He said there was the danger in India of poverty being deified. Mrs. Ghandi made "Abolish Poverty!" her political slogan. But more than empty rhetoric is needed where famine stalks and malnutrition rages. Leaning over communal water taps are emaciated bodies, children's jutting ribs - the pariahs of humanity sunk in the runnels of filth.

At noon we left Calcutta, the city in need of incense. We were off to Darjeeling on India Airlines to go as far as Bagdora, then a seventy-mile drive from there to the mountain city.

Our driver and good guide was J. B. who took us masterfully over the narrow road with its contorted turns. At times we crisscrossed the tracks of the Toy Train that picks up its passengers as it chugs along. The train trip takes seven and a half hours; we would arrive in about two and a half.

Ascending the Himalayas, we were surrounded by its perpetually snow-clad peaks. Shafts of sunlight fell over the deep ravines. In the small villages and rural areas is more poverty, filth and dung surrounding huts of grass, mud, and matting but in the clear air of this altitude, none of it seemed as abject as in the city. Rice and tea are terrace-planted, forests are dense with pines, and peach trees are in bloom. The glades are ablaze with tall red rhododendron trees. At last we reached the Mount Everest Hotel at 8,000 feet and had some fifty steps to climb, straight up, to our room.

Hot tea and biscuits were served to us and the channel coal fireplace, as in all the rooms, was cheerily burning. There was no central heat anywhere and our Florida bones were reacting to the intense cold. In a vase on the mantle, however, were blossoms from a golden rain tree.

Long ago, this place was a summer refuge of the British and it retains much of its colonial charm. Dinner, eaten by candlelight with three fireplaces blazing in the room, was simply super: roast beef au jus and Yorkshire pudding just like my mother used to make!

We were up at 4:30 and out at dawn to go the twenty miles by jeep to Tiger Hill to photograph Mount Everest and Kanchangjunga from 8,600 feet. We had a cold but exciting panorama of the whole Himalayan range waiting for Eme's camera.

On the return trip we visited the Ghoon Monastery and the market square where we purchased Darjeeling tea, known as the best in the world, to bring home. We had passed up Ceylon's famed tea to stock up on this.

When we started down the mountain a day later, big green ferns dominated the scene along with banyan trees, and farther down were the deciduous forests. Where water cascaded into rippling pools, washings were being done and children were frolicking.

At Bagdora J. B. cleared us through customs and we returned to Calcutta overnight before leaving on Thai Airlines for Bangkok and Singapore. At the Calcutta Airport we met our U.S. Counsel, Robert Breneman, who said that if all the dead and dying in the streets of Calcutta were counted in the census the population would be fifteen million instead of nine million. Robert Goheen, our ambassador to India, was attending a meeting at the Oberoi Grand while we were there.

One of the most thought-provoking books describing India's deplorable impasse today is V. S. Naipaul's *India, a Wounded Civilization.* In it he writes that India has no identity beyond the tenuous ecumenism of Hindu beliefs; that its crisis is not political nor simply economic, but that these are only aspects of the larger crisis which is that of a decaying civilization where the only hope lies in further swift decay.

On boarding Thai Airlines the women received orchids, and on leaving everyone was given kites. Ours were saved for our Texas grandsons, Tim and Chris. In Bangkok we transferred to Singapore Airlines where the stewardesses wore long brocade gowns with matching slippers. In a spotless DC10 we were first treated to rolled and perfumed washrags, then, to good food and service.

On landing, we were in a whole new world. Singapore! Green, shimmering and immaculate where you're fined $250 for littering and $50 for spitting. Years ago Singapore was practically a slum, but the island has been made into a garden city. Trees and shrubs were imported and much of the jungle and swampland of the lowlying areas reclaimed. Singapore has sea and air routes among the most important in the world - linking the Indian Ocean with the South China Sea and the Pacific beyond. It has a population of 2.5 million, of which seventy-six percent is Chinese and fifteen percent, Malayan.

Our first jaunt was a morning cruise by motor launch around the harbor where every conceivable type of watercraft, large and small, can be seen. At Sentosa, the island resort, we stretched our legs with a walk through the gardens down to the sea.

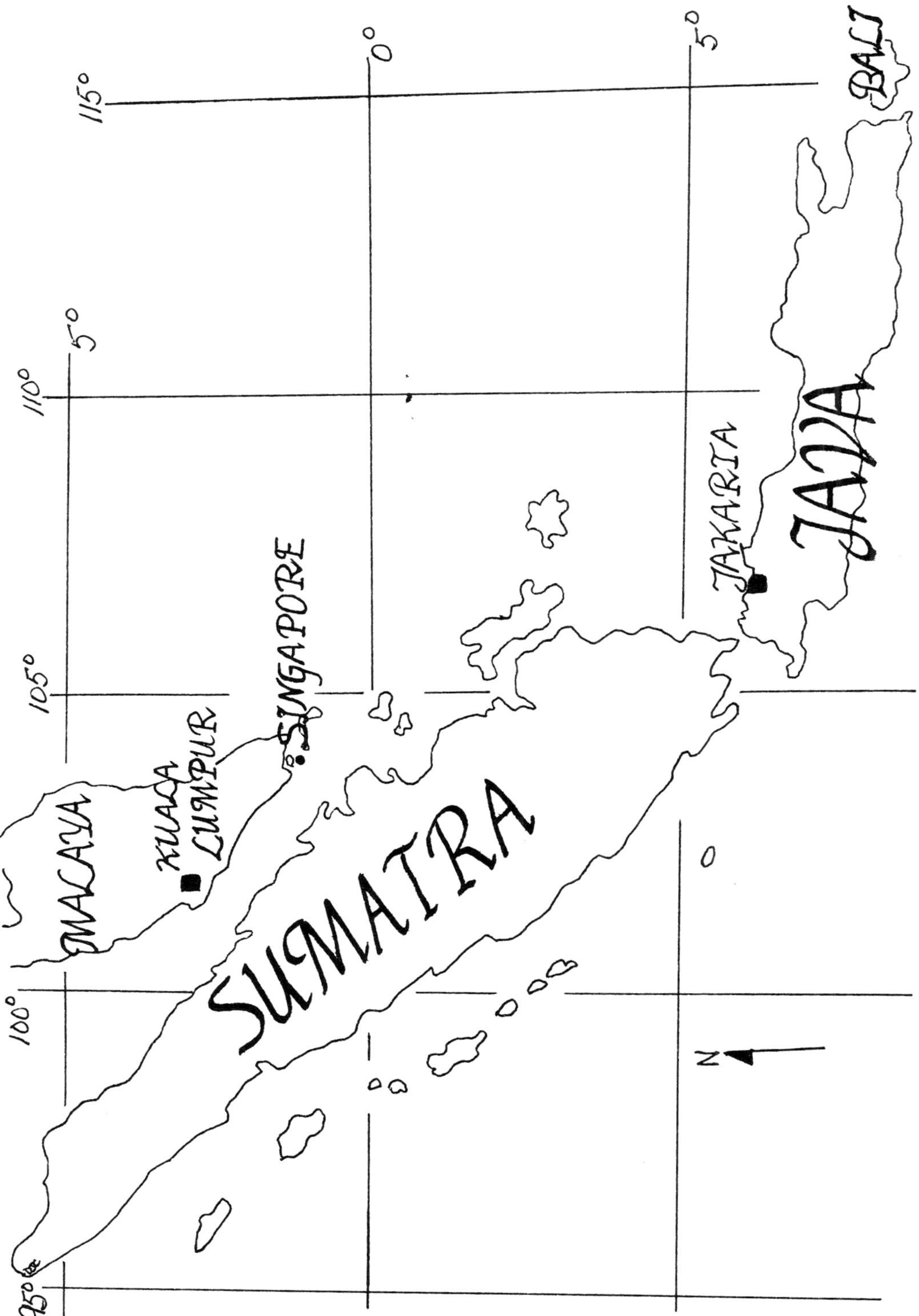
SUMATRA
MALAYA
KUALA LUMPUR
SINGAPORE
JAKARTA
JAVA
BALI
95°
100°
105°
110°
115°
0°
5°
5°
N

Next day we visited the Jarong Bird Park and the Singapore Handicraft Center which was within walking distance of our hotel, the Marco Polo of Chinatown, destined to be torn down to make room for high-rises; and the Botanic Gardens, a project of Sir Stamford Raffles, the founder of Singapore and an avid naturalist. At the Tiger Balm Gardens, we took startling pictures of the bizarre and somewhat garish collection of stone and plaster statues depicting scenes from Chinese mythology.

The restored home of Sun Yat Sen during his residency here is now a library, called Sun Yat Sen Villa, and a statue in front of it is dedicated to his memory.

On another morning our driver, Gopar, took us through Customs and across the causeway to Malaysia. This is a country of twelve million people and thirteen states — seven with sultans and four with governors. We saw the famous Abu Bakar Mosque and the Sultan of Jahore's palace on 500 acres of ground. We were lucky to have as our guide the grandniece of the former sultan, Maria, who dangled the keys to the many enticing locked cupboards in the palace. Her granduncle had been the only sultan to have his own army of 400 for official escort. Inside the locked glass cupboards are more silver and gold place settings than the eye can value, but certainly enough to feed thousands. Afterwards, Maria took us to a batik factory where we selected a handpainted red print for our granddaughter, Stacy.

Back to Singapore and a few random comments: The university here is free to those who finish six years of elementary and four years of upper schooling. The Prime Minister is Chinese. One of our greatest joys here: tipping is prohibited. Singapore, in most regards, has a very Western atmosphere. English is universally spoken and understood.

The following day it was time to leave for Djakarta, the capital of Indonesia. We flew Garuda Airlines, which practically has a monopoly on air traffic in that country. After a short stay in Djakarta, we left on Garuda for Denpasar, Bali.

Bali provided a most fitting finale to our trip. We found a perfect "fall apart" setting, a veritable paradise where the people are most hospitable and even the sea is soft-spoken. For six days we sunned and swam, dined and danced. The Bali Hyatt Hotel is on thirty-six acres abounding in flowers, fruits and singing birds. There were two pools for swimming, as well as the sea, tennis courts, bicycles and a three-hole golf course. I loved the geese honking about the place and they often settled quietly under our lounges as we sunned by the pool. There were ducks on the pond with a new batch of babies in decorous file behind them, and water lilies responded to the sun's rhythm, opening and shutting on the pond's surface.

We dined outdoors and indoors in a specialty restaurant built on four levels. The open-air theater offered daily performances by Bali's marvelous dancers.

Bali is a haven of beauty and relaxation with white beaches running along the bright blue waters of the Indonesian Ocean, with swaying palms, vibrant-hued flora and a fertile green country-side. Alas! Foreigners are not allowed to live here over thirty days.

Their flamboyant ceremonies are guided by the Hindu-Bali religion, much different than that practiced in India but still a ritualistic lifestyle.

At night we were mesmerized at dinner by the monkey dance, performed by 100 men and a girl, and by the Ramayana Ballet.

The soaring pitched roof of the hotel lobby is made of beams covered with thatched elephant grass. There are no walls, just a stupendous view across the garden and down to the sea.

Bali, just east of Java and eight and a half degrees south of the equator, is divided east to west by a craggy chain of volcanoes. Soaring above the island at 10,000 feet is Mount Agung. Most Balinese on this very clean island are farmers and stock breeders, but they are better known as artist-dancers, musicians, weavers, sculptors and painters.

Mr. Oka was our driver and guide on the several trips we took around the island by car. As he drove he told us pertinent facts about the communal way of life that provides help for one another so that no one starves, although he claimed that anyone who is diligent can make a living there. Violence is despised, he said. Geese provide both meat and eggs. No dung is burned for fuel. The rice fields belong to the community and irrigation is regulated by a complicated system of bamboo pipes which automatically close and open. Much bamboo is used here but we learned that it grows three feet in twenty-four hours!

There are 7,000 temples in Bali and we visited several. We saw, too, the caves where the Japanese lived and stored their supplies during World War II. Two days after Hiroshima was bombed, Bali declared its independence.

We stopped at an open-air theater to enjoy an hour's performance of the Barong and Kris dance, vividly depicting the eternal struggle between good and evil spirits. Continuing on, we saw beautiful carving being done, batiks being hand-patterned, artists working in oils and silversmiths fashioning all kinds of jewelry.

We lunched at Peneloken, a hilltop spot with a sweeping view of the thriving rice paddies, the sparkling green valley below and the distant mountains of Batur, an active volcano regarded by the Balinese as a threat of the gods. A religious commune has lived on the shores of its crater lake from time immemorial even though some years back the volcano violently erupted, burying over 500 of the people.

Dozens of children blocked our passage back to the car, badgering us to buy postcards or religious trinkets. I wanted postcards, and they had hundreds to look through, but I picked out ten quickly and scooted into the car before other small vendors joined the group.

Within a quarter-mile of the hotel was a series of fine small restaurants where we gorged ourselves daily on fresh fish — often gourami, lobster, or shrimp — at the price of $4.00 for a complete dinner.

The Balinese consider their island a gift of the gods and we came to warmly appreciate their feelings.

Leaving this happy Indonesian island, we arrived midafternoon in Hong Kong. After a five years' absence, we found it much changed, having gone mostly down hill with too many additional high-rises and excessive pollution. But even down-hill, Hong Kong will always be exciting and we browsed old paths, savoring them all, before returning home.

Chapter 4

When all the pre-travel planning is done and you finally find yourself in line waiting to be off, you solemnly repeat to yourself Art Buchwald's "Tourist Prayer":

> "Heavenly Father, look down on us, your humble obedient servants who are doomed to travel this earth, taking photographs, mailing postcards, buying souvenirs and walking around in drip-dry underwear. We beseech you, O God, to see that our plane is not hijacked, our luggage is not lost and our overweight baggage goes unnoticed . . ."

At least Eme and I weren't worried on that last point — our one bag each easily meets the acceptable limits. Our immediate concern, June 3rd, 1981, was getting seats for the long haul since Pan-Am was not taking advance reservations on overseas flights. Still, Eme and I were happy to be at the gate in Tampa, waiting to board a nonstop plane to Orly Airfield in Paris.

I always get a lift from the Tampa Airport because it combines utter efficiency with eye-and-foot appeal. Admiring it as we strolled, we casually glanced up at the Pan-Am posted schedules to learn that our flight, originating in Miami, was two and a half hours late! Since we were that much too early, for 6:30 p.m. departure, we had five hours to fill. We headed for Eastern Airlines Ionosphere Room.

Countless times we've blessed our membership in this club while having to dally at airports. We entered the private room, were greeted by the happy-faced receptionist, ordered a light drink and black coffee, spruced up in the well-equipped restrooms, read a magazine or two, left our hand luggage at the desk and made off for the Top of the Roof Revolving Restaurant in the International Hotel. The appointments and service in this attractive place are ultra and we dawdled over our dinner. As we were eating, thunder was brewing, lightning flashed and the rain ripped out with such gusto a minor tornado ensued. Back at the

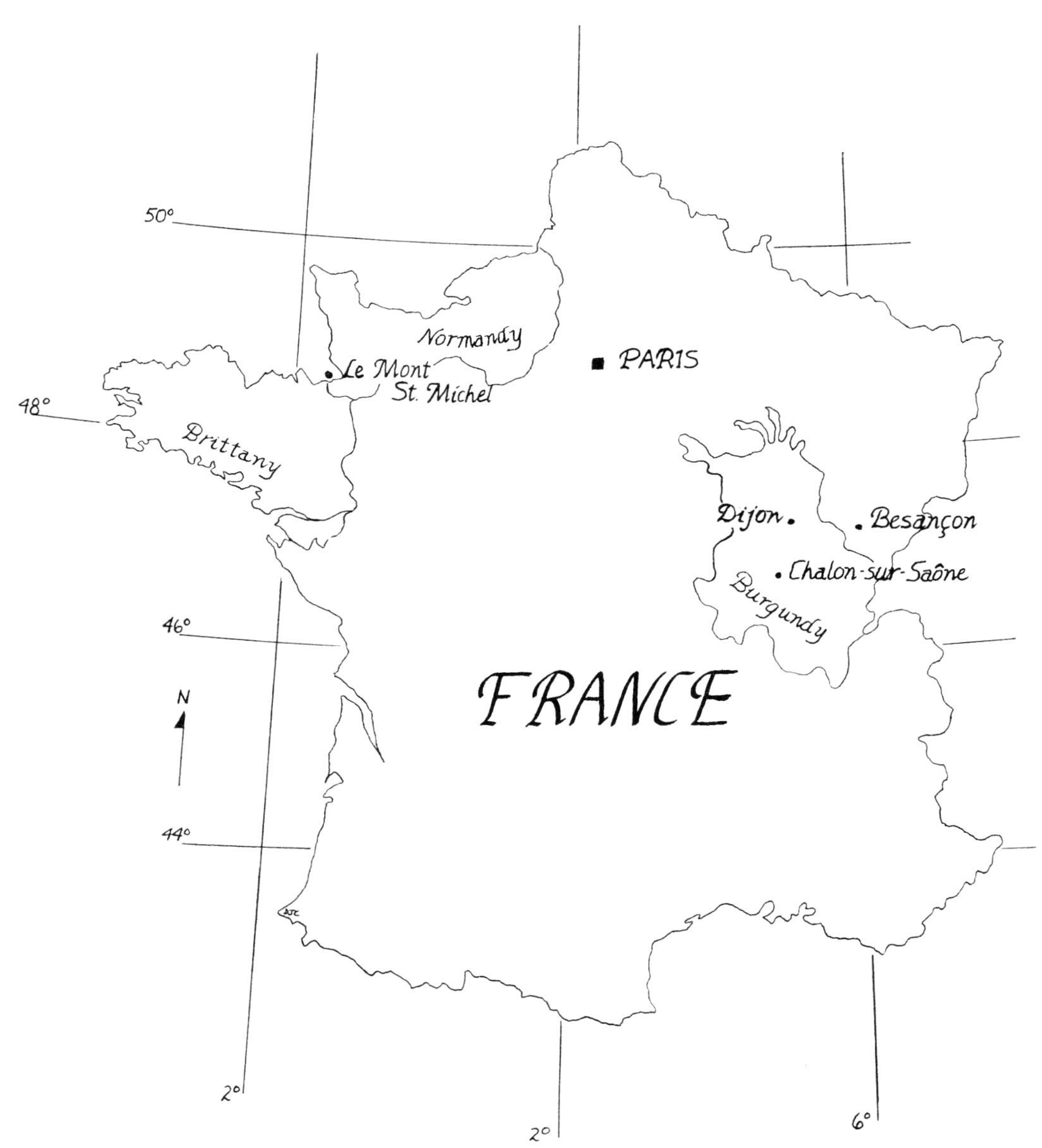

50°
48°
46°
44°
N
Normandy
Le Mont
St. Michel
PARIS
Brittany
Dijon
Besançon
Chalon-sur-Saône
Burgundy
FRANCE
2°
2°
6°

Pan-Am gate we learned Flight 82 had returned to Miami because of the bad weather. It was 10:00 p.m. when we at last took flight in a half-filled DC10.

At 11:10 our inedible dinner arrived and was returned untouched. We settled for a glass of wine and toasted the Top of the Roof. The *Wall Street Journal* had recently reported that Pan-Am had lost $141 million in the first quarter of the year. That was understandable. Our plane's walls, carpets and restrooms were grimy and unkempt. The service was perfunctory and the food, atrocious.

Six hours into the eight-and-a-half-hour haul passengers were bodily shaken and wakened for a "rousing good breakfast." "Rousing" was all it was. Eme said that had it been offered to prisoners, open riots would have broken out. But the coffee was hot, if feeble, and there was a slice of tasty fresh pineapple. In summation: the engines functioned well and we were mighty glad to have avoided Kennedy Airport. Our pilot smoothed us into a landing at Orly at high noon where, under sunny skies and balmy breezes, we were delivered into the arms of Paris in the late spring.

En route by taxi from the airport we drank in the familiar sights, unreturned to for a long time, and reviewed previous delights. At our hotel, the Royal Monceau, just a stone's throw from the Arc de Triomphe, fresh flowers greeted us in the lobby — giant pink glads and heather, long-stemmed yellow snapdragons wound with spider mums, blue shasta daisies and primroses, dripping from pewter, ceramic and glass.

Our twenty-four hour stint made hot baths and naps before dinner imperative. The small refrigerator in our room was well stocked with spirits and soft drinks, but, of all things, we picked Tropicana orange juice from Florida.

Ah, the French cooking at dinner! I know why Julia Child interned here. Given a pea, bean or onion to split, the French perform gastronomical miracles. Add a bit of *fromage*, a hock of *jambon* and *Voila!* All that's left to do is drool and dine.

My author-artist sister, Eunice, had hoped we'd get to see *The Book of Hours*, considered the most beautifully illuminated manuscript in the world. It is housed at Conde Museum in Chantilly, about twenty-six miles north of Paris. We headed there next morning by electrified train, swift as lightning and always precisely on time. But there were no signs in English and no one who spoke it. If you couldn't translate, you were out of luck.

The suburbs we passed through were cleaner than we had remembered and filled with high-rises and multiple dwellings. The country-side was green and lush with bloom; the forests dense and inviting. Gone were the days when a man's wealth was reckoned by the height of his manure pile. Synthetic fertilizers and modern machinery have canceled that.

Chantilly is at the edge of a dense forest beside the Nonette River and is known for its lace and porcelain, as well as its race track where the French Derby is held. Everything, including the museum, closes on racing days, and there are many of them.

The Conde Museum is in the Chateau de Chantilly. The elegant moat-encircled sixteenth century chateau of the Dukes of Conde is ringed with ornamental lakes, flower beds and 17,000 acres of forests. Inside are picture galleries with Raphaels, Renoirs, Van Dykes, Italian, French and Flemish paintings, tapestries to rival those of the Rockefeller collection in the Cloisters, gem-laden cabinets, exquisite furniture and stunning parquet floors. There are also ceramics, silver, gold and metal works, gorgeous Persian rugs, fireplaces that combine style with warmth, and a white marble statue of a girl by B. Chapin that entrances me. Her hair is in a French knot. Her folded hands are relaxed. A purse is slung over her shoulder under her cutaway jacket. Her expression is so natural I expect her to speak.

In *Le Cabinet de Livres* are some 13,000 volumes, richly bound in vari-colored leathers and printed on tissue-fine paper or vellum. We were miserably disappointed at not being allowed to see the *Tres Riches Heures* of the Duc de Berry. In the central glass case in the library are reproductions of this book's most famous miniatures, written and illustrated shortly after 1400 A.D., but because of its fragility, the original is no longer exhibited to the public. With sign language and woeful French, I arranged to meet with the curator who told us the book is lodged in a crypt surrounded by electrified windows and moved only by him once every two months or so — to keep it from moldering, I suppose. What a pity, that with all our modern methods, they can't display it under plastic or glass to let people admire it.

This *Book of Hours*, we were told, is a type of prayer book on 206 sheets of finely woven paper, eight by eleven inches in size. It opens with a monthly calendar of saints, illustrated with full-page scenes depicting landscapes. The margins are decorated with fantasy and delicate calligraphy. The text is French but the artists, like the Limbourg brothers, were German. Du Barry commissioned the most talented painters and illuminators to be found.

No one at the museum spoke a word of English, but fortunately, we could read some French. For awhile we tagged along after a French guide to eke out a few items of information. Intrigued with the setting,

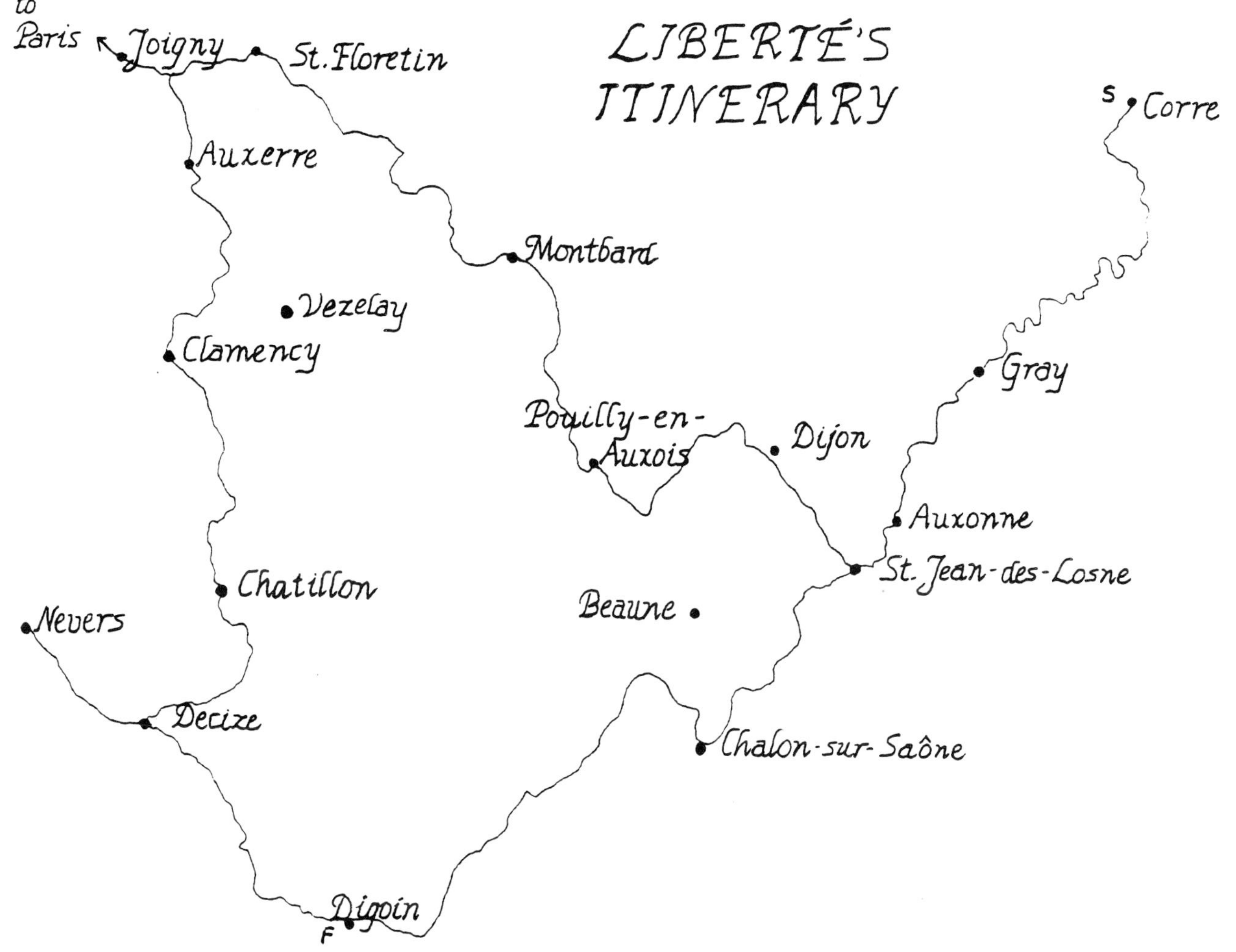
LIBERTÉ'S ITINERARY
to Paris
Joigny
St. Floretin
Auxerre
Montbard
Vezelay
Clamency
Pouilly-en-Auxois
Dijon
Gray
S
Corre
Auxonne
St. Jean-des-Losne
Beaune
Chatillon
Nevers
Decize
Chalon-sur-Saône
Digoin
F

Eme took shots of the park, gardens, stables and tennis court dating back to 1756.

We closed up the place at 6:00 p.m. to find there were no taxis to take us to the train station. It was shank's mare over cobble-stone streets, cars whizzing dizzyingly past. At last we saw a parked car with two women standing beside it and we trudged up to it on weary shanks. They were Dutch painters, rearranging their overburdened Renault and Allah be praised, they spoke English. We asked, if when they arrived in the village, they would send a taxi to get us. One measured me inch by inch and decided I was thin enough to fit in the rear of the car atop their folding chairs, suitcases, easels, oil paints and other miscellanea. I ducked my head and they sardined me inside, my head just clearing the car ceiling. Eme squeezed in between them on the tiny front seat. The car was visibly sagging as it took off for the Chantilly railroad station with these angels.

Next morning, we were off early to the Louvre and by noon we were rummaging through the book stalls along the Seine. Years before we had watched sidewalk painters completing their scenes of La Madeline, Montmartre, and these very book stalls, then purchased three of the paintings.

In the afternoon, those of us who were taking the Horizon Cruise on the canals of France were waiting in the lobby for our driver, Bruce. We were to drive 120 miles to the barge, Liberte, docked in Corre, riding in a specially-built Renault bus that would accompany us along the way.

Our trip got off to an inauspicious start with drizzling rain punctuating the miles. The flat countryside from Paris south was a welter of glistening green, meandering rivers and long trails of wood as we passed through Nemours, Nevers, and Bourgogne with its colorful flower-centered boulevards. The speed limit was seventy for private cars but only sixty for buses.

The road trip was over by dinnertime when Bruce drew up beside the Burgundy Canal where we spotted the freshly painted and immaculate barge, the Liberte, bicycles gleaming on her flower-fringed observation deck.

The captain welcomed us aboard and presented the crew. We were eight Americans sailing on a French barge with a crew of four peppy young Britishers and a French chef. Roger Collers, our captain, was all spit and polish for the proper occasions, and his chic but shy wife, Yvette, our gourmet cook. Nick was second in command; Caroline, our maid; and Bruce, not only the driver of the bus but the jack of all trades.

The other six Americans were Joan and Robert Michton of Merrick, New York — Robert, a cardiologist, and Joan, a physio-therapist; Sally

Our barge, The Liberte, entering a tunnel near St. Jean des Losne.

Beaune, the wine capital of Burgundy, France.

Buck Henry, TV and movie actor and screen writer, and Irene Ramp, with Time Magazine, who have two French "small fry" in tow, waiting to board The Liberte.

The Liberte in dock at Pouilly en Auxois, France; Buck Henry aboard.

Mont Saint-Michel, (built in the 8th century), now one of France's national shrines.

Interior of Chapel, Mont Saint-Michel.

First floor of the Louvre, Paris, France.

Chateau de Chantilly — 16th century — Chantilly, France.

Dijon, France, where the architecture wears many hats.

Black bronze statue in Vigeland Park, Oslo, Norway.

Author and Norwegian friends in Hammar, Norway.

A stave church in Bergen, Norway.

One of the 'walking streets' of Copenhagen.

Flower market in Bergen, Norway.

and Ralph Frank of Beverly Hills, California, who had recently sold the Lowry Salt Company; Buck "22" Henry from Los Angeles and Irene Ramp from Manhattan, New York. Buck, of course, was the movie and television actor and script writer of shows going back to the Garry Moore Show. He wrote and acted in such memorable movies as *The Graduate*, *Catch 22*, and *Heaven Can Wait*. He was modest, droll and affable. Irene, a reporter for *Time* magazine, had a willowy, wandlike figure, a winning smile and a sharp-as-crystal wit. Both added sparkle and substance to the sun-deck and dinner table discussions.

The Liberte had room for only ten passengers in one suite and four staterooms, carried its own bus for side trips, and bicycles for all. The amenities included a teak-paneled library, stereo, well-stocked bar and wine cellar.

I'm provoked I didn't start sooner taking pictures of the food; it had the touch of epicure and genius combined. Every dish looked as if it was lifted out of the pages of *Gourmet* or *Better Homes and Gardens.*

On the first morning we were awakened by the sounds of an old-fashioned brawl. A large barge, the Dunkerquois, was blocking all traffic at De Port Sur Saone where the Liberte was docked. Roger had asked the barge to move aside so the Liberte could come about. The Dunkerquois captain had replied with a hard slap to Roger's face and a volley of oaths, saying he would not budge an inch on a religious holiday. It was Pentecost, he reminded Roger, who was but a third the size of the bullying barge master. To shorten a long story, nothing moved, nor did the police intercede. The law did state that no work need be done on a religious holiday. Roger later learned that this particular fellow spent more time in jail than out. All day the Liberte sat dockside while we bicycled and lay in the sun.

In the afternoon, however, we drove to Besancon with Eme and Buck champing at the bit, eager to watch the French Open tennis match on television. Much of that section of the country has the orderly green look of Switzerland. The Jura Mountains in the distance are heavily wooded. The Charollais cattle munch in the grazelands and a walled city we passed recalled France's history.

Besancon still retains the triumphal arch Marcus Aurelius erected after Julius Caesar captured the town in 58 B.C. It is the center of France's watch-making industry that was founded by the Swiss. The Citadel, perched above the Doubs River, is an imposing fortress with its high-peaked lookout guarding the city. Much work has been done to restore and beautify this ancient walled edifice which houses the Popular Museum, the Museum of the Resistance, and one of natural history. We meandered around the premises several hours before returning to the boat.

Unlike American waterways flanked by roads and blaring signs and littered with trash, many of France's rivers present the rural landscape completely unmarred. So it is with the Soane River — not even a towpath intrudes. The eye picks up the red tile roofs and church steeples in the distance, the miles of soft forests, feathery bushes and lime green meadows, tiny flowers splintering through the rocks, assorted ferns, flashes of wings and birdsong even in the rain. Often the barge had to inch its way through long tunnels or locks until it was once more in the clear.

Part of the river's allure is its restlessness and varied personality. It was extremely peaceful to stand on deck in a spit of rain, a small wind whipping, and watch the unfolding panorama.

Some tall weeds we passed looked like parchment and I thought of Emerson's words, "A weed is a plant whose virtue has not yet been discovered." We'd soon be docking and could ride our bikes through small villages and explore the countryside, cheery with sprinkles of flowers and foliage, knowing that at a lock along the way the Liberte would catch up with us.

Arriving at St. Jean des Losne and the beginning of the Burgundy Canal, Bruce drove us to Bourgogne in the afternoon. Along the way the roses, on trellis and bush, were a multi-hued mosaic. On the Cote d'Or are cliffs, gorges, and mountain torrents sloping precipitously to the valley of the Saone where the famous vineyards, many of them walled, stretch for miles and miles. The vines are kept low and trimmed, not like grandmother's over-the-fence type, and it takes about five years for them to fully mature. So important is wine making in this area that there are schools devoted to the art, and a museum housed in the Hotel des Ducs. We toured its cool cellars, tasting a goodly number of samples.

Baune, where the museum is located, is the wine capital of Burgundy and is also famous for its historical treasures. The fifteenth century Hotel Dieu, built for the poor, is both a hospital ward and church. In one part of this structure, remarkable for its unique architecture and fabulous varnished tile roof, we filed into an air-conditioned room to view Van der Weyden's masterpiece, the Last Judgment. Covering an entire large wall, it's a double-faced painting on wood, full of subtle impressions expressed in vivid color, shadow and light.

We returned to the barge in time to pedal our bikes on many towpaths. We watched both men and women — it takes two of them and hard work — open locks and earn their $300 a month. Some were most voluble (in French only) and able to give directions and tell many stories. Some had garden-fresh vegetables for sale. We biked past a small church and up to a charming old chateau. Cautiously we squeaked open the huge iron gates. Thin glossily groomed whippet dogs met us in friendly fashion. A face appeared at a shuttered window but no one came out. Roses were everywhere, bent cypress trees with mistletoe balls festooning them. Geese ambled in straight file; cattle speckling the far-off pastures, frogs twanged in the ponds and birds thrummed in the trees. A sense of utter peace pervaded. We strolled a bit revelling in the pastoral scene before high-tailing it back to the Liberte.

Leaving our pleasant moorings in the afternoon, Bruce drove us through nearby villages to Dijon. The roadway, through endless rows of poplar and plantain trees, shows rural France at its most prosperous, comfortable and picturesque. A Mercedes in every garage is no lie. The houses are spacious, built around courtyards with attached vaulted cellars, and have well-groomed lawns and landscaping.

Dijon itself has a quarter of a million people. So numerous are its churches that this ancient capital of the dukes is known as "the city of 100 bells". The town is the gateway to the finest wines in the world and is also the world center for the mustard abroad we're told wouldn't pass muster here. (I couldn't resist that one.) It bears little resemblance to the hot, piquant, bright yellow, real McCoy.

Dijon's most striking landmark is the Cathedral of Saint Benigue highlighted by massive twin towers and octagonal belfries. In its heyday wealthy Burgundian dukes built their palaces here and contributed many of the city's art and architectural treasures. The outstanding monument is the Palace of the Dukes of Bourgogne, now the Hotel de Ville, housing the offices of the municipal government and a renowned museum.

The city's architecture is fascinating. One building with many parapets atop, looks as if they all were wearing hats. The chimneys especially intrigue me; none are plain and straight, but multiple, with stacked, geometric, or very decorative exteriors.

The air show had been on all weekend and we saw French pilots who were training Egyptians and later watched the planes maneuvering in various formations.

Then it was back to the barge for our final farewell dinner aboard. To say it was festive is to put it mildly. With Captain Roger in the seat of honor at the table, we did our usual justice to Yvette's delicacies and the various decanters of wine in all colors. Assorted cheeses were passed at the end of the dessert course, some decorated with flutes and flowers on top. One that was frosted squeaked when we cut into it and revealed a toy mouse, earning the laughter of all.

Next day, after an early breakfast aboard, we would go our separate ways. With thanks given to the genial crew, it was then au revoir to all.

Six of us — all but Buck and Irene — drove back to Paris via a different route, after which Eme and I returned to the Royal Monceau Hotel. After dinner and a walk on the Champs d'Elysee, Eme and I returned to our room in time to receive a phone call from Buck and Irene, traveling in the south of France. Because they hadn't been up in time to say good-by, they wanted to wish us well. Their call warmed us greatly, making us realize that we had made some thoughtful and interesting friends.

In the morning we were eager to be off to a place we had always wanted to see, the Mont Saint-Michel.

It was a long trip, eleven and a half hours, but the bus was a very comfortable one with reclining seats and a guide who spoke excellent English. Leaving the city, we admired the forsythia and bridal wreath bordering the median of the four-lane expressway, the Ile de France in the Seine, next the forest of Versaille, and then the Dreux River from Paris to Normandy.

Hedges fenced the fields of lower Normandy; massive plantings of barley greened the roadside. Plantain trees, with leaves resembling the maple, lined either side of the road. Most of the houses were stone with brick chimneys but the oldest were made of clay and stone with thatched roofs.

We lunched at Digue close to the dyke and were treated to a Michelin three-star restaurant meal of many courses and all the trimmings.

Passing through Alencon, famous for its lace, we noted that most of the chimney finials are knobs, either square or pointed, and look like upended red tile pots. In Donjon, the granite houses are austere. Most of these villages were bombed during the Second World War and have been reconstructed. In Dinan, eighty percent of the houses are rebuilt.

Climbing steadily we approached the Mont, first named Tombe, which was once surrounded by the Ceci Forest until a tidal wave struck in the seventeenth century, destroying most of the trees. As we passed, the tide was out; the day was calm and clear on which to contemplate this fantastic wonder.

The abbey was built in the eighth century after the Bishop of Avranches claimed to have seen Gabriel in a vision and been instructed to construct a chapel on this rock. For many years the Tombelaine Island on which the abbey stands was isolated, but a paved causeway has brought the rush and crush of tourists. After climbing 100 steps of the often lacework-like stairways, we wandered around the sloping passageways along the fortified walls. Standing on a gigantic rock in the sea, the monastery clusters around the church with the town at its feet, surrounded by ramparts and towers once needed to protect it from the greed and covetousness of princes.

The Gothic part of the abbey is its marvel. From below one can see the strong buttresses, and from above, the conical roof and subtly stained glass windows of the Guests' Hall and the thirteenth century refectory. For centuries the monastery withstood wars and weather, but by 1800 the monks were gone and the island became a prison. Now it is a national shrine. Decorated wooden fences enclose the beautiful gardens. Inside, the flamboyant choir loft is all light and grace. Each room adds a new dimension of beauty. We were given a good bit of time and leisure to enjoy it and the High Street behind, where there is a quaint flower-strewn church, a hotel, and shops lining the promenade. An aura of artistry crowns this dreamy pyramid of pageantry. It was midnight before we returned to the hotel.

Early next morning we took the subway to the Louvre, just two blocks from our hotel. It was fast, efficient, and cheap. Unlike New York's subway system, it is extremely clean; there's no litter and no graffiti on the walls. At the Louvre station are attractive vases and valuable pieces of sculpture in glass cases. Guess how long these would last in New York! We were waiting when the museum doors opened and glad that this was the day scheduled for a da Vinci exhibit.

The da Vinci miniatures and the Mona Lisa are protected by glass. I don't understand how the Venus de Milo, left in the open, stays in such good condition, but I did notice there was very little touching of it. Marcel Proust, the French writer who influenced world literature, said, "Thanks to art, instead of seeing a single world, our own, we see it multiply until we have before us as many worlds as there are original artists." We especially enjoyed the French and Italian schools of painting, but were disappointed the Corots and Monets were closed to the public.

In late afternoon we visited La Saint Chapelle, which, like the Louvre, is worth a return visit anytime. This absolute jewel is surely one of the glories of France. Built as a shrine in 1248 by Louis the Crusader, it is crested with multiple delicate spires and houses an illuminated manuscript of lapis lazuli and glowing gold. Its exquisite array of stained glass windows are breathtaking. It also contains the personal chapel of Marie Antoinette.

As the Rogers and Hammerstein song has it: "The last time I saw Paris / Her heart was warm and gay. / I heard the laughter of her beat / In every street cafe." A cafe was where we spent the last moments before the sun went down on our last day in Paris. We returned to the hotel for dinner and packed for early morning departure on Air France for Oslo,

Norway.

Speaking of Air France leads me to retract much of my nastiest criticism of our international Pan Am flight. The Mictoms, who were barge companions, flew Air France from New York to Orly. Tightly crammed with no leg room into an absolutely full 747, they were handed two plastic sacks, containing dinner and next morning's breakfast. "Eat whichever you choose at any time," they had been told. A tour director we met in Copenhagen said he'd never heard of such an outrage on an international flight.

Anyway, it was Air France we were on, leaving Charles de Gaulle Airport. We were handed breakfast in a plastic bag upon boarding but over the loudspeaker the captain's voice commanded, "Don't eat until you're invited to." This being a flight of only several hours we didn't mind receiving the sack in advance, and the food was passable.

We checked into the Viking Hotel in Oslo to find some welcome mail. After unpacking we ambled along the walking street (no cars) to watch the artists and musicians at work, gawk in store windows and acclimate ourselves to the blustery weather. For dinner we enjoyed the most delectable fresh salmon ever spawned.

On a "Highlights of Oslo" tour, next morning, we learned that almost everyone here spoke English. The Oslo fjords jutting into the Atlantic Ocean dominate the scene. All kinds and descriptions of maritime craft were in the big harbor where the shrimp boats had just docked. According to our guide, Oslo has 460,000 of the four million people in Norway. We passed Amundson Square and visited the city hall whose interior is made of Norwegian marble. Displayed are pictures by the famed Ed Munch and the tapestries are by Lod.

It was nostalgic to watch the streetcars. We admired the beautiful linden trees in the park and smiled at the sign reading, "Don't step on lawns; summer is so short." At the Nobel Institute we learned that although the main prize is awarded in Stockholm, one prize is given here because Norway and Sweden at one time were united.

Near the ski jump we passed private homes, all made of wood because it is plentiful and because of its superior insulating quality. If any of these houses could be purchased, the least expensive would cost $300,000. The following year the world skiing championship competition was to be held here and a stadium to house 130,000 was being built. Fifty million kronen were being spent in getting ready, and most Norwegians, taxed and inflated almost beyond endurance, were not pleased. Close by were charming houses set in dense forests.

At Vigeland Park we stopped to see the unusual sculptures. The black statues are of bronze; the rest are of Norwegian granite. Crossing a

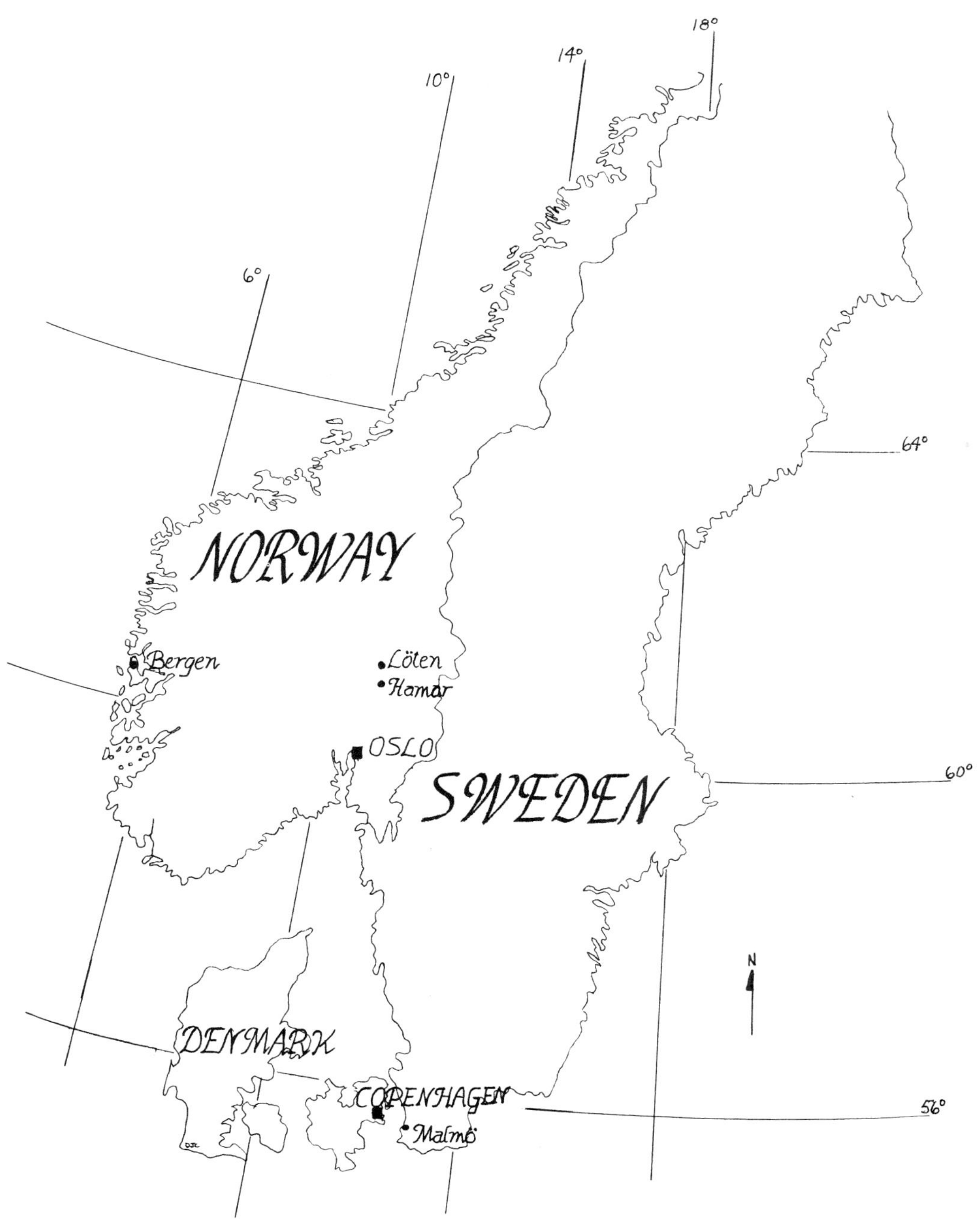
18°
14°
10°
6°
64°
60°
56°
NORWAY
SWEDEN
DENMARK
Bergen
Löten
Hamar
OSLO
COPENHAGEN
Malmö
N

small bridge over a waterfall, we found the little girl and boy statues and then the tiny waif alone. The "wheel of life" shimmers in black bronze. Golden rain trees sharpen the outlines of the figures.

In the museum, Viking ships made of oak are remarkable relics of the age. King Olaf Tryggvesson's ship was also his tomb (800 A.D.) and that of his dog, buried with him. In another museum we saw Kon Tiki, the raft Thor Hyerdahl and five companions drifted on for 101 days across the Pacific. Made of balsa, it was built as the pre-Inca Indians built theirs.

Dining at Englebretts, Eme tried reindeer meat but I ordered poached trout. At 11:00 p.m. it was still daylight.

At nine the next morning Dagney Berger and her daughter, Haldis, were at the hotel to pick us up. We met Dagney and her husband, Amund, twenty years ago in the Canary Islands and have corresponded ever since. One year Eme and I flew to Chicago to help friends entertain the Bergers because they couldn't come as far as Florida. Many times they had invited us to visit their farm in Loten, about eighty miles north of Oslo, and at long last we could accept.

En route we stopped at a charming place for lunch and were taken through a museum which marked Norway's independence in 1814 from Denmark and in 1905 from Sweden.

The Bergers own the second largest farm in Norway. It is only 300 acres, but farmland in Norway is scarce and priceless. Their specialty is dairy cows — 100 of them. The also have grazing land in the mountains and a summer home with about 200 acres.

The red-carpet hospitality they offered us was truly heart-warming. The first night, they gave a party in our honor. Fireplaces were lighted and the mellow wood-paneling glowed. Before the other guests arrived I walked into the living room to hear a voice say, "Good evening, I'm Steen." I was looking into the face of a real Hans Brinker with the blond silk hairbob, but this one was taller, handsomer and had no silver skates. A Dane, he was introduced as the oldest daughter's, Marta's, fiance. The three daughters, all lovely to look at, are Marta, Haldis, and Ingrid.

The following day we went to visit Dagney's sister and brother-in-law who live near Mjosa Lake. En route we stopped in Hamar where the Germans occupied schools and churches during the war.

An interesting fact about Norway is that the oldest child, whether boy or girl, inherits the farm. In Denmark, the youngest child inherits. Since Steen is the youngest of his family, and Marta the oldest in hers, this was presenting a thorny problem.

Our second stop, en route, was at Dagney's niece's house. Her husband owns a textile factory and we were invited to watch it in operation. After going through it I was invited to select any tablecloth I wanted. From there it was a half-hour ferry ride across the lake to Dagney's sister's house.

What a setting and what a house Solvel and her husband, Haakon have, surrounded by forest! Chestnut trees overhung the drives, lilacs spilled over the walks and red bullfinches sang in the blood beeches. The house was built in 1610 and was unutterably fascinating. But over and above all this wonder, Solvel showed us her private museum — ten well-lighted and decorated rooms in a red and white barn, displaying farm and home equipment dating back several hundreds of years. The collection, marvelously displayed, began as a hobby and had become an enterprise coveted by the state. Also at Solvel's we came to realize Norwegians eat about every hour and not mere snacks. It is strange that more of them are not overweight.

In the morning we went to the Bergers' mountain place where sixty-two cattle grazed. The road we traveled had been crossed the previous week by seventy-five elk. Amund Berger is one of 200 farmers who own all the forests of Loten. These are strictly controlled and there is a very strong and active farm council in Norway.

In this country one year of military training for boys is compulsory at age nineteen.

Going into the mountains we passed Elberun, where King Haakon, the father of the reigning King Olaf, stayed in 1940 on the first day of the German invasion.

At a museum where we stopped Dagney bought me postcards, and, as a parting gift, gave me a colorful signed tablescarf hand-woven by a cousin of hers.

That afternoon we reluctantly left Loten on the electric train for Oslo to make ready for our much-anticipated fjord trip.

For this three-day very comfortable bus jaunt there were twenty-nine. Our driver was Willy (pronounced Villy), and Annalisa, a political science student at the University of Oslo, was our pert bilingual (French and English) guide. Among our group were eight Spaniards from Barcelona, four Mexicans from Monterey, two Israelis, three from Capetown, South Africa, and twelve Americans.

Boats, boats, and more boats bustled in the harbor on the very cold morning of our departure. Mist was creeping over the low mountains, yet lilacs framed the doorways of the houses we passed and the markets displayed an abundance.

You can always tell a fjord (an arm of the ocean) we'd been advised, because it has seaweed growing in it. We passed a lake that had once been a fjord.

Norway is Europe's fifth largest country. Only three percent of it is cultivated; seventy percent is mountainous. It reaches as far north as Greenland and Alaska but its temperature is moderated by the Gulf Stream. With only four million people, the country has the lowest population density in Europe. There are no really big farms and no inheritance tax is assessed on a working farm. Milk, butter, meat, and cheese are subsidized by the state.

Annalisa established a few rules for the bus. We would be allowed a certain amount of time at each stop and anyone not back on time would have to sing as their punishment. If I were late, God help the riders!

"Skoll" is the Scandinavian word for "Cheers" but when you say it you must maintain eye contact — the idea being that there can't be anything underhanded taking place. You can buy beer in Norway if you're eighteen, wine if you're twenty, and hard liquor if you're twenty-three.

After telling us this, Annalisa passed out copies of Norwegian songs and the first was a drinking song about a farmer who goes out for a beer, and while he is gone, a student visits his wife. The moral is: Always take your wife when you go for a beer. Annalisa played a cassette to accompany us and we sang with abandon, "*Det var en god gammel Bondemann . . .*"

Norwegians aren't born with skis on, but they are wearing them by the time they are three years old. Cross-country skiing is the most popular variety.

We traveled through apple country before getting into the hill and lake region. The mountains were like soft ripples but got higher until the mist covered them and rain broke loose. Then back came the sun, lighting fields of oats, barley, wheat and potatoes. Potatoes are a staple and a national drink is made of them combined with caraway: aquavite.

There is free schooling from kindergarten through college in Norway. English, as a second language, is compulsory and children begin learning it when they enter school at the age of seven.

A refreshing thing about Norway is the lack of slums. The national pride is especially noticeable. Each section of the country has its own distinctive costumes for special occasions and national holidays.

The forests appear limitless, and seventy percent are privately owned, but no tree can be cut down without a replacement tree being planted.

We stopped for lunch and nobody was late getting back to the bus! As we journeyed through the Hemse Valley we could see snow on the distant mountains. As we climbed, we passed above the timberline into reindeer country and passed three waterfalls known as the Three

Sisters. The area reminded me of the rain forest on the Milford Track in New Zealand.

Hairpin turns braided the road. "There are only good drivers in Norway," Willy joked. "The others are dead."

Water from melting snow cascaded into streams below. Goats were everywhere — black and white. And we were in the land of the trolls. The mountain troll is the most dangerous, Annalisa assured us. It has twelve heads and the force of fifty men. It sounded like a match for Paul Bunyan. Some trolls hide during the day, she said, and if you trick them into the sun, they turn to stone, which probably accounts for so many stones along the way.

Grieg's "Piano Concerto in A Minor" (a cassette) silenced the chatter in the bus as we wound down the mountain side to Borgund. We stopped to see the inside of a stave church dating back to Norway's Catholic era in 1150. Its narrow shaped pieces of wood, poles and spires, with dragon heads atop, looked Oriental. In this ancient church, women had to use a separate entrance and only the elderly were allowed to sit. The arcade around the church was for lepers who weren't permitted inside and were passed bread and wine through a hole. Roman Catholicism decreased when Lutheranism became the state religion, but there is complete freedom of worship.

For a time we followed the banks of a rushing salmon river, the Laerdalelv. Salmon fishing here, where the whoppers are to be caught, is an expensive sport, costing $905 a day. People who own property bordering the river rent out sections at high fees for ten-year periods. The Atlantic salmon come from the salt water to spawn and the state feeds the streams with millions of salmon each year. The fish are caught with seines, gill nets, traps or by trolling with hooks.

At the south end of the river our bus boarded the ferry to cross to the village of Sogndal where we had dinner and spent the night.

in the nippiness of clear early morning, Eme and I, who had wandered off by ourselves to inspect the wharf, stepped onto a steamer, presuming it to be ours, for the four-hour cruise. Suddenly we discovered our mistake and hot-footed it up the line to where our good guide and fellow passengers were waiting to take off. It was biting cold and windy on the top deck but the scenery compensated for any discomfort.

This was the Sogne Fjord, king of all Norway's fjords — its longest and deepest. Stretching halfway up the west coast, it is 110 miles in length, and 650 fathoms or 3900 feet deep. As a fjord penetrates the countryside, dramatic changes occur in the landscape. Rugged volcanic formations soar to dizzying heights but are almost outmatched by the breath-taking white-crowned glaciers. Giant waterfalls roar in the distance as they plunge over rock bluffs down icy slopes into the river gorges. Intermediate level slopes are greened with woodlands; farms teeter on cliffsides with orchards strung along like garlands. Closer to our ship, tugs brayed as they drew close while gulls and pelicans swooped and circled around.

Disembarking at Gudvangen, we climbed back into the bus to start up the famous (or infamous) Stalheim Road to Voss. The route, over a mile long, has thirteen curves and a 1 to 5 grade of elevation. Built in 1842, it is two-way but unbelievably narrow. Our bus, we learned with gratitude, was equipped with four sets of brakes. Those with rosaries began telling them; the others gritted their teeth and closed their eyes to oncoming traffic. All gave Willy a standing ovation for making it safely.

To lighten the tension Annalisa told us another of her stories. The Vikings discovered North America 400 years before Columbus set foot in the New World. When they greeted the locals, "Buenos Amigos", the Indians replied, "Skoll!"

Coming into Voss, a town of 5,000, we were entering one of Norway's most famous tourist areas. A gondola lift whisks skiers up the mountain in winter; where skiing gives way to salmon and trout fishing in summer, Voss has become the year-round "Tour Center of the West".

Knute Rockne, the renowned Norwegian-American football coach for Notre Dame, was born here; a memorial in his honor graces the square. The town is also known for its embroidery, hand-made to decorate national costumes and tablecloths. The first potatoes grown in Norway came from Voss.

Just beyond Voss is Ulvic, another resort village, that was our destination for dinner and the night. Approaching it we faced a spectacular sight, the majestic Queen Fjord, Norway's second largest. A number of our group concluded their trip at this point, leaving seventeen of us to continue on for the third day.

Cloudy weather stalked us as we left on the ferry next morning for Bergen. "It always rains in that city," we were told. Not too pleasant to look forward to!

Our bus rolled off the ferry and onto an extremely narrow main road where it had to pull to one side to let another car pass. A chemical factory was polluting the air. Electricity is cheap in this area and used for both heating and cooking, but there are no nuclear power plants in the country. Norway is the largest producer of aluminum in Europe, Annalisa told us. Other information she gave included the retirement age is sixty-seven and there is no unemployment in the country. The life expectancy for a woman is seventy-eight, and for a man, seventy-three.

Driving through canyons and tunnels, the bus headlights had to be on most of the time because it was raining harder. Annalisa taught us two more Norwegian songs then asked for volunteers from each country to lead the songs. The Spaniards contributed two rousing tunes and Annalisa led us in singing the Israeli national anthem. The American volunteers came up with "I've Been Working on the Railroad". The only South African among us, a delightful lady who supervises nurses in a hospital there, protested at having to sing alone, so she taught us a song: "Ai zika zumba, zumba, zumba / Ai zika zumba, zumba zay." Translated: "Lay him down, you Zulu warrior / Lay him down, you Zulu chief." Those on the left of the bus say: "Chief, chief, chief." Those on the right sing the refrain. It was hilarious.

While traversing the next mountain ravine with the Bridal Veil waterfall and more arm-of-the-sea magnificence, we learned three conditions were necessary to produce a fjord: a mountain range, a river bed, and an ice age. All of these came together in Norway a million years ago. When rivers dug valleys, the heavy ice cap burrowed deeper and deeper beneath the sea level. Along the coast, however, the pressure of the ice was lighter, accounting for the shallowness of the fjords' mouths. A mouth may be only 500 feet deep while the fjord's interior depth will measure 4,000 feet. The fjords never freeze, except in the remotest branches, because as the icecap retreats, salt water fills the enormous basins up to sea level. The salinity and the warm Gulf Stream prevent the fjords from freezing. The ice cap remains in the form of big glaciers that are Norway's reservoirs for generating power.

Arriving at the hotel in Bergen around 2:00 p.m., we took a short tour to acquaint ourselves with this city set among the grandeur of seven mountains. Both Edvard Grieg and Hendrik Ibsen were born here and there's a statue to Grieg in the park where concerts are held. Anita was our guide here and before we started she apologized for the rain.

Bergen is one of the country's oldest and most culturally-oriented cities. It is a leading fishing and shipping center, and cod liver oil is made here. Across the water is an island called Rosecrantz, home to 16,000 Dutch inhabitants. The ferry crossing takes a mere seventeen minutes.

In the old section of the city are wooden houses and meandering cobbled streets. We visited the Hanseatic Museum, housed in one of the oldest timber buildings. Furnished in sixteenth century style, it depicts the daily life of the Hanseatic merchants who came from Hamburg, Germany, and formed a league. The museum is also the scene of special parties, one of which was hosted by King Olaf.

St. Mary's Church, primarily Gothic in design and the oldest building in Bergen, was erected between 1130 and 1170 A.D. Lutheran now, it served Roman Catholics before the Reformation. Wooden houses in the old town are mostly occupied by artists but are so close together they present a very real fire hazard. The oldest school, built in 1740, is still in use.

Bryggen, the wharf, is a terrace of steep-gabled wooden warehouses along the waterfront. The market is busy and its colorful open-air fish, flower and vegetable displays are food for cameras.

Seattle, Washington, is the sister city to Bergen, and a totem pole in front of the aquarium is a gift from Seattle to her Norwegian counterpart. The Maritime Museum has intriguing exhibits of shipping from the Old Norse period.

The name Bergen means "Green meadow between the mountains". With 220,000 inhabitants, it is Norway's second largest city. It was vividly abloom with multi-colored rhododendron. A monkey-puzzle tree we passed was brought here from Chile. Bergen is fortunate, Anita told us, because it has more legacies than any other city in Scandinavia.

In the morning we took the funicular railway to the top of the Floyen mountain. The panoramic view is superb, embracing the picturesque city circled in the fjord, the mountains and the ocean.

By mid-afternoon, in a light rain, of course, we toured Grieg's house, five miles from Bergen. Leaving the bus at the foot of a sloping, winding road which was under repair, we walked a quarter of a mile up to the quaint Victorian summer home that was Edvard and Nina Grieg's. They called it Troldhaugen, the Hill of Trolls. The house is in an idyllic setting overlooking a lovely lake and surrounded by a park filled with pines, linden, and golden rain trees. Close to the house, geraniums sparkled in oval beds, and rhododendron were at the peak of color. Rows of beech trees along the lane have been trimmed and shaped to resemble old olive trees. A semi-circular window centered with a single rose is above the entryway to the glassed-in porch. Down a narrow pathway, bordered with pansies, is Edvard's one-room garden study where he did much of his composing.

Edvard Grieg (born 1843) and his wife lived in Troldhaugen for twenty-two years and both are buried here. In the realm of music, Grieg looms 100 feet tall, but in life he was only five feet in stature. Pictures show him in later life to have had a strong resemblance to Albert Einstein.

The original scores of the A-minor piano concerto, the Peer Gynt Suite, and two songs done in collaboration with Hans Christian Andersen are displayed under glass. The grand piano he used is in the living room and kept in perfect condition. Weekly recitals are given in the house. Nina was Edvard's favorite pianist.

Eme and I combed all the music stores in Bergen to find a cassette containing both the piano concerto and Peer Gynt, and found exactly one.

On our return trip to town our guide told us the Bergen Symphony Orchestra is 218 years old. Other statistics she gave are that four daily newspapers are published here; the main export is dried fish which is brought from all parts of Scandinavia and elsewhere for processing. You spend many years on a waiting list to buy an apartment in Bergen. Houses, in general, are woefully scarce but apartments are particularly so. Most of the house roofs are red tile imported from Holland with some use of slate. Taxes are high and inflation is worse than ours.

Bonfires were being prepared for the Midsummer Night celebration but the temperature was more appropriate for New Year's Eve. Hawthorn trees with rose pink flowers were in bloom along the streets.

The Hansa was one of the largest breweries we passed. Dr. Hansa discovered the bacillus of leprosy. The final note of information was that Bergen gets a minimum of eighty inches of rain per year.

Excitedly we waited at the Air France gate for the plane to Kristianson and Copenhagen. We were given no plastic bag for breakfast. It was explained that no food can be served on flights within the country. So at Kristianson everyone — including those at the end of their journey — was given plastic bags with lunches in them.

One happy thing happened while waiting for the plane. A Brazilian man waiting to go through customs inquired where we were going and when we said "Copenhagen," he made a suggestion. "Ask a cab driver to take you to the restaurant of the candles, St Gertrude's," he said.

That night we did just that, and found it to be the dining experience of a lifetime. In the cellars of a medieval monastery built over 500 years ago, the Danish architect, Anders Dyrup, created a restaurant in 1972. He insisted on preserving the old setting and atmosphere, restricting decorative materials to wrought iron, stone, old wood, religious paintings and sculptures of the period. There's no electricity — just the mellow glow of 200 candles.

We were ushered first into the library-cum-bar. Enchanting is the only word for it. Thousands of books line the shelves in the room. Ultra-comfortable Chesterfield leather furniture sits on elegant Oriental rugs. We sipped our drinks as slowly as possible and called for repeats to delly longer here.

We were given maps and diagrams of the rooms and, after our dinner order was taken, were asked, in which room we preferred to eat. It was a hard choice but, in time, we got to see all of them anyway, as I couldn't leave without inspecting everything including the circular staircases. In an intimate dining room with candles flickering on tables and walls, we ate on pewter plates with wooden utensils. Fresh flowers took on a jewelled auro; classical music played continuously.

The Scandinavian Hotel left nothing to be desired and we were refreshed by our five-day stay. A flock of mail awaited us; how good it was to touch base with friends and family! We had a beautiful view of an island of trees and water out front, a most comfortable room, and a well-stocked mini-bar refrigerator.

It was overcast the next morning but much warmer than in Norway. After a bountiful buffet breakfast in the hotel we took the Grand City Tour with Greta as our guide. The city was founded in the twelfth century and of the five million inhabitants in the country, 1.8 million live in Copenhagen.

Bicycles were everywhere and there were paths from them off every street and major road. The Carlsberg Brewery is one of the largest and all profits go to the city. In 1913, Carl Jacobsen, the founder of the brewery, gave the city the world's sweetheart, the E. Ericksen statue of The Little Mermaid which sits on a rock in the lovely promenade of Langelinie at the harbor front. Inspired by Hans Christian Andersen's fairy tale, and sculpted of bronze, she is periodically washed by the waves and dried by the sun. It seems incredible that twenty years ago someone lopped off her head, but such is the case. We found her likeness in Swedish glass and brought her home for safekeeping.

We watched the changing of the guard at noon, but they were not wearing their brilliant red uniforms which are kept for special holidays or for Queen Margaret visits. They were dressed in black and white tops and blue and white trousers.

We found it interesting that the American and Russian embassies are separated by a cemetery. Three lakes crisscross the city.

In the afternoon we wandered their wonderful "walking streets" where no vehicular traffic is allowed, where musicians and artists hold forth, and youth wears its denims stretched as tight as muslin round hams.

In the famous Ilums Bolighus store, possibly the world's most superb showcase, Eme and I separated with arrangements to meet in the lounge. When I didn't appear, a clerk asked Eme if there was something he was looking for. Eme answered, "I've lost my wife."

"How lucky can you get?" the fellow moaned.

There is no crime here and it was safe to walk the streets, day and night. In late afternoon we went to the Tivoli Gardens where Walt Disney is said to have found inspiration for some of his ideas. This is not only in the heart of the city but it is the heart of the city. The 135-year-old pleasure garden covers twenty acres and is much more than an amusement park. There are free concerts, good theatre, ballet, supervised playgrounds and illuminated plants and flowers. It boasts numerous restaurants and cafes, and we were fortunate to get the last reservation at the Balcony which has excellent food and a view.

It is even more difficult to get an apartment here than in Norway. Our guide told of one person waiting twenty years to get one. The city simply grew too fast.

The Danish pastry was all you'd expect. Like the Greek tissue-layered baclava, it melts in your mouth. After over-indulging in this and smorgasbords all through Scandinavia, Eme said if he were Catholic he'd run right to the confessional.

A tour we took called "Round the Horn" had to be the world's best travel bargain. We rode a clean, comfortable train to Elsinore, home of Kronberg Castle and the setting for *Hamlet*; crossed by ferry to Helsingbord, Sweden, where we lunched at the Grand Hotel on plaice — platter-size flat whitefish, the most succulent I've ever eaten; rode a Swedish train to Malmo, Sweden, with its excellent shops; and then enjoyed a marvelous forty-five minute hydrofoil ride back to Copenhagen — all for $11.00. The train route to Malmo was strewn with wild red poppies and white daisies; seagulls clustered around the hydrofoil.

Elsinore, dating back to 1200, is one of Denmark's oldest towns. Although Hamlet never lived here you find his castle, grave, and a statue of him and Ophelia on the grounds. The real Hamlet lived in the seventh century in the pre-Viking era but his life closely paralleled that of Shakespeare's Hamlet. Kronberg Castle was a disappointment to me; I'd built it up much differently in my mind. The cannons on the ramparts were intact, the towers were graceful, but its renaissance interior and smelly moats left me cold.

It was fun walking into the city. We envied the cyclists and longed for our ten-speeds back home. One fellow intrigued and delighted us, simultaneously playing the guitar, harmonica, castinets and drums.

Suddenly we heard bands playing and saw coming, a block or two away, a marching parade. Onlookers crowded around and we too were agog with excitement. Balloons and flags waved and large posters atop long poles waved in rhythm to the music. Unable to read the placards, I clapped with a number of others and kept time with my feet while Eme captured a number of shots with his camera. As the parade passed from view I asked a bystander what the celebration was. "They are protesting for gay rights," he said.

We lunched at the Salad Bar on Stroget, Europe's longest walking street, and after a casual afternoon, had dinner in the Crown Room on the twenty-fifth floor of our hotel. The view was splendid, the music for dancing, dreamy, and the menu superb.

Unbelievably, the sun was shining as we left on an eleven and a half hour trip to Odense and Mr. Andersen's fairyland. We'd be covering part of the 250 miles on a large ferry that holds up to 1,000 people and almost as many cars.

Odense is the third largest city and one of the oldest communities in Denmark, dating from the ninth century. It has two faces: the one of the fairytale streets, houses and teeny shops; the other, industrial. Hans Christian Andersen was born and lived here until he was fourteen. The museum, which was his house, is filled with manuscripts, copies of his books and a collection of his drawings.

Our guide was Edith, who added a good bit of humor en route, including a demonstration of how Americans awkwardly manipulate eating tools. One of her truisms was, "Carrots must be good for your eyes; you never see any rabbits wearing glasses."

The barley here is used both for feeding pigs and the production of beer. The "landrace" pigs have one rib more than other breeds. This is also home of the Brown Swiss cattle. The startlingly yellow fields we passed were not mustard but rape, a plant whose leaves feed pigs and sheep, and whose seeds are squeezed for lamp oil.

At Rungsted, a village about halfway between Copenhagen and Elsinore, we passed the former estate of Karen Blixen, known better as Isak Dinesen. Here she spent her last years and is buried under a large oak tree. This much-admired Danish author (relish the magic of her prose in *Out of Africa*) was Hemingway's favorite.

Edith took us to visit a quaint house on a small farm of a friend of hers. Its thatched roof glistened in the light rain. Grass and straw makes for the snuggest roof thatch, but I liked best, one at Odense that was sprinkled with violets.

A river and a lake run through Odense. In these waters Andersen saw the beautiful swan and an odd duckling. "The Ugly Duckling" is really his autobiography. His complex started with his too big feet and too big nose and no doubt extended to fear of officious critics. Pining for appreciation, he turned these so-called handicaps into tales of Red Shoes, Little Mermaids, Match Girls, Naughty Boys, Thumbelina — and other enthralling childhood stories. He made silhouettes and designs as an artist and songs, novels and fairytales as a writer. Andersen loved top hats, and any chimney sweep who wore one was tops with him. He was a close friend of Charles Dickens. His 157 fairy tales have been translated into twelve languages. The Royal Doulton figurine of Danny Kaye as Andersen, displayed in the museum, is startingly lifelike and appealing.

It was a long absorbing and fun day, but as Edith remarked on the return trip, "With a bad driver you'd have no memory to take home."

We took another day to leisurely explore the environs of Copenhagen. We admired its many smooth gray-barked beech trees emblematic of the nation. Cutting down any of them is prohibited. The ships were out in full sail and the streets full of small cars. The cheapest one to be purchased, the Citroen, costs about $8,500.

We were due to leave on Scandinavian Airlines at 12:40 p.m., but due to an air traffic control strike in London, take-off was delayed until 2:45. The airlines cabled the Cramers in Mount Dora for us, telling them not to meet our plane. On board, the steward explained about the safety jackets with batteries that burn ten hours if immersed in water. Fortunately, they weren't used on this trip. The flight was filled but we had good seats and smooth sailing all the way.

Arriving in New York we found there were no connecting flights available to Orlando other than one landing at 2:00 a.m. We stayed over in an airport motel and returned to the airport early the next morning to get seats on a Pan Am flight and enjoyed tasty Danish rolls at Pan Am's Clipper Club.

The flight was crowded, every seat taken; children were spilling out into the aisles, luggage crammed everywhere, and we didn't have the seats assigned to us. I went to the stewardess who was being harangued by two couples who'd been sold the same seats, to tell her the Clipper Club had made us reservations for seats other than what we had. Eme, standing by the other seats, was shaking his head at me, saying I ought to be able to see we were lucky to be on board at all. We sat in the "other" seats and then came a tap on the shoulder and a voice saying, "Follow me."

Into first class we marched and the next thing, tablecloths were spread and there was champagne in our hands. Melon and shrimp came as a first course followed by steak, button mushrooms, and spinach souffle for the entree and raspberry parfaits for dessert. Not until then was Eme positive about why he'd brought me along.

Chapter 5

The Canary Islands: Homer thought them the Elysian Fields, Herodotus called them the "Golden Apple Gardens", others labeled them the Fortunate or Blessed Isles, and on first seeing them twenty years before, we'd believed them to be Paradise — these Spanish islands lazing in the Atlantic Ocean just north of the Tropic of Cancer.

An old magnetism had drawn Eme and me for our third return, but this time we were exploring first what surely is not quite the most beautiful, but the most astonishing of them all: Lanzarote, the easternmost island, one we had not before visited.

There are thirteen islands, seven major and six uninhabited ones, in this archipelago that Spain acquired in the fifteenth century. Iberia is the only airline that flies directly from Miami to Arrecifi, the capital of Lanzarote, with touchdowns at Madrid and Seville.

On leaving Miami in the early evening of March 1st, the clouds were routine fluff and castle-building but, next day as we left Madrid, they were silver bands stretched over the long chain of the snowclad Guardarramas. Two hours later our plane was circling above Arrecifi, sixty miles off the west coast of Africa opposite southern Morocco, long enough for us to view the fantastic, monochromatic moon landscape below. It is mountainous, scored with ravines and huge craters, and layered with tuff, slag and ash resulting, we were told, from the last series of serious eruptions that took place in six consecutive years from 1730 to 1736.

The Canary Islands are entirely of volcanic origin and include active and extinct craters, lava fields and sandy desserts, as well as luxuriant valleys, virgin woodlands, beckoning beaches, spectacular scenic vignettes and the showpiece of its numerous mountains; snowcapped photogenic Teidi, 13,000 feet high, which in clear weather can be seen island to island, from Gran Canaria to Gomera.

Originally these islands, so varied in personality, were inhabited by

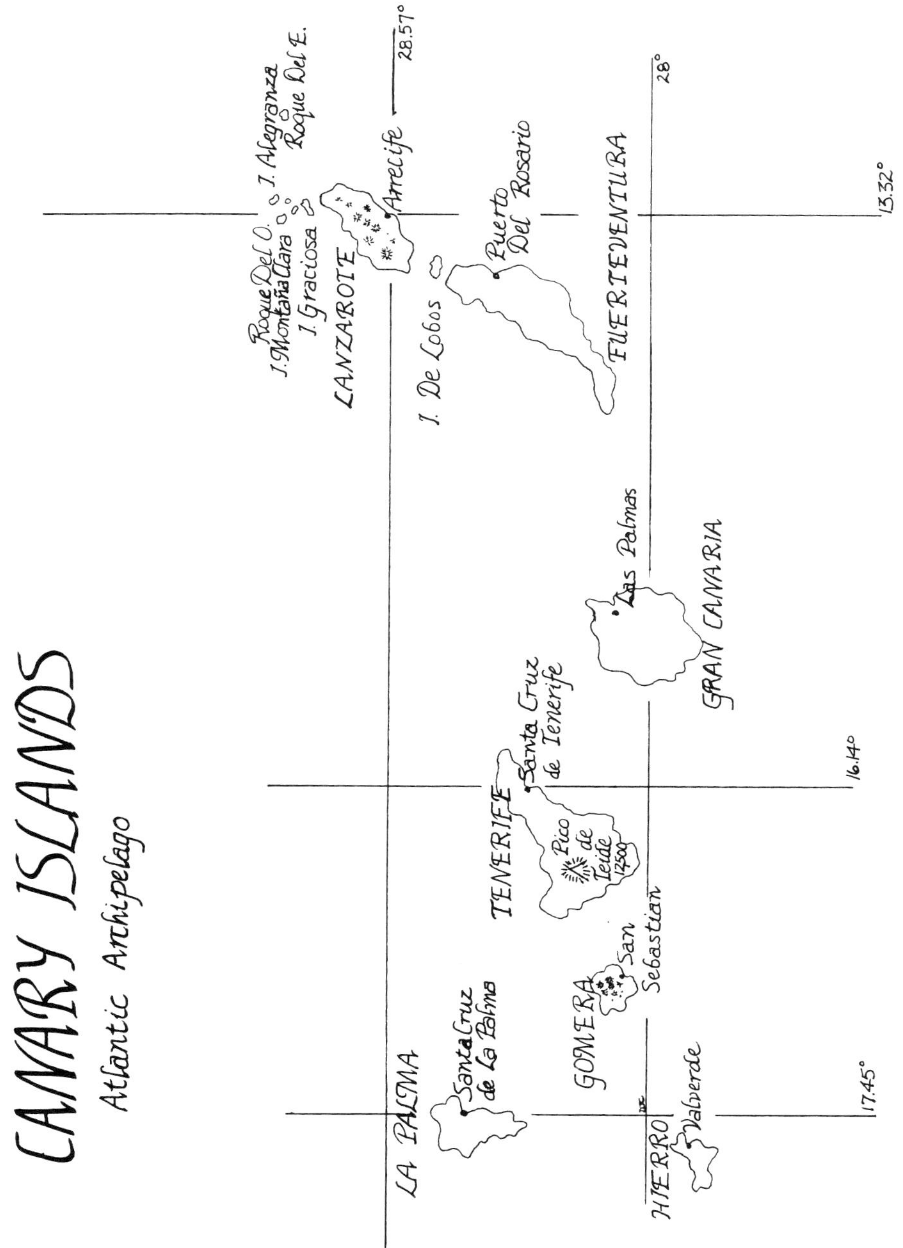
CANARY ISLANDS
Atlantic Archipelago
Roque Del O.
I. Montaña Clara
I. Graciosa
I. Alegranza
Roque Del E.
LANZAROTE
Arrecife
28.57°
I. De Lobos
Puerto Del Rosario
FUERTEVENTURA
28°
13.32°
Las Palmas
GRAN CANARIA
Santa Cruz de Tenerife
TENERIFE
Pico de Teide 12500
16.40°
San Sebastian
GOMERA
Santa Cruz de La Palma
LA PALMA
Valverde
HIERRO
17.45°

the Guanches, a tall, fair cave-dwelling people who knew nothing of boats but had an advanced social organization. In the Canary Museum on Gran Canaria Island, also in the Archaeological Museum in Santa Cruz de Tenerife, we had seen on our last visit, evidence of Gaunches civilization — their earthenware jugs and baskets, leather containers, and weapons. Only in Egypt, Peru, and here was true mummification practiced in ancient times.

Without stopping at the Canary Islands, Columbus would never have reached America. His ships anchored here for repairs, took on needed water and supplies and, in the *iglesia* in Gomera, he prayed before venturing into uncharted seas. On his four treks to the New World he took with him from these islands, sugar cane, fig trees, melons, oranges and lemon seeds, as well as chickens, goats and cattle. After his first base-touching in America and the Caribbean he confidently called them all "the Canary Islands of the Indies".

Many people think the canary bird gave its name to the islands, but the reverse is true. It was the islanders who called their small singer, actually more gray than yellow, the canary.

King of the flora on these islands, found only on two of them and growing spontaneously in no other place in the world, is the giant Canary dragon tree. Despite its closely-knit and spiked foliage, it belongs to the lily family and is a survivor from the Tertiary Age. The one at Icod in Tenerife is over 3,000 years old. The red resin of this tree was used by the Guanches in embalming.

One delightful boon in this archipelago is that it is completely free of snakes.

The seas around the Canaries, and particularly those extending between them, and the African coast are among the richest fishing grounds in the world. Our gourmet seafood dinners including Spain's national dish, paella, attest to that.

The drive from the beautiful airport of Arrecifi to our hotel was a shocker. When first seen, Lanzarote is overwhelming with its stark barren look of uncompromising terrain and utter desolation. Like an unmitigated catastrophe, innumerable volcanic cones teeter on endless brims of carbonized valleys — miles of nothing but fire, water, time and silence. Even words become a wilderness in describing it. Yet, there are striking contrasts everywhere from the black or ochre of its lava beds, to the intense blue of the ocean, to the white foam fringing its shores. Traveling north on the island (in all of them the north is always more fertile and less dry than the south), we stopped to watch friendly peasants digging in the life-giving cinders of lava in burned-out fields, a miracle of agriculture. In the depths of small cratered terraces thrive the grape vines that grow the exquisite Malvasic wine we sampled. Farmers spread a layer of fine volcanic ash over fields to absorb the night dew and retain the moisture and humidity needed by the grapes. Here also in this fine art of dry farming are produced the delicious watermelons, figs, tomatoes, potatoes and onions of the island, despite the fact there is less than five inches of rainfall per year. The peasant has persevered with his constant companion in labor, the camel. He scratches the earth with primitive implements — the Roman stick-plow — and digs funnel-shaped holes for planting. We watched one man at work in his black felt hat, his wife beside him with her white scarf, culling a living from this sea-tossed, stubborn earth.

In Lanzarote's brutal but exotic panorama there is an hallucinative impressive beauty; an invitation to repose here in direct ratio to the pervasiveness coastline is girdled with extensive beaches of fine golden, red, and black sands and coves hidden in the cliffs.

Our hotel, eight miles north of Arrecifi and about the same distance from the airport, faced the ocean and was a veritable oasis, set in green gardens among a sea of black lava. The hotel is a gorgeous white cantilevered structure surrounded by palms and grass, masses of bougainvillea, hibiscus and geraniums dripping from every balcony. It was designed by the famous architect, Fernando Higueras, and completed in 1977 after four and a half years under construction. He left absolutely nothing to be desired in this most extraordinary resort.

The marble-floored lobby leads to a large water garden open to the sky. Water cascades from four levels, fountains spray, giant ferns and imported palms rear cathedral high; ivy and geraniums entwine. Narrow grass walkways trail over pebbled lava and into cushioned coves. It is spacious, inviting, and entrancing.

The large and airy dining room overlooks the swimming pool and the bay. With soft lights and golden braziers aglow at each table it is a place of enchantment and romance.

Even the swimming pool reflects the genius of the architect. We swam around islands, under bridges, in deep and shallow water, and hopped into recessed coves at intervals. It is approximately four times the size of an Olympic pool.

Our spacious and attractive room had separate baths, tables set up for cards or writing, a mini-bar stocked with liquid refreshment, and a completely private huge balcony.

Eighteen entirely free facilities range from scuba diving, bowling and bicycling to wind surfing, archery and sailing. In addition, there was a nine-hole golf course, a nine-hole miniature golf course and five tennis courts. All considered, the rates were an outstanding bargain.

The hotel had seven national flags flying. When we arrived, an eighth was added: the American flag. Except for an occasional one from the cruise ships, there hadn't been an American here in over six months.

During our ten days on this island, besides exploring at random in a rented Colt Mitsubishi, we took two major excursions by motor bus that proved most interesting.

Arrecifi, built on a reef, is a picturesque town of 30,000. Its dazzling buildings, all made from volcanic ash and painted white, reflect in the deep blue of the sea. It's a clean town; sidewalks bloom with flowers and green palm trees, and gardens border the Redoubt Beach.

Our excursion to the north took us to the old capital of Teguise with its castle set on a volcanic cone; to Haira, the town of 10,000 palms and a splendid view of the nearby islands of Graciosa, a tiny fishing village with marvelous beaches. Throughout the trip we were more and more aware of the stunning contrasts between the terrible and the gentle. We passed quaint villages with thatched-roof homes and flowered walks, vineyards and fields of prickly pears, then came to barren lava lands and steep volcanic cones and were told we were driving over one of the eleven towns buried during the six years of volcanic upheaval. Looking at some of the wilder, more chaotic terrain, the earth seemed in perpetual torment. Weaving through weird formations of twisted lava we came to the Cave of Los Verdes, an immense underground gallery four miles in length (with some sections still unexplored) that winds from the volcano that created it to the sea. Our guided tour through this multicolored lava, many-shaped stalactites, green pools and mosses, all cleverly electrified, lasted one hour.

Also created in this eruption was the Grotto Jameos del Agua, our next stop. Through technicians and artists, this cave has been made into a fairyland. Down in the green pool at the bottom lives a primeval type of blind white crab, its origin unknown. The grotto has also been transformed into a restaurant and nightclub. Music, acoustically excellent, has been piped through the cavern. Canaries and other birds fly from the restaurant to the gardens at the other end. We sat sipping local wine and enjoyed it all.

On another excursion south on the island, we watched at La Geria the incredible devices that produce their wine. They dig craters ten to twenty feet wide and surround them with loose stone walls to protect the vines against the ever-present winds. The entire pit is covered with a layer of lava. Coming suddenly upon this area is startling: The acres of walled-in pits resemble a mammoth spread of Swiss cheese.

The scene changed as we passed a natural lagoon converted into salt flats. These are the largest salt pans on the island and the source of a great part of its riches.

The most spectacular feature of Lanzarote is Montana del Fuego — Fire Mountain — which has been burning since the eighteenth century. Look where you may, there's nothing but an endless sweep of lava, craters, and stark desert sands. In places the ground is so hot guides demonstrate how brushwood burns spontaneously and geysers spout when water is poured into tubes pressed into the ground.

Eme and I readied ourselves for a camel ride up the mountain of Timanfaya, 6,500 feet high. Camels, ungainly, unglamorous and sometimes cantankerous animals, are also patient, docile vegetarians and indispensable beasts of burden here. The camel we shared was a dromedary with one hump and wore a wire muzzle. We rode in wooden seats in a type of saddle slung over the hump. The rider weighing less rides on the right side, the other on the left. The camel (we hopefully dubbed ours Eureka) was lying down when we got into the open seats. We were told to hang on and beware as it lurched first to its knees then double-lurched to its feet. On wide, fat, squashy feet he plodded in cadenced gait on the zigzag path up the mountainside. Padding along in single file procession, we became acutely aware of the interminable stretches of black cinder sands and the awesomeness of silence. Only the rhythm made for reality as we reached the final ridge of Fire Mountain. Here, we were treated to an absolutely awesome view of 300 open, gaping craters that might well be remnants of the Big Bang. Eureka paused for photographs, shifting his cud in contemplation, then turned and obediently and slowly, but literally, hot-footed it down the trail.

After this trek we stopped at the village of El Golfo for a late lunch. First course in all village fare is a wonderful vegetable or fish soup. Often, after finishing this plus most of a loaf of hard-crusted fresh bread, we were ready to leave but couldn't resist either the entree or desserts. On one side of the Vermillion Mountain in El Golfo we looked below us under a volcanic cliff to see the lagoon separated from the ocean by a wide golden beach.

Water on all the islands is at a terrible premium. In Lanzarote, it has been especially so until the advent of desalinization a few years ago — with the help of some American money. Water sells for 150 pesetas or $1.50 for one cubic metre, plus transportation. About fifty million liters are used each day.

Stretched out on our balcony that night under a three-quarter moon as the sea sculpted the shore, the wind rustled, and the stars just escaped our fingertips, we decided this far-out island surfeits the soul. We wondered though, given the feverish building taking place, how long it will be before it sheds its Old World charm and joins the sleazy tourism elsewhere. Before that thought could jel, we left this shangri-la for our next stop.

Gran Canaria

It's hard to believe a fifty-minute plane ride brings such a transformation of scenery. We dropped down on the runway at Las Palmas, the capital of Gran Canaria, to catch the tempo and tab the changes.

The place was bursting at the seams. Like popcorn in an unlidded popper, tourism had exploded everywhere. Since 1979, we were told, the population of Las Palmas jumped from 275,000 to 400,000 people. The city covers the waterfront in a five-mile ribbon less than a mile wide and suffused with cosmopolitan color and chaos. Here we found the air contaminated by pollutants, traffic in snarls, and smoke billowing from manufacturing plants, ships, cars and motorcycles. The taxi ride from the airport to our hotel, Reina Isabel, taught us the traffic rules: (1) If in doubt, blow your horn and, (2) If street space is not available for parking, use sidewalks. Actually, cars and buses on these narrow streets have to use sidewalks for passing much of the time.

The port of Las Palmas handles the largest tonnage of cargo in Spain and is the third largest port in the world. It has an ordered look to it that the city surely lacks and is far tidier than the dirty and decrepit appearance of the urban streets. More building and more expansion is continually in progress. We were shown the new district that officials, ecstatic about, were calling "urbanization of the beaches". Their Gold Coast, of all things!

Growth here was, of course, inevitable. German money, while building, saw to that. At Maspalomas, the four-mile long beach in the south of Gran Canaria, there were apartments and rooms for 90,000 tourists and 30,000 more on Las Canteras beach. In a large bay within the city limits, the two-mile long beach of Las Canteras has very fine golden sand and is night-lighted for swimming. It is the drawing card for the people of Northern Europe who flock here in the winter. The view is toward the distant mountains surrounding it.

Our hotel was on the beach, a part of the Center City, facing the ocean and close to the Free Port's shopping section. No doubt it received its five-star rating because of this, and because of its top-of-the-roof swimming pool, sun deck and solarium. But for those of us royally spoiled in Lanzarote, it didn't quite meet this billing. Our balcony, though private, was tiny. Kleenex was doled out in sealed four-sheet packages. The electricity was temperamental and the faded oriental carpets, chipped marble, and frayed silk lamps attested to former better times. There was no chance of our going hungry, however; there were bars and dining rooms on five different levels.

Not far from Las Canteras beach is Santa Cataline Park near the dock of the same name. It's a small park but full of excitement. The main fascination is listening to the chatter of the throngs of people from every nation. We enjoyed drifting over there, day or evening, to catch the bustle and color, to watch the sidewalk painters and craftsmen at work and see, amid the trees and flowers, the diversity of merchandise displayed in the bazaars around the square.

Tiana is the main shopping street which follows through from the new urban district to the old section, the part with narrow streets, artistically decorated balconies and ancient mansions (the real Spain) dominated by its graceful Gothic cathedral and the museum housed in the governor's former home, Casa de Colon.

On our first day in this section we visited the museum, also known as Columbus House. Entering through the old spacious courtyard and sunny veranda, we were returned to another era. The doorways have decorative stonework, and the wall drawings depict the admiral's voyages. In the ground-floor, rooms are illuminated maps of his four voyages, his diary, and nautical instruments. In upstairs rooms are drawings of the Canary Islands at the time of the discovery of America, reproductions of Columbus' first three ships and reproductions of his flags and firearms. Other rooms display collections of paintings by Flemish and Italian painters and a fascinating exhibition of paintings that include some Goyas and sculpture on loan from the Prado in Madrid.

In the old part of the city, Vegueta, are wide balconies with delicate latticework, intimate patios and interesting examples of flowery Gothic architecture, including the sixteenth century cathedral with intricately designed tile walkways leading up to it.

An excursion to the north of the island had us winding through wonderfully fertile and varied landscape where, in Arucas, we saw cornfields, chestnut and popular trees, many kinds of fruit and blossoming almonds, as well as extensive banana plantations. Set among the banana trees and orchards was an amazing Gothic church. This is a city of well-tended artistically bedded gardens. A town of 30,000, it is known for its distilleries of brandy and bananas liqueurs, which we found both tasty and fiery.

The very elegant and unusual parador, one of Spain's super inns, was closed. Unfortunately for us, none of the paradors we saw on the islands was to open until May 1st.

A different tropical vegetation greeted us in the town of Agaete where there were date and coconut palms, mangos, avocados, pears, pawpaws and coffee bushes, extensive sugarcane plantations and a sugar refinery. The Mediterranean fly had attacked the orange trees and destroyed them, our guide, Benares, told us.

Benares spoke four languages — Spanish, English, German and French — all of them fluently. Had there been Italians on the bus, he could also speak that language. He drifted from one language to another with amazing facility. His English was faultless. He was born in Tenerife and graduated from the only university on the islands — at Las Palmas. Our bus was busily weaving up the narrow, twisty road, and as the driver was forced to pass another car, tissue paper could have filled the space between.

Coming into Moya, another sugar plantation center, we stopped to taste the famous Canarian rum and liqueurs — in very tiny glasses, I might add — also, the delicious Guia or "flower cheese" made from goat and cow's milk combined and fermented by the flower of the artichoke tree.

Our lunch at the tiny fishing village of Las Nieves was excellent. Custom in most communities requires three lunch courses and a supply of pitchers of sangria or whole bottles of the local wines.

On the return trip our guide took us through a banana plantation. Canary bananas are the tiny, sweet variety and sixty percent of them are exported to Spain. High walls protect the trees which must be planted between sea level and 1,000 feet. In this location three million trees were growing in an extinct crater. A new banana road had been tunneled through the mountains, passing over four bridges between here and Las Palmas.

The previous haunts of the Guanches were most evident here; their caves honeycombed the countryside. Some are now used to house cattle, others to hive bees. Some have been modernized with running water and electricity.

On a full day excursion to the south and center of the island we traveled first through a suburb full of luxurious homes, then through miles and miles of vineyards before coming to an oddity: Bandama Volcano. Here we photographed the only crater in the world where a small settlement of people lives year-round.

From there it was unforgettable scenery going up to Tejada where a parador is framed on its hill. From the highest point on a clear day you can see Teidi, white-capped and looming in the distance. Our day, as luck would have it, was overcast but we could see the two sacred mountains of the Guanches: Rogue Nublio and Bentaiga. The descent from here wound wickedly between peaks and valleys. One of Gran Canaria's outstanding features is the great ravines that drop from heights of 6,000 feet to the sea.

After lunch at Vallesco we continued on to the quaint, colorful and flowerful village of Teror, green with olive trees, and with a sanctuary in a grotto dedicated to the patron saint of the island. In the town were outstanding examples of the graceful and traditional latticework balconies.

Along the road were great masses of poinsettias, bougainvillea in a gorgeous magenta shade, wild buttercups and poppies. The Canary style houses wear red tile roofs, and most of them are painted white.

Our guide showed us the island's Mississippi River — a four-inch wide rivulet fretting down a mountainside. Much-needed water in Gran Canaria is furnished by 1,400 wells.

At San Mateo is a mellowed and typical old Spanish house, 260 years old, now a museum. Here we succumbed to the exquisite linen and fine lacework of the islanders and found a three-yard length of pale blue table cloth to take home.

Las Palmas' main industry is cigars and cigarettes, and from what we saw, every man and woman and many of the children smoke them. Practically all Europeans do, too. The countries from which most tourists come are Germany, Scandinavia, Belgium, England, Spain, Italy and Switzerland. Americans are scarce.

Tenerife

Iberia Airlines was waiting for us and in forty minutes we would be in the place that inspired our love affair with these islands, Puerto de la Cruz, Tenerife.

It was a goodly distance from the airport to our hotel, and this gave us the first glimpse we almost feared to take. It had grown, all right, but not in the disheveled way of Gran Canaria. We tabbed a few familiar haunts along the way.

Our hotel, Ybarra Semiramis, faced the ocean and beach with a swimming pool and sauna on its sky top. In this very modern structure the entrance and lobby are on the fifteenth floor.

A giant black and white chessboard with chess pieces three feet high is part of the patio setup next to the tropical gardens.

We picked our way through various parts of the city — taxis are cheap here — browsed through a museum and lunched at Tenna where we drooled over the paella.

Tenerife is the largest island in the archipelago. It has enormous contrasts, from moonscapes to lush landscapes. Through its center runs the mountain range that culminates in the peak of Teidi, the highest point in Spain. Extensive areas are cultivated and the flora is profuse. The beaches are both black and golden sand.

Santa Cruz, the capital, has 200,000 inhabitants. We found it still beautiful with parks, gardens and white buildings, but with much busier streets, new roads leading to it, and scads of new building projects in progress. It is the Washington, D.C., of the islands, the seat of the captain generalcy of the Canaries. The city's plazas slope down to its busy port. In the Concepcion Church is kept the Cross of Conquest and banners captured from Admiral Nelson.

As well tended as ever was the Botanical Garden, built in 1788 between La Orotavia and Puerto. It houses exotic plants and trees from all over the world. Puerto de la Cruz has a number of natural pools, and along the shore an artificial lake was being built.

Leaving Puerto it was slightly hazy at sea level, but hopefully, it would clear when we reached the mountains. It was an especially exciting day for us because we were to climb Teidi, something we'd always wanted to do.

Our excursion bus barrelled up a new road past unexpected sights. The highway was lined with blue jacaranda, eucalyptus and royal palms. Higher up were cork oaks and aspens and still higher it became almost fully pine-clad. Finally, we came to the dense groves of prickly gorse at Las Canadas, the gigantic natural crater some twelve miles in diameter. It has been declared a national park and is more than 6,500 feet above sea level. The rocks in it are of variegated colors.

We left the bus here and those not faint of heart trolleyed the rest of the way by funicular. A long line of people waited, only partially under cover, in wind blowing at a clip and little sun shining. The funicular tickets cost $3.50 each. There were two trolleys, each holding thirty-three people. We swung wide over the chasm! WOW! And climbed to 12,500 feet. The total length of time to go that distance was ten minutes. Once inside, Eme positioned himself at the front for good picture-taking. We got off at a small refuge on the side of the mountain and were sold hot chocolate with brandy in it. That really warmed us! We were wearing too light clothing for this trip, but it was the warmest we had packed.

Fortified with cheer and determination, the wind licking around us, we started, on foot, straight up for the last 500-foot climb to the top of Teidi. How glorious to have finally made it all the way, to be able to doff our caps to the white-capped one we had so long admired, and to throw a snowball to celebrate. With teeth chattering we crawled our way back down, and, after another outdoor wait, were glad to get back inside the bus where the strains of a Vienna waltz played on a cassette. We wound down the mountain to hot food and lunch at the Bambi restaurant in Orotavia.

Another day in Puerto de la Cruz we spent in town, part of the time in Casa Iriarte, the 300-year-old Canary mansion with galleries surrounding a patio devoted to the crafts of the islanders. We watched them embroider and do the open lacework, handtool leather, carve wood and ivory, filigree silver and gold, and do the marvelous damascening of Toledoware. One man doing the latter had spent twenty-five years in Toledo before coming here to continue his craft. All products were for sale at prices more reasonable than elsewhere.

The house contained a huge exhibition of maps, perfectly scaled model boats and tall ships. It is unique in its presentation of the history of Tenerife as it relates to the sea from its ancient history over stepping stones to the New World and the present.

One of the attractive aspects of Tenerife is the walking trips, delightful either high up or in the coastal areas. How rewarding are the ever-changing views. Tenerife has been called "a basket of flowers in the sea". Almost every kind of flower is here — alive and well. We were content, between touring, to loiter at a few of these favorite spots.

Gomera

This was to be another first on these islands for us: traveling by bus to the south of Tenerife and then by car ferry to Gomera, where we'd never been.

The road south was a good one and a big achievement, tunneled through part of the mountain to Los Christianos. Our bus followed us on board the ferry for the one-hour crossing. "I must remember you to be back at the boat by 6:10 p.m.," warned our bus driver, Manuel.

We docked at the capital of Gomera, the port of San Sebastian. Of 22,000 inhabitants on Gomera, 7,000 live here. There was a lovely twenty-seven room parador on the island, but it wasn't open either. Back in the bus again Manuel began the climb up the mountain over rugged terrain. Looking back, we had a captivating view of the harbor and the parador. With very little tourism in Gomera, the island has been left natural.

We were snaking up this road to see a very special virgin forest. The road, if you can call it that, was built by Franco's political prisoners from

Camels and passengers descending from Fire Mountain, Lanzarote, Canary Islands.

Finest example in the world of tree-covering of the Tertiary Age — centuries old forest of laurel, cedar, and pine on the island of Gomera.

Teide Volcano — 12,500 — Santa Cruz de Tenerife, Canary Islands.

Author and husband, ill dressed for the trek, slushing in the snow on Teide, 400 yards to the summit.

Our Hotel Las Salinas, a veritable Shangri-La on Lanzarote, Canary Islands.

1936 to 1939. As a hair-raiser, this was first rate. All in the bus voted Manuel the "mettle" of honor because he'd learned the road to the breadth of a hair and the length of a whisker. Some bends were cavelike trenches. As we went higher and higher, it was a quieting sight to see, on both sides on the road, this magnificent stand of centuries old Canarian laurel trees plus Canarian cedars and pines. United States botanists visit here often because this forest is the finest example of the kind of tree-covering during the Tertiary Age. Our guide pointed out the gorgeous ireca arbora trees which have white blossoms with red centers and grow to a height of fifty-five feet. At the peak of the mountain, 4,450 feet, are tabiba plants from Portugal and cactus from Mexico. The tabiba plants are green and yellow and look somewhat like dwarf dragon trees.

Returning, we looked down into fertile valleys planted with tomatoes, bananas, and date palms, although the base of the mountain itself is barren. Steep ravines cut through the island from all directions.

Back in San Sebastian we had a late lunch and looked forward to a treat promised by our guide. We were to hear "silbo", the whistling language that is on its way toward disappearing. It had been passed down from father to son, and children learned it along with their native language. Until the telephone made it obsolete, it was the best method of communicating across the ravines, from one village to another.

A message is preceded by a call for attention from the sender and an answer from the receiver is the equivalent of "Ready". The only whistling language in the world, each modulation represents a letter or syllable.

After lunch the demonstration began. One young man stood in the room we were in and his partner stood, sometimes in the next room, and sometimes outside. Anyone could ask a question in Spanish and have it relayed. By waving my arms excitedly I got first chance. I asked him to have his partner bring me a full, unopened bottle of uncarbonated mineral water. In less than three minutes it was put in front of me. Someone asked to have the lights in the next room blinked on and off, and they were. Another asked for a kiss from a pretty girl and one came out to comply. One woman, a little the worse for wine, insisted the young man had something in his mouth besides tongue and teeth, so he came close to her to prove her wrong.

We had many funny experiences on the islands with their own various languages. Very little English was spoken anywhere. One night I called room service and in my best Spanish asked for some very ripe sliced tomatoes. What did I get? Toothpicks! Another time Eme, who doesn't speak Spanish, asked room service for a mixed salad. "What kind of dressing do you have?" he asked. There was dead silence, then a voice replied, "One moment, sir, I'll give you the housekeeper."

We remembered to be back at the ferry by 6:10 for the four-hour trip back to the hotel. There was one more day of browsing in Tenerife and it was time to trek home.

Again, Iberia treated us to an ultra-comfortable DC10 flight to Madrid and then on to Miami. We arrived intact, but our luggage didn't. We had to wait two days at home, in Mount Dora, for it to catch up with us. And when it did, U.S. Customs had cut the chained combination locks off our bags and discarded them, although Iberia passed our lock combinations on to them. So, it was the old story: Win some, lose some. But how could we complain after such a happy trip.

Chapter 6

Time magazine stated in a recent book review, "The disease that affects so many tourists to China is romanticism and naivete." True, because tours, in general, tend to homogenize the personal experience of travel with 'just what the doctor ordered' fervor, and tourists often superimpose their Western stereotypes on a foreign country and return from it spreading the contagion of wide-of-the-mark cliches.

"Sorting truth from facts" is one of China's new slogans and is especially pertinent to tourism. Most of us arrive in strange lands with preconceived impressions. John Fraser, the Canadian author, thought, as a child, that it should be easy to tunnel all the way through the world and pop out at the far end right into China. My hold-over was from Fifth Grade geography when the teacher pulled down the big map over the blackboard, took her pointer and said, "This morning we'll be traveling to a far-off land, and we'll be peeking in on Peking." The class tittered but my seatmate and I, at our ink-welled desks, doubled up in a fit of giggles. Little did I know how long it would be from that first faint glimpse to a real look at the least accessible country on earth. And the teacher's reference to peeking couldn't have been more apt because China has always been a secretive country and a loner, not just since the rise of communism, but in ancient times when emperors sought to insulate themselves and their territories from foreign encroachment and barbarian taint.

Too many have wanted to relate, by camera or print, only the good in China, not the real. When James Reston of *The New York Times* went there for the first time in 1972, he reported: "They are engaged in one vast cooperative barnstorming." If China could do that — broadcast its views and stage its opinions — how blest the Chinese would be. They had a recent breather and hour of glory though, as Fraser, an eye-witness, vividly described it, during four months of 1979 when Deng Xiaoping, China's premier, gave free reign in Peking to the poster

BEIJING
(PEKING)
The Great Wall
CHINA
Xi'an
Shanghai
Chengdu
Guilin
Kunming
TAIWAN
Guangzhou
(Canton)
Nanning
Hong Kong
35°
30°
25°
20°
130°
125°
120°
115°

makers. Hungry for recognition they came to the Xidan Democratic Wall which stretches 200 meters in front of a bus station. They came by rail, by bus, on foot from near and far, cautiously at first, then openly, to add their calligraphy to huge posters (pinpointing their protests, airing their grievances) before pasting them up on the Wall. Great crowds jammed in lines, rubbing elbows and snarling traffic, waiting to read and digest the posters. Then, as unpredictably as the privilege to write and be heard began, so was it unceremoniously taken away and the ban clamped on again and tightened. Yet, something in the air had cleared and hope was definitely alive.

In the United States, the love affair with China started with the New Left in universities and grew to a crescendo in 1966 at the time of the Cultural Revolution, the most massive political upheaval of the twentieth century which, in the long run, accounted for the massacre of her culture. The Chinese Communist Party has admitted it was a disaster, but at the time of its conception by Chairman Mao, it was construed as an heroic effort to rid China of its class distinctions and economic disparities.

In China a new system of spelling has evolved called Pinyin, a word that means blending sounds, and which is supposed to aid foreigners phonetically in learning the language. But, like trying to teach Americans the metric system, it's hard to cope with once you've been familiar with the old ways. So, with well known names in this account I'll keep the familiar spellings as follows:

Old Spelling:	New Spelling:
Peking	Beijing
Canton	Gangchow
Mao Tse Tung	Mao Zedong
Chou En-lai	Zhou Enlai
Sun Yat Sen	Sun Zhong Shan Ling
Deng Xiaoping	Teng Haiao-ping

To appreciate the country better and our venture more, Eme and I have enjoyed a copious amount of China reading and the following are some of the gleanings:

The history of the world's oldest continuous civilization began more than 5,000 years ago. Its country is 90,000 square miles larger than the United States and is landlocked, except for its eastern seacoast. The world's highest mountains rim its southwest and west borders; the Mongolian Desert and a frigid frontier are shared with Soviet Siberia on its north. One billion people live in China today — one out of every four of the world's population. The greatest part of its population crowds in the fertile valleys created by the Yellow, Yangtze, and West Rivers.

These are the people who invented paper and printing, silk and porcelain, compasses, important aspects of medicine, bronze casting (never matched since), paper currency and gunpowder, and a complete counting system a thousand years in advance of Rome's. These are the people that titillated the curiosity of the world, the ones who, in the thirteenth century, Marco Polo couldn't write fast or glowingly enough about and thus, on his return from Kubla Khan's court, earned from his fellow Venetians the title of "man of a million lies".

These are the people whose exquisite landscape painting was conceived centuries before Europe's and whose poetry is a way of life. Over half of all their literature is in this form and they themselves consider it one of their greatest achievements.

Their outstanding philosopher-sage was Confucius, born in the sixth century B.C. He spelled out the Golden Rule for them, and it was he who suggested that lighting a single candle was better than cursing the darkness. Confucianism was remarkable because it was considered appropriate for the problems of everyone from emperor to peasant. It took on the role of a father concerned with all his children. It was bound to neither church nor religion but spoke for the common concerns of all through ethical principles based on learning. Confucius made ancestor worship and filial piety the keystones of Chinese civilization and, for twenty centuries, his tenets and ethics dominated social and political thinking.

His rival and contemporary was Lao-Tsu who influenced a minority of the people by preaching the mystic philosophy of Tao, harmony with nature.

The third major spiritual source was Buddhism, imported from India in the second century A.D. Although alien to Chinese modes of thought (by denying family obligations) it dealt with human suffering and destiny, about which other Chinese philosophy had nothing to say.

During the legendary period of China's ancient dynasties, life changed but little and slowly through the centuries. Culture and deference to Confucius maintained the feudal order and helped develop a strong attachment to clan but discouraged personal innovation. This tempo sufficed until the eighteenth century when, after Manchu power dwindled, complacency set in as irrigation systems collapsed from neglect, corruption spread among officials, taxes and rents skyrocketed, and revolt and famine became common. Records of the time show people in some districts reduced to cannibalism and peasant leaders burned alive by the authorities.

At this time the industrialization of the West was disastrously felt in

China. First came the traders, then the missionaries who set up hospitals and schools and introduced new concepts in science and law and stressed the value of the individual — the very ideas and ideals that had activated the French and the American revolutions.

China's revolutionary spirit sprang from the age-old struggle between landlord and peasant, between the class that claimed the land (and through its monopoly of education controlled the government) and the working peasantry — eighty percent of the population. The latter paid the heavy taxes, provided soldiers for the armies, suffered from inadequate shelter during floods and famine, and stagnated in ignorance and poverty.

For 100 years, from the time the British defeated the Manchu troops in the Opium Wars (1839), China continued to lose face and suffer one gross humiliation after another. Country after country wanted what it could get for the taking. China was sliced up like ripe fruit and the spoils divided. The French and English sacked Peking, Russia took Port Arthur and parts of Manchuria, Germany took Kiaochow, America insisted on the "Open Door" policy of trade, and Japan (1895) drove China from Korea and seized Formosa (Taiwan).

Foreigners took control of customs and treaty ports, a monopoly of transport, and finally the right to locate Western-owned industries on Chinese soil. This was the straw that broke the camel's back. It ruined village industries with factory-made goods, increasing the common people's hardships and embittering them. Anti-foreign riots started in a China that was prostrate. As the Manchu Dynasty passed into oblivion the man who picked up the pieces was Sun Yat Sen (1911) who devoted himself to establishing a constitutional government somewhat along Western lines. Sun's followers staged revolts in Central China; the whole country then followed suit and a republic was proclaimed with Sun as its president.

In 1917 China entered World War I on the side of the Allies. The Versailles Conference proposed that Japan take over Germany's territorial and trading position in China as a reward for her participation in the war. Violent student rioting, in protest, broke out in Peking.

The result was electrifying: Intelligentsia and peasants united in a move against foreigners. This revitalized Sun and his Nationalist (Kuomintang) Party which, after his death in 1925, was commanded by Chiang Kai-shek. Serving under him was a communist political chief, Chou En-lai. At this time the communists were but a small minority, but Chiang, having ties with the landlords and business classes, looked upon this Left with growing fear. Finally, he turned on Chou in an effort to purge all Left-wingers. According to U.S. Government reports he killed hundreds of thousands, all without trials. Chou En-lai and his followers fled to the hill country.

History proves they benefited by being pressed into the wilderness where they were joined by other Red groups, one led by Mao Tse-tung. Mao outlined a method of defeating the landlords. The policy won the affection of the peasant majority and cemented the friendship of all the communists who slipped through the Nationalist lines in 1934, and embarked on the 6,000-mile Long March to safety in the north. Of the 100,000 who set out on the Long March through excruciating hazards only 7,000 reached Shensi province. Many, ravaged by disease and hunger, had to eat bark and drink their own urine to survive.

Chiang Kai-shek decided to hold part of his army in reserve, not committing the whole of it to the conflict with Japan but continuing to blockade the communist-held areas. This weakened his already-frail standing with the people. He refused to give the communists any representation in government and became the despair of his American advisers. In 1949, he fled his homeland to Taiwan. America had poured millions of dollars in aid into his lap, much of which found its way into his personal coffers.

The communists won the civil war because they took the part of the peasants against landlords, not because they had the backing of Russia. Chairman Mao told Edgar Snow (*Red Star Over China*) in 1936, "Whoever wins the peasants will win China."

As Steve Allen points out in his book, *Explaining China*, "To have a monolithic view of Communism is to be seriously misled, but Americans have held fast to this view of World Communism."

Despite the sins of communism and many of Chairman Mao Tse-tung's purges and failed programs, the experiments that survived in China made its communism and national life distinctive. Mao unified a torn-apart country and, because of him, one billion people enjoy a much better life than did previous generations. "Don't wake that sleeping giant," Napoleon said of China, but Mao did just that. Under him an illiterate nation did an about face, becoming a ninety percent literate one. Women were given equal rights and peasants were given small plots of the "good earth" to till.

John Fraser, who, in 1979, was sent to China as the Peking Bureau Chief of the *Toronto Globe*, says he found the people far better off than before the revolution, but that there were still plenty of beggars in rags and human beasts of burden, in contrast to the political elite in chauffeured cars, shopping and eating in places open only to them.

Mao's heirs have inherited low productivity, a high crime rate, monstrous over-population and underemployment, but as Dennis Bloodworth states in *The Chinese Looking Glass*, "Mao's one great unexceptionable achievement was restoring the all-important 'face' to China that the barbarians had torn away." The term barbarians includes all foreigners.

China detonated its atomic bomb in 1964. In 1967, just twenty-six months afterward, it achieved atomic fission and exploded a hydrogen bomb. The same step took the United States over seven years.

In 1971 the People's Republic of China, long denied the privilege, replaced Taiwan in the United Nations. In 1972 President Richard Nixon made his historic breakthrough to United States fellowship and peace with China.

W. Scott Morton says in *China, Its History and Culture*, "What shines out in contemporary China is a sense of purpose, of progress and of pride."

When the Central Committee met in 1981 it praised Mao as their "great proletarian revolutionist" but regretted the ideological and political errors he'd made during the last two decades of his life. After his death and in the resulting political turmoil, the famous (and truly infamous) Gang of Four took over. These included: Jiang Qing, Mao's widow; two Shanghai radicals; and the vice-premier. Their reign lasted one month before they were arrested and incarcerated for conspiracy to overthrow the government. In the summer of 1977 Deng Xiaoping was reinstated to power and position. The Gang of Four had been the actual perpetrators of the Cultural Revolution which the Chinese people, especially the intellectuals, believed had made their country a laughing stock and a degenerate nation.

It was Premier Chou En-lai who finally restored to honor and power many prominent victims of the Cultural Revolution, most notably Deng Xiaoping. He used the prestige of his office in the last four years of his life (he and Mao died in 1976) to establish the Four Modernizations of: Industry, Agriculture, National Defense and Science-Technology, slated to be attained by the year 2000. Under Premier Deng Xiaoping these programs have progressed on schedule.

Our Horticulture Tour took off for this fabled land under the leadership of our good friend and guide, J. Barry Ferguson. Barry was our leader when we backpacked on the Milford Track in New Zealand and it was his wit, savvy and unwaivering enthusiasm that made the trip so memorable. Barry is a horticulturist, landscape artist, and well known on television and the lecture stage. One of his projects in New York is having charge of the Botanical Gardens. A magazine article called him "the man with flower power." Add to that word power and extraordinary art and skill power and you come closer to listing his special charms.

Eme and I felt fortunate to be on this China tour with him and with our friends of long-years' standing, Barb and Miller Sherwood from Michigan, whom we talked into going along. Since the Sherwoods were a bridge game ahead when we last trekked with them in South America, and were no doubt hoping to add to that handicap, they accepted without hesitancy.

Eastern jetted Eme and me from Orlando to Kennedy Airport the evening of August 29th. An overnight at the Hilton refreshed us for our meeting with Barry, the Sherwoods, and the rest of our group of twelve for the next day's 12:45 p.m. takeoff on Japan Airlines for Tokyo.

Japan Airlines does almost as good a job of pampering its passengers as Singapore Airlines. On a completely filled 747 we were well taken care of, and the plane was immaculate. Takeoff through a white-frosted blue sky was prompt. Most of the passengers were Japanese people returning home.

The Sherwoods (our fellow travelers on the Galapagos trip three years before) were a mighty welcome sight as was Barry, effervescent as always. Our tour members included three from New York, two from Massachusetts, two from New Jersey, two from Michigan (the Sherwoods), and three from Florida, Eme, myself, and a woman from Sanibel. In Tokyo we picked up the other member of our group, a Californian.

After using the warm washcloths passed out by the gracious Japanese hostesses, we were given rice paper napkins and small bottles of Bordeaux, then settled down to the inexorable rhythms of engine drone, good food, reading or a movie if we wished, occasional isometric exercises and rapport with our fellow travelers. I watched a Japanese child across the aisle self-consciously struggle with two forks held upside down to eat and thought to myself, "I should do so well with chopsticks!"

Our first touchdown, eight hours after leaving New York, was a refueling stop in Anchorage, Alaska. We bought postcards and stretched our legs a bit before takeoff in a low diffusion of weepy clouds spread over very rugged terrain. The captain pointed out the Bering Sea and Kamchatka as we passed over them. The weary bunch of us deplaned at 5:00 p.m. at Narita Airport in Tokyo to meet the final member of our group, Audrey Summers from Los Angeles.

We had just finished going through customs when whom should Eme and I see on the other side of the gate but Karl and Hiroko Dyslin of

Peoria, Illinois. Our nephew, Karl, we hadn't seen in fifteen years. Only that morning he'd received our letter saying we would be overnighting in Tokyo, and he had come to meet us. He has an import-export business and alternates between his Illinois and Tokyo homes. It was a wonderful treat to meet his wife and take them to the Narita Prince Hotel where we were staying, and then to dinner at the top-floor restaurant. They introduced us to exotic Japanese dishes, both the contents and the method of attack. Eme is a natural with chopsticks and enjoys eating with them. I'm definitely a dud, but credit me with sticking with these elusive prongs for the entire trip. It was late when we said good-by and Eme and I numbly found our way to bed.

The Narita Prince Hotel is beautiful, with every conceivable amenity — many that American hotels don't offer.

After a leisurely breakfast chosen from a picture-postcard array of the freshest and most colorful delectables, we were off again to the airport for the one-hour flight to Osaka. As we skimmed the runway we looked up at the cabin movie screen to see, by Aero-Video shots, the takeoff of this JAL flight. It was a thrill, never having seen one before, to watch our plane gaining speed on the ground and taking off into the fair skies. Soon after we could see, through the window, the shoulder of Mount Fuji nudging the distant clouds.

On September 1st we wished Miller "Happy Birthday". We'd skipped saying it to Eme on August 31st because we lost his birthday crossing the International Date Line.

Reaching Osaka, a city of 2.7 million people, we wandered outside the airport among masses of bonsai trees and artistically trimmed ginkgos. Our guide was really as sweet as her nickname, Sugar — short for Osaka. We started our sight-seeing in a minibus — just the right size car for us — going to Kyoto, sixty miles distant, where we would stay two days.

Nara, the first small city we came to, was Japan's first capital. There is much evidence here of antique traditions. We visited the East Temple which the Japanese copied from the first Chinese capital. Their national religion, Buddhism, was also imported from China and in Kyoto there are 1,900 Buddhist temples. Nara claims the largest Buddhist temple in the world, built in 1750.

The Japanese actually synchronize their religions, Sugar explained. They marry in Shinto temples, bury their dead in Buddhist temples, and find nothing amiss about celebrating Christmas. There are no images in Shintoism. At one Shinto shrine, Sugar told us, the proper procedure is to "close your eyes, make a wish, clap hands twice and drop a coin in the offertory so your wish will come true." One of the most amazing statistics

Sugar gave us was that forty percent of the young still have "arranged marriages", and want it that way.

The Japanese houses seen along the way were made of wood with red, blue or slate-gray roofs. As we started on the expressway we were going through the mountains. Rice fields were abundant; many farmers get sixty-five bushels an acre with the average yield being forty-five. There is actually over-production since the younger generation doesn't eat much rice. Everyone in Japan over sixty-five receives free medical attention.

Stopping in Nara Park we visited a Shinto shrine and inspected the stone statues; many round squatty ones lined the steps and winding trail. Set in the midst of a thriving bamboo woods, 1,000 deer roam this forest. Sugar told us the origin of an American expression. She said no one in Japan was allowed to kill a deer and if a dead one was found in front of someone's home, he would be buried alive for the offense. Finding one, a homeowner was quick to transfer it to his neighbor's front yard, and that was called "passing the buck".

In Kyoto, a town of 1.5 million, we stayed at the Hotel Miyako. In the sky room that evening we had a most appetizing dinner and a superlative view of the city. We would find food and drink terribly expensive throughout Japan.

We had a more commodious bus the next morning with Sugar in charge to brighten our sightseeing. She had already taught us *okini*, the Japanese word for thank you, and *ohio*, which means good morning — an easy word to remember for those of us who had lived there.

Our first stop was at Nijo Castle, built by the first shogun in 1603. Its thirty-three rooms were filled with marvelous carvings and the ever-so-fetching "nightingale floors". When one steps on these wood floors a clamp underneath moves up and down and a bird-trill sound is reproduced by friction between the nail and the moving clamp. Kanoi artists have put gold leaf on their paintings displayed here. The Japanese depend on shadow for natural effects with no color added. The feudal lords ordered much damascening done. Tokugawa shoguns controlled all feudal lords between 1600 and 1867.

I liked Sugar's use of plurals: "we'll go there togethers." About Buddhism she said: "with it you get a peace mind." As with Christian denominations, she told us, there are some 100 kinds of Buddhism. And "the small ties you see on bushes are for bad wishes." Her most astute philosophical observation: "It's simple to know the tenets of religion, but hard to believe in them."

Outside the palace are neatly trimmed grounds that require thirty men about three months, twice a year, to contour and maintain. And the flowers are coddled, too. Chrysanthemums and ripples add design to the roofs. The nearby bamboo forest is hushed tranquility.

Back at the hotel we enjoyed an afternoon at leisure with the Sherwoods. We got into our swim suits and discovered an unused pool on the seventh floor (two huge ones were at ground level). We ordered lunch with wine and afterwards swam and played bridge, each winning one rubber with thirty points difference to date.

It was early dinner and bed by nine because our wake-up call was for 4:00 a.m., for a 5:30 departure on JAL. Sugar greeted us with "Ohio" and taught us a song called "Sakura" meaning cherry blossoms. No matter how tiny the streets or humble the dwellings we passed, everything was painstakingly neat.

Japanese written characters were created from the Chinese alphabet and both languages are read from top to bottom but the lines run from right to left on the page.

At the airport we got out of the limousine and Sugar said good-by, telling us to "please all stay right heres. I bring the porter before I go." She did and the limo, and Sugar, departed.

I not only stayed "right heres," I stopped dead in my tracks — my trip was about to end before it began. I had picked up my tote bag but left my purse, passport and all, on the limo that had joined dozens like it in the milling crowd of the busy airport. Sugar was gone and we had exactly two hours until our plane left for Shanghai. Not speaking the language and unable to find anyone to understand English, I was mistakenly sent up two floors and down four, from one place to another by Japanese personnel trying to make out my speech and panic. An official finally got my message translated for me at the limousine counter.

Meanwhile, Eme thought I was under the charge of an English-speaking assistant and worriedly waited for me to return. Barry was getting our boarding passes, and although he tried to contact me, my erratic up-and-down flights made him miss me. In one of my cross cuts I finally found him, and he stemmed my trembling lip with a firm "don't worry" handhold to rush me back to the limo counter. But the official who'd taken me there had left. As we were running toward the counter a Japanese boy came racing toward us holding up my purse. I grabbed it and kissed him. Not until I saw Eme, fifteen minutes before boarding time, did I throw my arms around him and let the tears sprout. Perhaps I needed this lesson early. My compatriots, who were all sympathy, said it taught them a lesson, too. We checked one another from then on and almost everyone of us, at one time or another, left something behind.

I learned here, and later, not only the group's capacity for empathy but of the members' compatability as well. We had with us another horticulturist besides Barry, a computer expert for NASA, the wife of the music critic and columnist for *The New York Times*, a computer trouble-shooter, a semi-expert bird spotter (who loaned us her binoculars for use in field, museum, and opera), a geology major (Barb), several businessmen, and Edith. Her full name was Edith Meiser and she was eighty-four!

Edith was tall, willowy, smooth-skinned, with light blond hair softly waved and short. She had nice teeth and dancing blue eyes. At one time she and her husband ran a radio station and took all the major dramatic and speaking parts. She had been a star on stage, screen and television, playing with Katherine Cornell and Helen Hayes. With a melodious voice, mellow sense of humor, and instant recall she made for very good company. Her large lace-straw hat was a standout in a crowd and she used an elegant parasol as a cane when needed. Standing under it for sunshield in her high-fashion outfits, she might have been a model for Renoir. The fact was she had so many charming outfits we suspected her modest-size suitcase had secret compartments. "Just let me do my own thing, Darling," she would admonish anyone wanting to give her an arm up or down steps, and she flatly refused any help with her totes or luggage, saying she hadn't come to be a burden to anyone. We grew to love her and look out for her.

Some of us were a bit knowledgeable in Chinese. Bonnie Shattuck, the thirty-four year old computer troubleshooter, was by far the most proficient, having taken a five-week university course in it. The Sherwoods had been tutored in basics and phrases by a friend in Michigan who was from Shanghai.

The Chinese language presents a thorny problem to foreigners. I know the old saw about not teaching an old dog new tricks, but I'm convinced a new dog is equally hard pressed to learn even to bark in Chinese. Three weeks before leaving I bought the neat little "learn Chinese" book written by Mary Chiang, and sent for the speaking cassette. It came a week later and proved indispensable for tuning the ear to pronunciation since there are tens of thousands of Chinese pictographs and only 100 syllables with which to pronounce them; one sound can represent over 100 characters. On top of this, the tones — and there are four of them — completely change any syllable's denotation. And, on top of that, there are eight major dialect groups with "Peking" spoken by seventy percent of the people. Guess why only a pittance of the "foreign invaders" ever conquered the native tongue!

At 10:30 a.m. Flight 971 was off and again the passengers watched the movie of our plane in actual takeoff. Two hours later we were drifting down, readying for landing, into the country a *New York Times* article described as: "Powered by muscle and fueled by sweat," and waiting to exchange our hellos for "nihao ma's," which translates, "Hello. How are you?"

Shanghai is one of three cities directly administered by the Central Government. It is the largest city in Asia and the second largest in the world. Its shores touch the East China Sea on the south bank of the world's third longest river, the Yangtze.

Getting a first glimpse of this fabled land we saw it was a green world outside and the temperature was 82 degrees.

On the minibus with us, as we left the airport, were our local guide and our national guide — the pattern throughout the entire trip. All travel in China is monitored by the China International Travel Service and often the exact itinerary and hotel reservations are not disclosed until the tourist arrives in China.

Mr. Chen, our national guide, would be with us during our entire stay to translate, smooth over difficulties, and travel with us city to city until we left. Clean-cut, nice looking, smiling and slim, he had earned everyone's fondness, admiration and respect by the end of the trip. The father of two children — a boy sixteen and a girl of twelve — he was a dedicated party member whose wife worked with him in the office.

We passed rice paddies, wheat and cotton fields, and rows of plane trees, known as Chinese parasols, that led to our hotel. The Hengshan Guest House, a fifteen-story structure, was renovated in 1980 and boasts 220 air-conditioned rooms and suites. In drawing for room numbers Eme and I were lucky enough to get a suite.

As we started off on our sight-seeing that afternoon, it was hard to believe this city began as an eleventh century fishing village and is now home to nearly twelve million people. Early European traders flocked here and you can see their architectural influence along the Bund, the wide avenue and legendary waterfront beside the muddy Hangpu River. A second river, the Wusong, also runs through the city. The harbor is China's largest port.

The streets made us feel at home with their resemblance to Western ones: massive banks and hotels line them opposite the wharves. No longer known as the Bund, the section is called Zhongshan Road East, and some of the most imposing buildings belong to the government. Trolley buses, a few cars, and zillions of bikes filled the avenue.

We stopped at the City Museum which has one of the outstanding art collections in China. Besides the paintings, sculptures and ceramics, the bronzes were especially fascinating. China has never been equaled for its bronzes, and some of the ancient ones date from 1900 B.C. Tools, weapons, instruments of torture, food and wine vessels, literally breathe their history and artistry. One warrior and a horse from the Qin dynasty (220 B.C.) found in the Xian excavation of terra-cottas, is on display. A closeup of the intricate details is entrancing. On one floor, old colored, crackle-glazed pottery covers an entire section along with beautiful blue and white Ming vases. China was reputed to be, because of the chinaware she early introduced abroad, "the land of porcelain".

We went through the Trade Fair at the Shanghai Exhibition Hall, an attractive building with a reflecting pool in front. One section contained all industrial products, the other displayed countless articles for sale.

The streets in this buzzing metropolis are remarkably clean and the number of people, utterly incredible. Despite all we had read, seen or listened to, Eme was totally unprepared for this influx of people or the white-shirted, curb-to-curb students wanting to walk with us and practice their English. I met many interesting, smiling Chinese this way. The children loved having their pictures taken and often the parents posed them for us.

In one morning of sight-seeing we visited the Botanical Gardens. After being given a brief account inside a pavilion, we wandered through a fifty-acre section of the total 168 acres open to the public. The garden has 5,000 species and exchanges seeds and species — the main ones being camellias, azaleas, and orchids — with thirty countries. Their bonsai tree exhibits have won prizes in many countries. A greenhouse was under construction for tropical plants. Traditional gardens and fruit orchards were not yet open.

On a short visit to the zoo we captured on film the rare giant pandas (thirteen in all), the red-crowned cranes, and golden monkeys.

Later we stopped at the bright saffron-walled Jade Buddha Temple, built in 1882. No cameras were allowed. Here we saw the exquisite Burmese white jade statues, one sitting and one reclining. Other ancient Buddhist statues, sutras and paintings were also on view. Some worshipers still attend and a dozen monks live in the temple.

Our lunch at the Park Hotel was a mouth-watering gourmet feast with dozens of choices in spanking-clean surroundings.

On a catamaran we cruised the Huang Pu to the point it joins the Yangtze River. Here, the Yangtze is fifty miles wide. Much ship building was going on in this tremendous harbor because of oil recently discovered in the China Sea. Natives and tourists waved from Chinese and foreign ships as we passed. There were huge barges of coal, and almost every size boat, including many junks and tankers. The wind whipped up a light breeze and a cassette on board played Vienna waltzes. On the return trip we kept warmer inside and played a little

These life-size terra cotta warriors and horses are part of the thousands in the recently discovered and excavated Chin tomb. Picture is courtesy People's Republic of China. Unauthorized pictures taken here are immediately confiscated by on-duty guards.

Section of the Great Wall of China, at Badaling Pass.

Facsimile, in color, of the gray terra cotta soldiers found at the dig of Xian tomb, where cameras are forbidden. Figures show some of the ethnic groups, their hair styles, and costumes.

Faces of the Sani people of Kumming are as vibrant as their dress and bazaar crafts.

bridge with the Sherwoods while Mr. Chen offered a bit of advice on "misplays".

After a multi-course dinner at the hotel, we went to an auditorium to see Chinese gymnasts put on a spectacular show worthy of the Olympics.

It was "nihao" (pronounced knee-how) from Mr. Chen next morning. Wide streets and friendly crowds — in every direction we were wedged in. Pedestrians swarmed like a miniature Milky Way and bicycles flowed like a river. Perhaps the people seemed more numerous because of the uniform white shirts worn by most men and women. The children wore colorful outfits and we were told adults are now able to buy patterns and colors too. The busiest shopping street is Nanjing Road. A park, large stores, small shops and hotels jam-pack it. People here work six days a week and shop on the seventh, so, in the holiday convergence, breathing space is at a premium.

Celebration of the Twelfth Congress of the Party was in progress all over the nation. Red Banners and streamers decorated buildings, lampposts and streets.

For dinner at the hotel we were served, lazy-susan style, soup and countless appetizing dishes, plus good crisp apples to eat later.

At 4:00 a.m. excitement wakened me. I got up to window-watch and listen to the murmur of night noises. From the living room windows I followed the trolley-buses skimming along, the honey carts (foot-pushed, wheel barrows), the bike-pedaled ones hitched to trailers and the motorized flatbed, stacked-can ones. There were the light feet of an occasional jogger in white shorts, the silent pedals of the two-wheelers, the constant background drone of cicadas, and the bent-over or steady-gaited pedestrians carrying sundry loads. Only an occasional horn tooted.

Before 6:00 a.m., because I couldn't go back to sleep, I was out on the streets in the warm, humid air, where I met Barry and the Sherwoods also ambling and taking pictures. Tai Chi exercises (shadow boxing) were being done in the park opposite the hotel, as on almost every street and by every age individual from the slow strokes of the elderly to the ballet or acrobatics of the young. Early shoppers walked along with market purchases in their hands — chickens lugged by their feet offered no protest. The streets were overhung with plane trees, like our sycamores. Workers with small straw brooms were already out sweeping the gutters, and sprinklers were cooling and cleaning them.

During the day Shanghai bustles with trade and industry. Its 8,000-odd factories make everything from White Cat detergent to Spring Thunder radios, as well as autos, elevators, and sewing machines. New

living-quarter highrises are everyplace and more are going up daily. The largest indoor stadium, in China, with 18,000 seats was built here in 1975. The city is also known for its medical achievements and its surgeons have become famous for being able to re-attach severed limbs and digits.

I had the misfortune to develop a cold and Mr. Chen, who also had a touch of one, helped me buy two face masks to wear. I'd hoped not to contaminate the others, but such was not the luck; almost everyone took a turn at getting it.

Before leaving Shanghai and en route to the airport we visited the Yu Gardens. This exotic layout of colorful ponds, tiny bridges, rockeries and winding paths was inspired by a famous landscape artist of the late Ming dynasty, Zhang. The garden is divided into three parts, separated by dragon-spined walls. The pavilion in the center of the lake was once a teahouse called Willow Pattern. The outline of the Huxinting or pavilion is the center motif of the well known blue and white willow pattern underglaze porcelain, which is still made and was once Shanghai's symbol.

Readying for departure, we realized you can't be an American in China for even a few hours without feeling an all-out friendliness. One of the joys of this country is: "No tipping allowed." You don't feel anyone is obsequious because of expectation but that the help you get comes willingly and with a smile.

An old Chinese proverb says, "Keep a green bough in your heart and the singing bird will come." We had hoped that after a year of Barry's dickering, and with Mr. Chen's help, we would get to see Guilin, so we were keeping that green bough where it belonged. Our sightseeing at an end in Shanghai, Mr. Chen counted heads and said, "Zhou ba!" Let's go!

On the way to the airport Mr. Chen stopped at a restaurant to buy lunches and beer for our flight on China Airlines. We could eat them either in the waiting room or aboard. We found later which was best: Quarters on board were plenty cramped and Chinese domestic planes were mostly of a long-past vintage. The ubiquitous (but we were told excellent) beer or a sickly-sweet orange drink were the only beverage alternatives — not only on the airlines but at most meals too. All the tea in China? We seldom saw or were served it.

On the minibus, after our arrival in Peking, Mr. Chen introduced Mr. Wang, the local Chinese leader. Barry, of course, was the one who had to make all important decisions and smooth everything on both sides of the fence. He was happy to have such an intelligent and flexible man as Mr. Chen to work with.

Of one thing there was no question; we'd been guaranteed (for over a

year) of staying at the Diaoyutai State Guest House, probably the most luxurious accommodation in China. The villas in the compound numbered twenty in all. Ours was No. 11 and we were the only ones in it. Former President Nixon arrived the next day and was in No. 18. During our four and a half day stay we passed his place daily and saw the long black cars lined up in executive formation.

The State Guest House has its own security; no one unvouched for or without a pass can enter the gate. It has its own post office and small store in Villa No. 3. Situated in the western suburbs, this place was formerly an imperial palace. Built over 800 years ago, it features one of the famous gardens of Peking. After the founding of the New China, the old garden was given a new look. In 1959 it became the state guest house for heads of state or government. The various villas have art treasures of different periods. The grounds are graced with stone bridges, a pavilion and lake in the compound, meticulously kept lawns and colorful varieties of flowers and shade trees along the winding walks. Our accommodations were so plush, combining all modern amenities with Chinese styles, we pinched ourselves wondering when the bomb would fall.

On our first evening we were given a welcome-to-Peking banquet. The napery and table setting was elegant; the superb dinner included: For appetizers — minced chicken with radish, lettuce root salad with mandarin oranges, sauteed cucumber and small ravioli with orange sauce; Then — soup, noodle pancakes, deep fried with rice angel hair, very large fried prawns, dumplings in sauce, noodles in sweet-sour sauce, salad of lettuce-root balls, carrot balls, and monkey head mushrooms, fruit salad in sauce, honeydew slices, cream-decorated layer cake and watermelon balls. Many toasts were given with wine and tiny glasses of maitai, their national drink, which is pure liquid lightning. Each of us was presented a gift of a beautiful pure silk brocade.

Early next morning we left in the minibus for a short stop at the zoo which in the Ming dynasty was an imperial park. Today it houses 3,000 animals including Mr. Nixon's gift, one of the two musk oxen still alive, and it has a fine outdoor bird sanctuary. The giant panda, native to Sichuan province is here. George Schaller, we had read in the *Orlando Sentinel*, is one of the few scientists to have seen this rare panda in the wild because it is so reclusive and isolated, living in the inaccessible mountains of southwest China.

Our next major stop that morning was at the Summer Palace, the recently restored summer residence of emperors. The grounds cover nearly 700 acres of parkland with Longevity Hill, its prime scenic view, northward and Kunming Lake, south. The lake, a great favorite of the

city dwellers for boating, swimming and skating, occupies almost three-fourths of the total park area. At the edge of the lake is an elaborate marble boat. Bronze lions, a unicorn, deer, and a phoenix — the symbol of immortality — adorn the courtyard. After entering the walled grounds through a red gate, we passed numerous buildings, all with such poetic names as "The Hall of Jade Billows" or "Bridge of Embossed Ripples". The structures were formerly the royal apartments, and some still contain precious art objects and antique paintings. The glazed tiles of gold on the palace roofs, shimmering in the sunlight, have their own lyric swing.

On top of Longevity Hill, overlooking the lake, is the 'Listening to the Orioles" pavilion restaurant and interesting shops. At lunch we sampled velvet chicken, fried fish in sweet sauce, corn pone, and winter melon soup. The Chinese serve soups last, almost like a dessert course.

After lunch we were poled in boats on Kunming Lake, crossing it to reach our bus which had gone round to meet us. It was an absolutely perfect 75-degree day, sunny and bright, with scenery to match. We were keeping that green bough in the right place.

On the road again, we viewed fields of taro and whole tracts of rice. The huge sunflower plants are the size of trees. Next to the Botanical Gardens was a private ginkgo grove. Barry was bringing the administrator of the gardens all kinds of cactus plants and seeds from America as a gift.

After sampling the local cuisine at a neighborhood restaurant we went to Exhibition Hall to watch a performance by a special ensemble — a celebration in song and dance (with vibrant costumes) in honor of the Twelfth Congress. The Seagull ballet was pure excitement of utter grace and breathtaking precision.

Another balmy morning found us in the Forbidden City, the Imperial Palace, which is actually a maze of palaces containing 9,000 rooms, located in the center of Peking. We approached it by a lake and wide moat, entering the gray crenelated walls around it through the southern side at Meridian Gate, the longest and most imposing of the four gate openings in the wall. Inside, the tentlike basic design of the buildings is unusual: raised on platforms, the roofs are supported by pillars, not walls. These golden roofs are spellbinding, undoubtedly the most gorgeous sight in the Forbidden City. Their gently turned-up ends are decorated with ceramic figures; the most prominent motif, the dragon, is a symbol of the emperor, the phoenix or peacock, of the empress. Beside the palace is an artificial, rather unimaginative garden.

For five centuries the Forbidden City was the emperor's throne, the center of the world closed to all commoners, but now open to all, it is the

Imperial Palace Museum, housing an extensive array of architecture, ceramics, fabrics and art. Many of its rare valuables were confiscated by foreign troops; many were taken to Taiwan; but the Chinese communists, realizing the genius of the work, want to preserve it despite the apparent contradiction of imperial exploitation versus national treasure.

We climbed the three flights of stairs leading to the Hall of Supreme Harmony, but the emperor never did. He was carried up the carved center ramp on a litter. The hall was built in 1420 and became the site of the rigid "Palace Examinations." Successful candidates became "scholars"; graduates were appointed to high positions.

The Forbidden City combines very ornate figures with those rich in simplicity. The variety of treasures in the various buildings is amazing. It would take weeks to explore all the dozens of palaces and gardens, but just scratching the surface, the impact was overwhelming. As Marco Polo said of China's wonders, "But I have told you only half."

Afternoon found us in Beihai Park where Kubla Khan had his palace on a lake in the Round Town, but little remains of his time here. The Bridge of Perfect Wisdom linking Hortense Island to the lake is one of the park's landmarks and on the island is the White Dagoba (Tibetan style) built in 1651 in honor of the Dalai Lama after a visit from him. Strolling through the pleasure gardens helped us realize why they're so popular with urbanites who can also boat and swim in the lake. We came back from the stroll on the subway for 10 cents apiece. It was clean, free of graffiti, and had immaculate stations.

At the Restaurant of the Five Fragrances we had dinner. As always, washcloths were passed first and small paper napkins were rolled in the glasses. We did justice to two kinds of shrimp, sesame dumplings, and their famous five-cube dish — five kinds of meats and vegetables cubed. They kept piling dish after dish on the table until either counting or eating was impossible.

That evening we gussied up to go to the opera. Edith, in a flowing outfit, could be spotted as a box-seat first-nighter anywhere. The performance, as a whole, was enjoyable; the first act, outstanding. We could easily have skipped the nasal, high-pitched singing but the dazzling costumes were worth the price of admission. Completing the Oriental picture was the use of stylized ritual and odd instruments. Turnout for this opera astounded us — a completely full house of both young and old Chinese coming just for drama (no violence). But the timing of the swords in Act One was a real spine-chiller; the expression on the girl's face (the victor), a triumph.

We returned to the hotel still thinking of this as well as of the

excitement ahead. Another day of days — we were going to The Great Wall!

During the one-hour bus trip we passed through a number of communes where the vegetables growing included beans, cucumbers, eggplant, chard, Chinese cabbage, chives, onions, corn, and coriander, which is used as a garnish instead of parsley. Rice fields were everywhere, terraced or flat. We traveled a narrow two-lane road with a ridge of hills in the distance and on either side, orchards of apples and pears with melons and grapes heavy on the vines. We passed a free market where, when commune quotas are filled, an individual may get cash for the rest of his produce, such as tobacco, sesame, peanuts, dates, pigs, and so forth. Irrigation has helped the communes by pumping water through canals to the fields. Water buffalo are used for plowing, hauling and for food. Sorghum is grown in the highlands and used in making maitai.

Beyond the hanging rocks above us we could see branches of the Great Wall. A train whistled past: the Siberian Express that travels between Outer Mongolia and Peking. Wild morning glories were thriving; the countryside was awash with them in every color. Cosmos and daisies lined the winding trail. Yellow squash and hollyhocks added to the picture.

Along the way we listened to a recorded talk on The Great Wall. Like the pyramids and hanging gardens, it has been considered one of the four great wonders of the ancient world. Here in the Yanshan Mountains we scrutinized the masonry of such a gigantic engineering feat that the contemplation of it is stupefying. The wall stretches over one-twentieth of the earth's circumference. At the Badaling Pass, where we were, its gray granite blocks tower twenty feet into the air with five-foot parapets crowning that, and a paved road wide enough for a half dozen cavalrymen to gallop abreast. The wall is clay or earth facing with brick gates topped by watch towers. Had Robert Frost been able to survey all its original 1700 miles of sinuous and undulating rhythms he would have hesitated to write: "Something there is that doesn't love a wall, / That wants it down." The Chinese definitely want this one up and keep it in good repair all the way from the Gobi Desert to the Pacific Ocean. It is their tourism drawing card, the only visible manmade earth sight from outer space, and now as always their symbol of culture, unity, and greatness.

It may have been erected in the third century B.C. to please the vanity of the boy wonder and emperor, Ch'in, from whom the country takes its name. It was he who, tearing down parts of the protective walls around a flock of warring, multi-languaged states, brought the people

together by giving them a common written language and a common administration. He built highways and dug canals to link the empire. And his wildest inspiration was to conscript labor, criminals and prisoners of war, as well as many from the intellectual elite, to build this great wall running east and west across the entire border. All north of the border was considered "barbarian" lands and all south of it was China. His plea to his subjects to spur them on was that these crenelated ramparts dizzyingly scaling mountains (in spots at impossible angles almost two miles high), looping through valleys and plains, plunging into gorges and crisscrossing rivers, would keep out marauding armies and Mongolian tyrants.

Many of the 25,000 watch towers, forty feet high and measuring two bowshot lengths apart, still stand. (Paul Revere would have appreciated these.) From them, with smoke signals and flares, soldiers could spiral a message across the empire in twenty-four hours. In its heyday one million men garrisoned these ramparts. Little did they realize that by the hundreds of thousands they would eventually die on the job from disease, exhaustion, and hunger, and be buried in the foundation along with the too-slow workers who were buried alive beside them.

The kingdom Ch'in expected to flourish for 10,000 generations actually held together only three years after his death, but The Great Wall survived and later emperors enlarged it to its present length of 3,700 running, zigzagging miles.

At Badaling Pass we climbed every inch of the way to the top in a whipping wind and peered out through the watchtower, listening for the raiders' hooves.

After this indelible experience our feet retreated, and we ate our box lunches contemplatively. En route back we listened to a cassette before stopping to go through the Ming Tombs carved out of solid rock in the fifteenth century. Thirteen to sixteen Ming emperors chose to be buried here, just north of Peking. Through the central archway we went, to the first of the thirteen tombs through the Dragon on Phoenix gate. Beyond the gate is a huge stone tortoise, symbol of longevity. It is the beginning of the famous avenue of animals: lions, camels, elephants, horses and several mythical beasts — all of which we covered photographically.

We had our first feast of Peking duck that night at the Big Duck. It was brought out, before carving, for our inspection and approval.

After dinner we went to hear a friend of Barry's lecture on "Modern Chinese Art". She showed us her home — an apartment adjacent to the Peking Hotel. She's an Italian, married to a Chinese, and had a handsome and beautifully-mannered fourteen-year-old son as well as a shy young daughter. Her painting-displays were lovely and showed the

comparison between ancient and modern Chinese art.

The *China Daily* newspaper announced, in a front-page article, that Peking's birthrate was down one percent — less than ten per 1,000. Birth control has been written into the Chinese Constitution. The municipal government passed regulations giving benefits to young people who marry or have a child late. Men who marry after twenty-five or women, after twenty-three, get twenty-two days leave. Every one-child family will receive a monthly five-yuan subsidy until the child is fourteen. The sixty yuan is equal to the monthly pay of an average worker. In the countryside, one-child families receive two shares of private plots and 400 extra work points toward cash awards.

The resolutions on the new Party constitution adopted by the Twelfth Congress was cause for great celebration. Our Mr. Chen, who lived in Nanjing, expressed his happiness over them. The national flag was prominently displayed: five white stars on the big red-star field. The white star in the center represents the Party; the four surrounding it represent the workers, the peasants, the petty bourgeoise, and the national bourgeoise.

There is a Friendship Store in every city and we shopped at Peking's looking particularly for jade. A common misconception is that jade is always green, whereas it can vary from being colorless to blue, red, gray, black or brown, as well as apple or emerald green. Jade sings when struck, I learned. It feels smooth and slippery to the fingertips when polished. We found a special piece for Cindy. Jade is found in riverbeds, especially in Khoton, and some is mined or dug out of mountains. Today the work is mechanized and stone is not just material for jewelry but also used in industry. The Chinese call jade "the stone of heaven" and prize it above diamonds.

Wandering in the Square, we got the feel of its massive structures and memorials. Tien Anmen is the largest public square in the world. Some of the buildings around it show the stark frigidity of Russian influence. The Gate of Heavenly Peace, of heavy stone with wooden roof, is dominated by an immense portrait of Mao Tse Tung, whose impact on world history is immeasurable. An enormous memorial hall in his name was completed in 1977.

We were enthralled by the bike population here — 3.5 million of them — the largest in the world.

Like schools of fish, they swim around the flat streets (a paradise for them) and float through the oceanic crowds. Flying Pigeon and Phoenix are the most popular brands and Eme and I got to inspect several carefully. I liked hearing the tinkle of their bells and seeing the riders stack their purchases, packed in nets or lotus leaves, in the baskets or

across their backs.

This city, home to nine million people, has fifty institutions of higher learning. It is the country's greatest repository of monuments and ancient treasure. We were aware here, as in Shanghai, that there is no place in China to be alone. I know Mr. Kodak must love us, and China, too; there's a picture around every corner such as: seats of moppets' pants are intentionally split (without benefit of underwear) for quick curbside action; kids ride piggyback on their father's bikes; pedal vehicles come in all sizes; babies ride in bamboo perambulators (like glorified supermarket carts), and the evening's dinner may be flapping its wings while being carried home by the feet.

After an early breakfast we were off in the bus for the airport and Xian. We saw many brick plants en route. From the lowliest hovel to the largest building, brick is used. Mr. Wang said precast concrete is also being used for the new housing for the masses. There was a good mixture of silver poplars, pines and seedling acacias along the streets, and the willows were trimmed to resemble hula skirts.

Because of the dust, wind, smoke and ever-present pollution, Peking is known for its respiratory ailments. Unfortunately, Eme got both a cold and a cough while there.

It's impressive, as you leave this ancient city, to realize it is where Peking Man roamed, 500,000 years ago. Remains have been found in a nearby cave. It's also where the People's Republic of China was proclaimed in 1949.

We left on China Airlines, on a four-engine turbo-prop (a pure antique). The belt was broken on Miller's seat so they tied all six-feet three-inches of him in with rope. Quarters were so cramped we could scarcely move. No announcements were made about seat belts or smoking; Chinese characters flashed on just once. The mid-morning snack was a small bucket of orange ice with a wooden spoon — very refreshing. Also, a tray was passed with foldup fans for everyone.

In Xian the minibus and our local guide, Mr. Ma, were waiting for us. It was hot, very humid, and the dust seemed worse than in Peking. On a tree-lined boulevard from the airport to our hotel, plane, willow, poplar and tung predominated. The tung trees, from which tung oil comes, has large leaves and purple flowers. Most of the houses we passed in this city of 2.8 million were the traditional style with courtyards.

We touched base at our hotel, the Wei Bin — the same name as the river here — long enough to use the facilities and were promptly off for a museum, city and countryside tour. The first commune we passed outside the city has, Mr. Ma told us, 23,500 people, 5,000 bikes and 1,500 sewing machines. Most peasant houses have three rooms: a center room

for eating, one room for sleeping children, and one room for sleeping adults. Thanks to adequate rain the crops are rich and plentiful: cotton, corn, wheat and sweet potatoes. Ninety-five percent of the people in the northern part of the province live in caves and sleep on kangs, straw-type mattresses. School is compulsory from seven to sixteen and primary school is held for the three-to-seven-year olds.

Settled since the paleolithic era, this city is the capital of Shangai province that was, intermittently, the capital of the whole empire for over 1,000 years. Once dripping in imperial splendor, it is now a model of the PRC government's efforts to create new centers of industry. Ancient walls surround the city, and wide avenues, laid out in criss-cross pattern, are pleasing, but the new urban developments are stodgy high-rises.

We were in the southern district at the Neolithic Museum housed on the grounds of a former temple of Confucius. It has an impressive collection of historical relics: Persian and Byzantine coins, beautiful glazed pottery horses figurines from the Tang tombs, exquisite murals, bronzes and ceramics. Its centers of attraction are the gallery of ancient stone carvings and the library of 1,000 steles that record the evolution of the art of calligraphy.

The bell tower of the town, built in the fifteenth century, has a two-story wooden tower with graceful arched roofs. The third floor we climbed to had a fine view of the city and of the Drum Tower one block away, built in the Ming dynasty.

Our dinner in a local restaurant that night was early enough for us to make a 7:15 movie. The picture was pure propaganda but good photography, and had cheery pictures of the great progress China is making toward its goals of the Four Modernizations.

We headed fifteen miles east, next morning, to Hot Springs, a place used by royalty as early as the eighth century B.C. This is where Chiang Kaishek was captured while trying to escape up the steep trail behind the pavilion.

Three miles east of this spot we approached the archaeological find of the century, the tomb of Ch'in Shi Huang. The mound over his tomb, forty meters high, can be seen from Xian. The tomb itself had not yet been excavated, but a nearby pit showed lifesize terra cotta warriors and figures carrying real arms. This museum, built to house and display what has already been excavated, is just north of the mound, known as Pit No. 1. Down eleven long rows, with still unexcavated runways in between, we walked back and forth as well as around, to better view this marvelous, compelling array, this incomparable sight spread before our eyes. It left us staring and speechless as we circled the huge, domed

arena to witness such an astounding exhibit of art. The pottery figures of infantrymen and horses in front of their royal war chariots are lined up in battle formation, as if awaiting commands, in the red soil of the pit. Figures of the soldiers and their servants stand six feet tall. The warriors in armor are no doubt generals.

Men and horses are realistically modeled of fired clay. Heads, hands, and bodies, we were told, were made separately and are hollow inside, whereas the feet, legs and arms are solid. The hair is so vividly sculpted it is like that of a living person. Originally the figures were painted in bright colors, but most of the dye is now faded. The metal weapons are real, as are the wooden crossbows and arrow bags, spears, knives and hammers. Some of the warriors wear tunics with waistbands or knee-length jackets with short sleeves; some wear stocking caps, other puttees. Some of the leather armor is intact. One man wearing a leather vest kneels with a crossbow. Horses have flying manes, knots in their tails; ears are forward with forelock between, and some seem to be panting. Other heaps of battered statues lie, as yet unrestored. On the ground are strewn arrows in bundles, free of their quivers.

In 221 B.C. Ch'in, founder of The Great Wall and the first empire, went on probably the most extensive ego trip in history. Fearful of assassination and hankering for immortality, he lived in easy luxury and incredible splendor in a palace a mile and a half long and one-half mile wide. He switched sleeping places nightly, rotating among his other 270 less regal abodes within an area of sixty miles, all connected by tunnels. His tomb was as sensational as his dwelling and took thirty-six years to complete. It was then covered with a hill so ingeniously concealed it wasn't discovered for twenty-two centuries and then only by accident. Farmers digging wells near his mausoleum in 1974 unearthed one of its subterranean vaults. In it was what we were feasting our eyes on. In battle array, a whole handmade life-size army of some 6,000 archers and soldiers, with other charioteers pulled by teams of horses and all cast in painted terra cotta, are the bodyguards ready to serve their master in the afterlife. He was buried in 210 B.C. So definitive are the features, hair styling, mustaches and limbs on the various figures, it has been easy to pick out the minority groups in the bodyguard lineup.

Only Chinese archaeologists and restorers have been responsible for this tremendous presentation.

Pomegranate and peach trees surrounding the tumulus, Mr. Ma told us, were planted so that the already sunken earth will sink no further.

After several hours of viewing (at times with Mary's binoculars) we left this unforgettable scene to have lunch in town. It was a many-dished, piled high, appetizing one. The spring rain noodles Eme could

eat endlessly, along with lotus pods and fresh dates.

What a joyous day this was. It was the Sherwoods' forty-fourth anniversary, and the wonderful news was passed through the bus that we'd been given permission to go to Guilin. That green bough in the heart really had worked magic.

Meanwhile, we were off to see the Big Wild Goose Pagoda, a square brick building seven stories high that houses the Buddhist sutras and the Sanscrit texts brought from India by a monk. There are 248 steps to the top of the temple and it was well worth the exercise up the spiral staircase for a super view of the city and the promise that those of us who made it are assured longevity.

Next, we went to see two factories, one for making cloisonne, and the other for reproduction of clay figures and warriors of the Ming dynasty. We could buy products, if we wished, in either one.

En route back to the hotel Barry pointed out the blue-black drongo birds with swooping tails winging through the poplars.

Hurrying to dress, we helped the Sherwoods set up the wedding anniversary cocktail party, featuring our wine and theirs bought in Peking. The hotel gave us a lounge for the occasion and we'd invited the bus driver, Mr. Ma, Mr. Chen, and all members of the group. The guests supplied the appetizers from their "rainy day" rations. Each one brought something they'd saved — a few American pretzels, a can of peanuts, mints, a few cheese crackers, and some seaweed tidbits served on Japan Airlines. Eme and I had arranged with Mr. Chen to order a big (and it was a simply delicious) decorated cake that said "Happy 44th." We saved this surprise to have at the end of dinner.

Another day, another city! We were up at 5:00 a.m. to leave for the airport at seven, en route to Chengdu. Tai Chi exercises were being practiced in every block. Telephone poles were made of cement because wood is scarce.

We ate our box breakfasts in the bus and flew China Airlines on a rare Ilushun-14 Russian plane, vintage 1940, that held thirty-two people. Luggage couldn't come on the same plane, it followed on a later one. No food was served on this two-hour flight, but a tray of pretty pink mirror-comb sets were passed out. In the front of the plane, the altimeter was on one wall, a clock on the other. We had seat belts but no life jackets, masks, or the like under the seats. Without pressurization, it was murderous on the ears.

In front of the Chengdu Airport were formal gardens. The gardens were a mass of bloom and fragrance. Barry identified the lovely hedge as serissia. Miss Cheng Lei, our local guide, was there to meet us, but a dim and dreary day greeted us.

It was rice-cutting time and the growth was profuse. There are two crops a year and we followed the extensive paddies all the way to our hotel, the Jing-Jiang, near the river of the same name. We didn't linger at the hotel because no luggage would be arriving for some time; instead, we started sightseeing.

The countryside was full of olive trees, oleander, eucalyptus and loads of flowers. Bamboo grass and taro were thriving and the boulevards were ablaze with canna blooms and crepe myrtle.

Chengdu is the capital of Sichuan province, the most populous one in China with 100 million people. The Tibetan population alone is more than a million. The city is watered by the Min and Tuo rivers and is meticulously cultivated. The population of Chengdu is over three million. Once surrounded by a wall, this looked like a charming old city. Most of the houses were built of wood with an overhanging upper floor like Tudor ones. The Tang Dynasty poet, Tu Fu, lived here and of his hundreds of lyrics, one stands out in my mind.

Since I am poor, all I can provide
Is the wine in the old jar.
If you are willing to drink with my neighbor
I shall ask him to come over the fence and
join us.

I wished we'd had Tu Fu's address.

We made a stop at a tree-shaded zoo where a number of pandas were the main attraction, then continued on to the Precious Light Monastery, a Buddhist temple from the Tang Dynasty. A dragon screen and two red sandstone lions marked the entrance to the temple. In a reception room, tea was served in ten-century-old china mugs with a Tang dynasty pagoda painted on them.

We lunched at Cassia Lake Restaurant, rather dirty and noisy but with loads of choices of food — some quite spicy.

The plumbing facilities in most restaurants and public places were atrocious and generally filthy. Practically none had Western-type toilets for women and many of the floor-type wouldn't flush. Invariably the floors were wet and imbedded with dirt. There was running water but no towels and seldom soap. In our hotel in Xian the bathroom floor was so cruddy Betty Morzenti scrubbed theirs with the cloth laundry bag and soap, and Miller wanted a brush to work on theirs. The beds and linens were clean but bathroom floors got no attention. This isn't because help is scarce; they just ignore it. With China hankering for more tourism, they must make an effort to rectify this, but I knew of no diplomatic way to get this over to Mr. Chen.

We had a half-hour break after lunch for sauntering and picture-

taking. Eme and I inspected the long lineup of Zhong-Zow bicycles. Locks were built-in under the seats. They cost 151 yuan, about $76, one merchant told us. Tires are big and bikes are heavy to withstand hard use. One sign above the main street said in English: "Plan your family for a better future."

Bamboo trees were everywhere and we went through a bamboo factory that "knits" the wood. We saw the various pieces of furniture made from it.

Dinner was in town that night. In some restaurants, when we could forget their sanitary habits are not ours (nor are the Europeans' for that matter) and concentrate on the imaginative gourmet cuisine, hot pepper and all, dish after dish after dish of unique foods, all was well. Invariably in local restaurants meals were served us on the third floor. It was as if they reserved the first two floors for the natives. The trouble came later if, as we were leaving, we saw the way the dishes were being washed: dumped into two medium size dishpans of water sitting on a shelf and wiped.

"Nihao," Miss Cheng Lei greeted us next morning. She was not very proficient in English but tried hard to please. It was a gray, overcast, damp day with a welter of clouds milling around threateningly as we left.

There was a queue-up at the meat shops; rationing was still in effect to some degree. This was the noisiest town we'd driven through; there seemed to be more traffic here with the constant honking of horns and bell-ringing of bikes.

Fields of squash and winter melon lay ready for picking. The rice had been sickled and was stacked like small teepees in fields and spread out for miles. Some winnowing is still done by hand. The rice was yellow but after threshing would be white. Water buffalo help with plowing, threshing and hauling. All rice is hand cut, then spread to dry on bamboo mats that must be taken up on rainy days. The mats lined the highway, miles and miles of them, often on both sides of the road.

Chengdu province has more silkworms than any of the twenty-nine provinces in the country, so, of course, has more mulberry trees. Trees are often planted in the rice paddies. For good silk you must have good cocoons. The genuine silkworm comes from China and has spread all over the world. Not until monks smuggled silkworm eggs across Asia to Byzantium — hiding them in bamboo — was the 600-year old monopoly ended. When, years ago, China exported silk west in caravans, about which Marco Polo tells, it was a luxury trade. Now there is cross-breeding of the cocoons and increased production. The Party has planted six million mulberry trees to feed the silkworm larvae. The

proper leaves must be selected for the best silk dyeing. By 1980, 154 tons of new silk were being produced annually.

The mist turned into a steady drizzle and Miss Cheng Lei, to entertain us in the bus, sang a song, "Son of the Husband". We knew instantly she had missed her calling. Beautiful to look at with a moon face, she had a truly beautiful voice. She told us she also danced — folk and ballet.

We stopped at the Shaolin Temple, a Taoist one dating from 256 B.C. The rain had almost dried as Eme sat under shelter on a top step of one building to change film in his camera. He might as well have been putting on a magic show. Little by little the crowd stopped to watch him, gathering closer and closer, nudging for a better view, until he was completely surrounded with wide-eyed, curious Chinese.

Our multi-course lunch included a 1,000-year-old egg. Eme finally got me to taste it and it wasn't too bad, just a little rubbery. Edith remarked as they kept pouring in with dishes from the kitchen to overload the table, "This gets to be just like the Chinese water torture."

In the afternoon we saw a most important project here — the irrigation system. This engineering marvel dates back to 250 B.C. and was built to divert and check the waters of the Min River which flows down from the mountain, and at one time, flooded the valley. The system channels the water into irrigation canals and, since being expanded in 1949, irrigates over 6.5 million acres. In the exhibition room of the pavilion we saw a slide show tracing the history of this technological wonder.

A Taoist temple, built up the side of a hill, has a magnificent view of the whole river valley. From here you can see most of the modern parts of the water conservation project.

While on the bus Mr. Chen told us about Taoism, one of the three religions here, the others being Buddhism and Christianity. Mr. Chen is an atheist but spoke objectively about all religions. Lao-tsu, founder of Taoism, lived 2,400 years ago and was a contemporary of Confusius who emphasized the place of man in society using ethics and the Golden Rule. Taoism advocated utter simplicity in living and preached that Tao, The Way, was the cosmic order of nature that couldn't be grasped by intellect nor put into words.

The route to the temple was pure fascination, through a ginkgo forest where hundreds of butterflies (Barry said eight varieties) fluttered and a circuitous trail was punctuated with waterfalls, small pavilions and gardens. Almost every turn of the winding path brought a gasp of delight. Barry pointed out the Asian anemones and japonicas, purple and pink.

Our hotel, the Jing-Jiang Guest House, named for one of the local rivers, was comfortable. Built in 1956 by Russian experts, it had a well-appointed lobby-shop, post office and, as in most hotels in China, same-day laundry service. On the outside it had a somber Soviet look but its dining room was cheery.

A twenty-one course banquet served us there was an exotic delight. The table settings featured rose petals floating on green ferns and white napkins folded in the shapes of animals in our water glasses. I copied the menu:

Cold Courses: (1) Fried fish; (2) Tea smoked duck (camphor tea); (3) Lettuce and bamboo shoots; (4) Cubed rabbit and red pepper sauce; (5) Centerpiece basket with handles of mandarin oranges. Inside were duck sausage slices, hard-boiled eggs, Chinese money slices, mushrooms, and sausage spread on a bed of flaked fish. (6) Dried bean curd and mushrooms; (7) Beef slices in hot sauce.

Main Courses: (1) Abalone in sauce: (2) Hot spicy noodle soup (spaghetti noodles); (3) Large squares of winter melon with shrimp inside and a mild sauce over it; (4) Tiny spring pocket rolls served individually stuffed with a mild sausage; (5) Dumplings (very thin crust bag) with bok choy and vegetable filling; (6) Pigeon eggs in sweet and sour sauce; (7) Steamed duck with Chinese caterpillars; (8) White fish with whole cloves of garlic and mushrooms; (9) Side dish of flour pastries; (10) Sweet and sour pork (lots of tomatoes); (12) White fungus and fruit broth; (13) Soup with broth and bok choy, sweet red pepper, bamboo shoots and fish balls; (14) Rice. Red wine, beer and maitai liqueur were served throughout the meal and fans were presented all.

Before leaving for Kunming I took camera street scenes while Eme went to the bamboo forest to photograph some of the 128 varieties there. A young man on a bike stopped me near the curb to talk and practice his English. I was soon surrounded by some thirty others who also wanted to show what English they knew. More kept coming and smiling, crowding in for a word. We Westerners furnish the Chinese a good bit of entertainment.

We then took off on a prop plane holding forty-eight that was clean and had a cute stewardess aboard. Mr. Son, our local guide, met us in Kunming. He pointed out the main thoroughfare — East Wind, a wide two-way boulevard — that divides the city into two parts. The streets are picturesque and quiet. There's a huge outdoor arena for Tai Chi exercising and there was a bombardment of color around it in geraniums, oleanders, hibiscus and mums. The two million residents enjoy year-round good weather, Mr. Son said.

Our hotel was the Spring Lake, rather new and most commodious. It

Author and husband at impromptu party in Xian given in honor of their friend's anniversary.

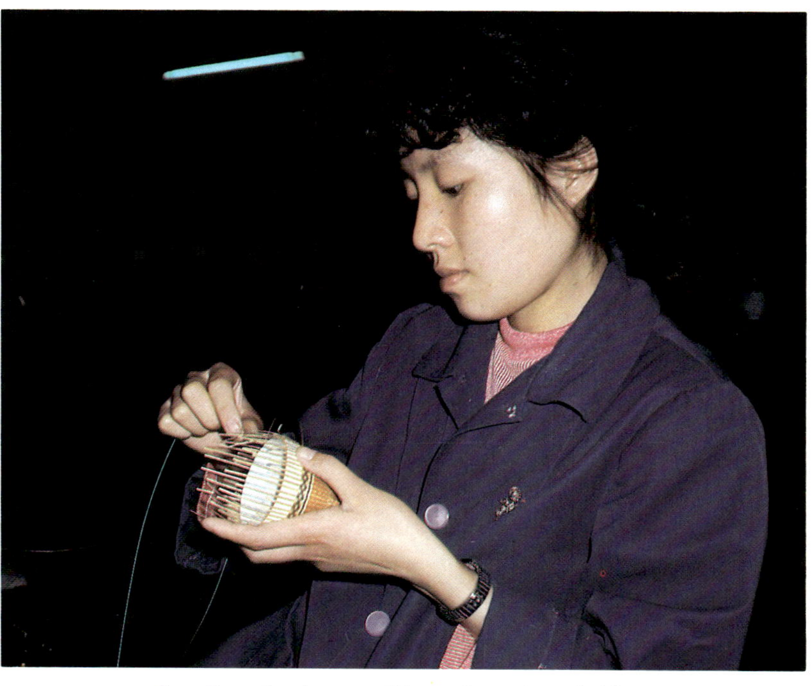

A craft worker in one of the pottery shops in Xian.

This great bronze Foo dog is one of two that flanks the Hall of Supreme Harmony in the Forbidden City.

A specimen of the detailed work on the curved golden roofs in the Forbidden City.

One of the magnificent bronze urns flanking the Meridian Gate of the Forbidden City (circa 1300).

A kindergarten class in Kumming.

The fascination of a lake in Shanghai for a small child who wears the typical rear-open-for-easy-access pants.

In Shanghai, where there are more bicycles than in any other city in the world, this bicycle holds much more than human freight.

Just north of Beijing, off the route to the Great Wall, are the Ming Tombs. Beyond is the famous avenue of stone animals and twelve humans (honor guard for the dead emperor), this, one of them.

Rice is dried and harvested right on the thoroughfares of Chengou.

A Chinese artist in Guilin.

Our travelling companions, the Miller Sherwoods, examining an exquisite urn in the Forbidden City.

The dramatic karst mountains of Guilin — as seen from the Li River.

has shops, bar, post office, and most courteous, pleasant service. The dining room was sparkingly clean and the food scrumptious.

Next morning, instead of visiting the Golden Temple Palace and Black Dragon Pool park with the others, I stayed to wait for a doctor who was coming to see Eme and Barb. It was the best time to take a break from the touring, if need be, because we were to leave next day for an overnight trip to Stone Forest. Mr. Chen stayed with me and called the doctor. Eme's cough was deep, as was the congestion in his chest. Barb had the regular cold symptoms. Dr. Zhaon arrived and insisting on an electrocardiogram for Eme, set up a portable device between our bedroom and bathroom. He gave Eme a shot in the hip for infection and from his own pharmacy, some antibiotic pills. Total cost: $5.00. Barb got a shot and pills from him. Total cost: $2.00.

In talking to Mr. Chen while waiting, he admitted China over-mans jobs to substitute for underemployment. But he was hopeful about the future, feeling that everyone was aware of the Four Modernizations (industry, agriculture, science technology and defense) and sincerely striving for them. He said he felt the pot was boiling and things were really perking in today's China.

At 8:30 a.m. the next day we headed for the Stone Forest, eighty miles away. Mr. Son pointed out, at a branching of the road, that the right led to Burma and the left — the one we were on — went to Vietnam. The best tobacco in China is grown here, also sorghum. White egrets combed the rice paddies and the tiny rice-flower birds we saw are eaten by the natives.

Pear trees were loaded and corn was planted right in the orchards. The red earth was like Georgia soil. Scarecrows wore orange hats and red peppers were stretched for drying. The acacias had only yellow flowers, but eucalyptus, Barry told us, blooms in a rainbow assortment. A huge dam here is used for irrigation. Overloaded water buffalo wallowed through the mud of the fields. Ninety percent of the grain raised — buckwheat, rice, millet, wheat — the government sells overseas, but in case of national disaster, gives it to the people. Bauxite is mined here for manufacturing aluminum. Coal is also being mined with the result that pollution is dreadful. The reforestation program was begun in 1958.

We passed the former base of the Flying Tigers where a narrow-guage railway runs nearby. The Flying Tigers were a part of the U.S. Air Force under Generals Stillwell and Chenault during World War II and flew supplies from India over the Himalayas and Tibet into Kunming.

In the lounge of a fairly clean pit stop, Chinese walnuts, like our big English ones, were served in bowls with nut crackers, as snacks with the tea we were offered.

In a village we saw people pole-balancing buckets on their shoulders to collect the harvest from the fields. Chickens scratched in yards and roads. Wide-rimmed strawhatted workers dug diligently outside their huts of mud and straw. We glimpsed the precipitous gorges and looked up at hydrangeas clustering the caves in the mountains and along the overhanging rocks. Rice plantings were held to precise, square carpet patterns. A passing hoopoe bird with black and white striped wings and orange crest delighted our bird spotters, Mary Emerson and Barry. Tiny ponies trundled along the road. Dozens of lime kilns dotted the near hillside indented by waterfalls. Anemones whitened the rocks and terraced planting added to the montage.

Leaving the Vietnam (360 miles away) road we entered the Stone Forest area and saw three dogs — a rarity, but goats romped everywhere. The working kilns close by made bricks the natural choice for all houses. Rice and tobacco were the main crops in this village adjacent to the Stone Forest Hotel, a rather primitive one where we stayed. The whole village had brick houses. The lotus pods grew huge. The panorama of rice was in varying colors of ripeness. Goats romped. Bouganvillea brightened the Stone Forest Hotel, a rather primitive one where we were to stay.

We spent several hours in the Stone Forest, an extraordinary sight of limestone columns and towers, some as tall as California redwoods, rising vertically from the ground in thick formations. From a distance they resembled a forest of pines. Barry described it as "like being in a giant Bonsai forest." Marine fossils are in the limestone whose age is estimated at about 270 million years. It was under water at one time, part of a great sea.

Poisonous snakes swished through the forest and Mr. Son advised us to stay with the group and follow him or risk the consequences. Caverns, pools and pagodas offset the twisting path we followed.

After dinner at the hotel we attended an interesting performance of folk songs and dance by the Sanis. The Sani people have vibrant faces and wear bright colored (blue and pink, especially) woven robes. They live in the high mountains but some worked in the hotel and village.

After a good night's sleep under mosquito nets we were on our way, by bus, for a boat ride around Dianchin Lake. Ducks and chickens were out eating in the rice fields. They substitute for pesticides since they can be trained by stick and whistle where to go and what to do. There was applause for our driver's skillful manipulation of the curving, contortion-kinked road. We kept the green bough in our hearts that the soupy weather would clear up for our boat ride, and the closer we got to the lake, the brighter the weather got!

Everyone has to plant three trees on the barren hills, we were told. Each commune is given its quota. The big government forests, far north of where we were, are filled with Korean pines. There were lots of amaranthus along the route, green stalks with showy bright red flowers; seeds are used for oil. Many brick kilns were steaming. The sweet olive trees scented the wayside where a hotel was being built by the French.

We boarded the boat just before noon and selected our table in the dining room. The sun had come out and we were able to take pictures of other boats and lake scenes.

Mr. Chen, talking to us on deck, gave us more national facts. About four percent of the population are Party members, he said. To be acceptable, applicants must be citizens over eighteen, recognize the Party construction and pay dues. Those earning below 100 yuan pay five-tenths of a percent a month and those earning more, two percent. Members agree to observe Party discipline and work for the good of the Party. Only model workers are approved and workers can be expelled for mistakes. He mentioned that it was Premier Zhao who had invited President Nixon to China.

As we ate lunch they played all kinds of songs, including Christmas carols and Auld Lang Syne. There was a large, noisy Italian tour group aboard. When they got off, Barry chartered the boat to recross a part of the lake and dock at the park instead of making the trip by bus. This was a real joy and the peace was most relaxing. We sighted a whole flock of herons on the water. Men in junks had huge fishing nets open and others were beating the waters, hoping to entice or scare fish into the long stretches of woven hemp.

We dallied in the park and then returned to Spring Lake Hotel. Our windows faced the park where we watched children clapping hands, chasing butterflies, and turning somersaults. In their colorful garb they seemed happy and curious.

A special meal had been arranged for us by Barry, while he was yet in New York, at a Vietnamese restaurant featuring "Crossing-the-bridge" noodles — a twelve-course meal that for amounts and variety was almost our undoing. We entered through a revolving screen turnstile into a Chinese place with real local color to find ourselves the only foreigners there. A screen was immediately put up to shield the natives from us and us from the natives. They didn't start to cook our food until we sat down so, of course, there was some waiting. When it arrived they took down the screen so the people could watch us. They not only stared but carefully inventoried us from the bottom of our shoes to the top of our chopsticks. When we were leaving they stood, bowed, laughed and clapped.

Mr. Son told us the story of "Crossing-the-bridge" noodles. A young man went to school to try for a scholarship. He studied night and day and was so poor he went without eating. His girlfriend, sorry for him, walked across the bridge to feed him noodles. He won the scholarship and said he won because of her. She said no, it was because of "Crossing-the-bridge" noodles.

This special dish was brought in after umpteen preliminary ones had already been downed. What was being served was explained by Mr. Son and my face fell a notch with every new presentation. On separate plates we each received: finely shaved raw liver, raw buffalo meat, raw kidney, raw pork and raw fish. Accompanying these, a huge bowl of noodles was placed in front of each person. Lastly, a boiling cauldron was put beside each plate. We plucked with our chopsticks from each of the raw meat and fish offerings, dumped those into the cauldron with the noodles. When all was steamed to desired doneness, we ladled out enough to surfeit an army. I may never want another of these concoctions but I wouldn't have missed this one for anything.

Mr. Son was wearing a navy jacket which he called the Sun Yat Sen. It had replaced the tan Mao jacket, which indicated the de-emphasizing of the former dictator. Mr. Son was a perfect leader and story teller.

Staggering away from this feast, we went to a Japanese-made movie about this Yunan province with very good shots of the Stone Forest, of minority customs, songs and dance.

The Spring Lake Hotel where we stayed was topnotch, service was instantaneous and friendly and, of course, there was no tipping. After the movie we tried the disco room on the top floor where about forty people were gathered. The brandy sold for $1.75.

We got some shopping done in the morning and left for Guilin, a little before noon, in a British Trident. We had to wait a half hour while the pilot ate his lunch. We were given box lunches by Mr. Son and asked to save any uneaten food in plastic sacks he supplied. Aboard each flight of China Airlines we were given Chinese fans.

Guilin, as we approached from the air, looked like a soft satiny plain interlaced with rivers and lakes, yellow acacias, green fields and fantastic rounded towers of stone in a limestone fantasy.

Our hotel, the Li River, was the tallest building in this town of 370,000. It dominated the city and gave us, from the upper floors where we were assigned, an unparalleled view of the surrounding city and mountains. The lobby had a post office, bank, food store and good retail shop specializing in silks and local crafts.

After settling in, we went for a stroll to get our bearings and to take pictures. We learned that the unique Karst Mountains were formed on the bottom of the sea about 300 million years ago. Natural caves and caverns pepper the mountains. There are camphor and tung trees on both sides of the main avenue and the Li River sashes the city. There are thousands of peaks, many in clusters, and some of the more bizarre ones are 1,000 feet high. Trying to catalog the scene was a mesmerizing experience; the whole of it was elusive. We stopped to buy a big luscious-looking pomelo fruit, the size of a grapefruit, but found it neither ripe nor tasty.

It was a long bus ride to the boat dock for our much-anticipated trip on the River Li. Roadsides were filled with cassia and chestnut trees and we passed the Peach Flower River, a tributary of the Li Jang. Tangerines were ripe on the trees; brick kiln were being fired and a bridge was in the process of being built. The fish in the ponds were carp which could be harvested in a year.

Guilin gets a little snow in January, but otherwise is subtropical. The roots of the cassabas are poisonous but the other parts, we hear, make wonderful porridge and dumplings. Young groves were neat, the countryside wild, but the communes orderly. In a commune each family owns pigs and feeds them sorghum. Some 160,000 visitors come each year, and two more hotels were under construction. Half the tourists are Japanese.

Six years of English is compulsory in middle and upper school and students must pass it to enter the university. Russian is no longer taught and Japanese is the second language to learn. Six American exchange students were in Guilin at the time.

In a light mist the hills and mountains seemed unreal. Jute plants—green and white flowering ones—are used for making fibers. Orchards were loaded: oranges, pomelos and pears. Water buffalo, being herded down the streets, were muzzled so they couldn't stop to eat and hold up traffic. Buffalo live for fifteen years, we were told, and eat grass in winter as well as rice and drink rice wine. The Chinese don't eat butter; they use peanut, rapeseed and camelia oil to cook and to wash their clothes.

Guilin is over 2,000 years old. Ninety percent of this enchanting city was destroyed by the Japanese on the same day Pearl Harbor was attacked, and rebuilt by 1960.

Winding down to the dock we finally boarded the launch for our six-hour Li River Cruise. Your eyes sweep the spectacle, such breathtaking and gorgeous scenery defies description; it gives one a dreamy sensation of floating, such is the haunting quality of sea and mountains, mist and sky. From the top of the double-decker tour boat we scanned the stony crags, the inflections of the sun, fishermen plying bamboo rafts, peasants bathing their buffalo and loggers guiding long strings of casks through the rapids. From time to time we saw pavilions perched precariously on the cliffs and ancient temples recessed in caves. The buoys in the river were woven baskets heaped with rocks. Clouds dusted the peaks and the sun as it shifted, sparkled the smooth washed stone. Some rock formations looked like giant pine cones. The extraordinary thing about them is that they rise singly, as if out of nowhere, in round, oval, and even pyramidal shapes. Thick fluffy bamboo trees arched across the river. We spotted golden lilies (a very rare species). Barry called wildly to us to take note; he was really excited, having never seen them before.

The scenery varied throughout the afternoon, shadows, reflections and glowing lights gradually interchanging. One longs for a Corot or a John Constable to come and do justice to all this beauty, although the Chinese artists already have.

Leaving the boat, we stopped in the small village of Yang Shuo to shop the stores in tiny alleyways as well as on the main street. Most of us were sleepy and satiated as the bus pulled out on its final lap of the return trip. A new road was being built by hand and travel was slow. Persimmon and golden rain trees stippled the landscape, even as they do in Florida.

Early in the morning we left to view Reed Flute Cave which takes its name from reeds growing at the bottom of the hill used to make flutes. The illuminated stalagtites and stalagmites had a delicate coloring, reflecting the bizarre configurations outside.

We lunched in town and then were en route to see a commune, the Shiran Shan, started in 1958. It was our group's request to see one and since Mr. Chen had only one day to set this up, I don't feel anything was prettied up for our benefit. Each county has its own commune. We were visiting one of ten brigades in Shiran Shan. Mr. Yang was the head man and didn't speak English, so his remarks had to be translated.

First, he invited us inside the main office, a fairly sizeable one, and offered us tea. As we drank he explained the setup and bid us a warm welcome. The main crops of the brigade were vegetables and melons. There were 813 families living there — a population of 3,884 of whom 1,479 were able-bodied manpower and the others, the elderly and the children. On 200 acres, in addition to the farmland was a wine factory, foundries, and a fish-raising venture. The commune was set up for mutual help — a co-op. Water from the river was used for irrigation and sprinkling. Conditions had been steadily improving and production had increased each year so that the commune was yielding three times more than at the start.

The average annual income was 550 yuan, about $275, for all, including the leaders. Every family had its private plot on which to produce for its own use or to sell at free markets, after meeting the commune quota. Families can also raise turkeys, ducks, and hens. Under the new Party policy "the system of job responsibility" was being carried out. The land still belongs to the commune but families have the use of it. The new policy, we were told, has made people work harder and loaf less.

This brigade had one primary school, two clinics, 200 students and fifty teachers. Ninety percent of the children were in school. Brigade leaders distribute welfare to the less able ones in the unit. The leaders are elected by a show of hands. I asked if chemical fertilizers were used in addition to human and animal waste and was told yes, about one-fourth of it is chemical. Each family has its own house, and in the event of disaster, the government will replace a house and commune members help in its building.

We went through several houses which consisted of three or four rooms: two sleeping rooms, a kitchen, and eating room. Children's beds had colorful quilts and were hung with mosquito netting. Kitchens were tiny with big kettles for do-all cooking. Floors were bare and well swept. Some displayed knickknacks; there was a tape recorder in one home, television and radio in another; mattresses on beds; bicycles outside. It may have looked grim to some of us but as Ghandi said, "For those who are hungry God comes in the form of bread."

We inspected the clinic of the "barefoot doctor": medicine on the shelves, a small boy holding his stomach while waiting for help. We went through the foundries and looked over the farming setup in the distance and the irrigation system nearby.

While Mr. Yang was talking to us in the office, two workers brought out Chinese scrolls and paintings, hanging them in front, behind and around the sides of us. Many of them were more beautiful than we had seen in the hotels or the retail markets. I couldn't take my eyes off one scroll and neither could Eme. It was deftly done in delicate colors with an impressionistic background — a green bough with a golden bird perched on it, singing! As the others went outside and we were alone with the girl in charge, Eme and I asked to buy it. We wanted to present it to Barry as a gift at our farewell dinner two nights later in Canton.

At 5:00 p.m. we left the unique picture-book city, headed for Canton on a China Airlines flight.

Mr. Jian was our local guide who took us to the Nanku Hotel. Our room had a refrigerator, television, double lavatories and imaginative decor. It faced a lake and reflecting pool with hills in the background.

Canton is a very Westernized city built on a slope on the delta of the Pearl River. Its shopping district teems with craftsmen and tradesmen of every kind, and arcades of open-fronted shops line its busy downtown. The temperature is steamy and subtropical in this densely-packed place of 5.5 million.

The lifestyle was much more in keeping with Hong Kong than with the rest of the country. More visitors come here than to any other city in China. Streets are wide with bicycle paths running alongside. The hotels are huge. Sun Yat Sen, the first president of China, was born here and there is a statue to him in the square, as well as one commemorating the martyrs. We passed a number of beautiful parks. Banyan, casuarina and eucalyptus trees lined the streets.

On the night before our departure for Hong Kong, our farewell banquet was held, arranged by Mr. Chen at the Taotaoju Restaurant. Canton restaurants, of course, are world famous for their cuisine, a gastronome's paradise.

We held the dinner here because Mr. Chen could not cross the border to take the train with us to Hong Kong. One of the best known restaurants in southern China, this one was established nearly a century ago, and has a sign done by the famous Ching Dynasty scholar, Kang Youwei. It is noted not only for its tasteful decor but also for its many dining rooms and fine cuisine — known both inside and outside China.

Our menus were written in graceful Chinese calligraphy. Among the unusual things served at the banquet were magpie nests, winter melon soup, shrimp with green noodles, crab, chicken and peacock, pork and raisins, delicate fish and bok choy, teacakes, wine and maitai.

We offered many toasts, and Barry's off-the-cuff farewell was a masterpiece of good fellowship without being maudlin. Mr. Chen's was beautiful. We each knew that, with great dignity, a friendship had been established and sealed. In the People's Republic of China we had found friendliness unprompted and honesty endemic. We left with the certainty of keeping in touch with Mr. Chen whose full name is Chen Gen-Pei. Last names come first in China.

Our last day in Canton, the heat and humidity were excruciating. We had our last Western breakfast; all cities in China served us breakfasts of eggs in some form, toast, jelly, and sometimes bacon or sausage and fruit, but never fruit juices. The fruit that morning was leche which we thought was bland.

Waiting in the train station to board the train for Hong Kong — a three-hour trip — we all groaned about the extra luggage we had accumulated because of purchases. With a final handshake with Mr. Chen, who had a trace of tears in his eyes, we entered an immaculately clean diesel train that would take us directly into Kowloon and our hotel there, the Hong Kong Sheraton.

The ride was smooth and relaxing with good seats and plenty of leg room. There was a dining car but the Sherwoods and we opted to wait for a late lunch on our arrival.

As we said good-by to China, we voiced some of our thoughts. We feel China has great potential to complete her Four Modernizations — if not on schedule in the year 2000, then soon after that. We think she wouldn't have a prayer of survival without the strictest of disciplines and this, communism is giving her. Whenever she solves her population problem she can plan for a better future. We were impressed by the sincerity of innumerable youths we quizzed about their willingness to share the good and the bad for the sake of improving themselves and their nation.

As Clare Booth Luce said in an interview in *Geo*: "It is the height of arrogance and folly for the U.S. to expect every country will follow its ideological pattern. It's enough for people to be happy with the form of government they have, regardless of what it may be. If they're happy with it and believe in it, let them alone. Let them have it."

A Holt Executive Advisory said: "China's modernizations got a strong boost at this month's Communist Party Congress. Party strongman, Deng Xiaoping blueprints bold steps for China: there will be private enterprise in agriculture, and foreign investment in energy will be encouraged."

Customs and immigration formalities were minimal at the border and we were again in Hong Kong.

It was our fourth return to the place that has more exotic sights and sounds per mile than practically any place on earth — a dynamic and captivating spot but one growing almost literally out of bounds. Highrises everyplace and more being completed daily. In the sampan harbor, where junks elbow luxury yachts in the bay and where bargains are duty-free, it's hard to visualize what a few more years will do, building-wise, when almost every inch is already taken.

Although we'd spend another day in the city we held our formal farewell dinner the night before at the elegant Pink Giraffe Restaurant. We had a spectacular view from the top floor, of Hong Kong twinkling at night. Candles glowed on the tables. Cocktails arrived and we toasted first our inimitable leader, then a non pareil tour, and finally, all the members of the group. The food was excellent, the wine super. There was a good band to play for dancing. Barry danced first with Edith, then Miller and Eme cut in. Charming lady and what a good sport!

We had a buffet style breakfast at the hotel next morning, went shopping, and took the Victoria Peak funicular for the sensational view, while the Sherwoods took the Harbor trip they'd never been on. Later we lunched with their friend, Priscilla Liang, at the Mandarin Hotel. Priscilla's father works for Miller and he and his wife were born in Shanghai. It was Priscilla's mother who tutored the Sherwoods in Chinese. Priscilla, an attractive and interesting person, is a graduate of Oberlin and Radcliffe, and works for Merrill-Lynch in Hong Kong.

We went by ferry (25 cents) from Kowloon to Hong Kong but returned by taxi through the tunnel, which was a good bit more expensive. We had a delightful candlelight dinner with Barb and Miller at the Chesa Restaurant in the Peninsula Hotel, across the street from the Sheraton.

Next morning, we were off for Narita Airport in Tokyo and a four-hour layover before going on to Hawaii. On board JAL Eme was so adept at chopsticks he ate both lunch and dinner with them, but guess who enthusiastically embraced the silverware proffered on the same tray!

After plenty of walking at Honolulu Airport, we located Pan Am's Clipper Club and had time for orange juice and a bran muffin before our plane left for Kailua Kona on the big island of Hawaii.

We stayed at the Kona Surf and liked it immensely. The Sherwoods liked the salt pool but we preferred the fresh water. However, we all liked the accommodations, the scenery, the food, and our lanai overlooking the Pacific. Our first move after getting into comfortable clothes was to head for an ice-cream bar. Miller ordered a banana split and the rest of us settled for chocolate sodas — about the best ever. The sky was sunny, the weather hot, and it was so good to relax, now that our group was reduced to four with no schedules to meet.

My grandniece, Jennifer Kane, who lives here, called and although I could hardly wait to see her, fatigue forced us to wait till the next day. It was a joyous reunion with a beautiful young woman of twenty, we hadn't seen since she was nine. She arrived bringing tuberose leis to put around our necks and with a lovely oil painting she had done for us. We couldn't talk fast enough for the too-short time we had.

After a quick lunch, we went with her to see some of her father's restorations, art murals, and other work. Her father, Herb Kane, formerly from Chicago, is the island's leading architect-artist. Unfortunately, at this time he was in England on a project for *National Geographic*. But Jennifer, who works in an art gallery, showed us much of her art work done from the time she was in grade school. She drew a comic strip for the high school newspaper, has sold oil paintings, scratchboard art, paints marine animals on boat exteriors, and is a young lady of a dozen other talents including modeling. In 1982 she was chosen "Miss International Billfish", competing both on the mainland and the islands. She had reigned for a month of festivities, introductions by the governor and mayor and attendant meetings. She was a completely unspoiled and mighty personable young lady of whom we were inordinately proud, naturally!

She returned that night to have dinner with us and the Sherwoods. We had such a fun time reviewing family history and episodes we didn't want the evening to end.

In the following morning's *Honolulu Advertiser* it was announced that Kona coffee had their largest crop in twenty-five years — $4.4 million worth. But the restaurant got 95 cents a cup from us.

En route to Hilo we stopped at the Volcano House for lunch. Eme and I had taken this route several times. When we got to Waiakea Village, where we were staying, it was ablaze with flowers of every color and description. Impatiens grow high-bush size because of an abundance of rain. The elemandis flowers, like trumpet vine, were mostly in gold shades and the African tulip trees were burnt orange. There were loads of hibiscus, oleander, jacarandas and all tropical kinds.

In the coffee shop birds hopped in and out the open windows and customers were requested not to feed them. Ducks, mallard and muscovy, had a private pool.

Our deck faced the swimming pool and there was the recurring joy of simply lolling. This village, when we had visited eleven years before, was being designed and coordinated by Herb Kane. We played bridge, ate late dinners, and whiled away the evenings late into the nights.

We tooted around in the Sherwoods' rented car, lunched and shopped until time to leave for the airport after five days in the islands.

After arriving in L.A. at 11 p.m., we breakfasted next morning before the Sherwoods left for their winter home in Tucson. Eme and I collected our bridge winnings: 110 points ahead; thus, we had gambled our way to a plus five cents apiece. They presented us a rare and choice gift. In living color and ready for framing, it read:

Woman's faults are many
Men have only two,
Everything they say
And everything they do!

After seeing them off we returned to our room to find a message from friends of long years' standing, the Ivan Ryersons of Santa Monica. We stayed an extra day to have dinner with them and catch up on a two-year separation. They took us to Long Beach to eat in the Winston Churchill Room aboard the Queen Mary — a fitting finale to a memorable journey.

Early next morning Delta flew us to Orlando and the limo service from Mount Dora met us. We had been gone more than a month and in one short hour were at the most blessed of all earthly spots: home.

Chapter 7

A bomb threat is hardly an auspicious start for a holiday, especially when it comes at the JFK Airport in New York. To the passengers who had boarded South African Airways 747 to Johannesburg (and every seat including the stewardesses' jumpseats were filled) and were seat-belted, waiting on the ground for the motors to rev up and the big wings to leave tarmac for sky, the delay came as a double whammy. Most had spent part of this October 1st getting from their various states to New York and were already bone-weary at the scheduled takeoff time of 7:30 p.m.

Convivial to begin with, the exchange of pleasantries with fellow seatmates continued only a short while. Eme and I were to be part of a group of eighteen — fifteen Americans and three Canadians — to meet officially in Johannesburg where we would also pick up our tour leader, Hal Rice. Our destination: South Africa and Zimbabwe.

As our plane remained motionless on the ground after 7:30, first one hour, then two, passengers became restive, then irritated and frankly suspicious. After three hours on the ground those at the executive bar were partially stoned. Others demanded explanations. Into the fourth hour aground, it was getting plenty hot . . . inside the cabin *and* under the collar. An hour earlier, stewardesses had told us we were waiting for two passengers whose suitcases were aboard but who hadn't yet arrived. Another interval ensued. Captain Logan and his co-pilot finally emerged, down the aisle, and covered the length of the plane with smiles and assurances that safety is better than sorrow. None of us cared to argue with that.

When I asked why we didn't take off and return the suitcases on arrival in Johannesburg, the captain replied, "Madame, we don't know what is in those two cases."

They returned to the cockpit and there was an announcement over the loudspeaker: "All passengers will please disembark and identify his

SOUTHERN AFRICA

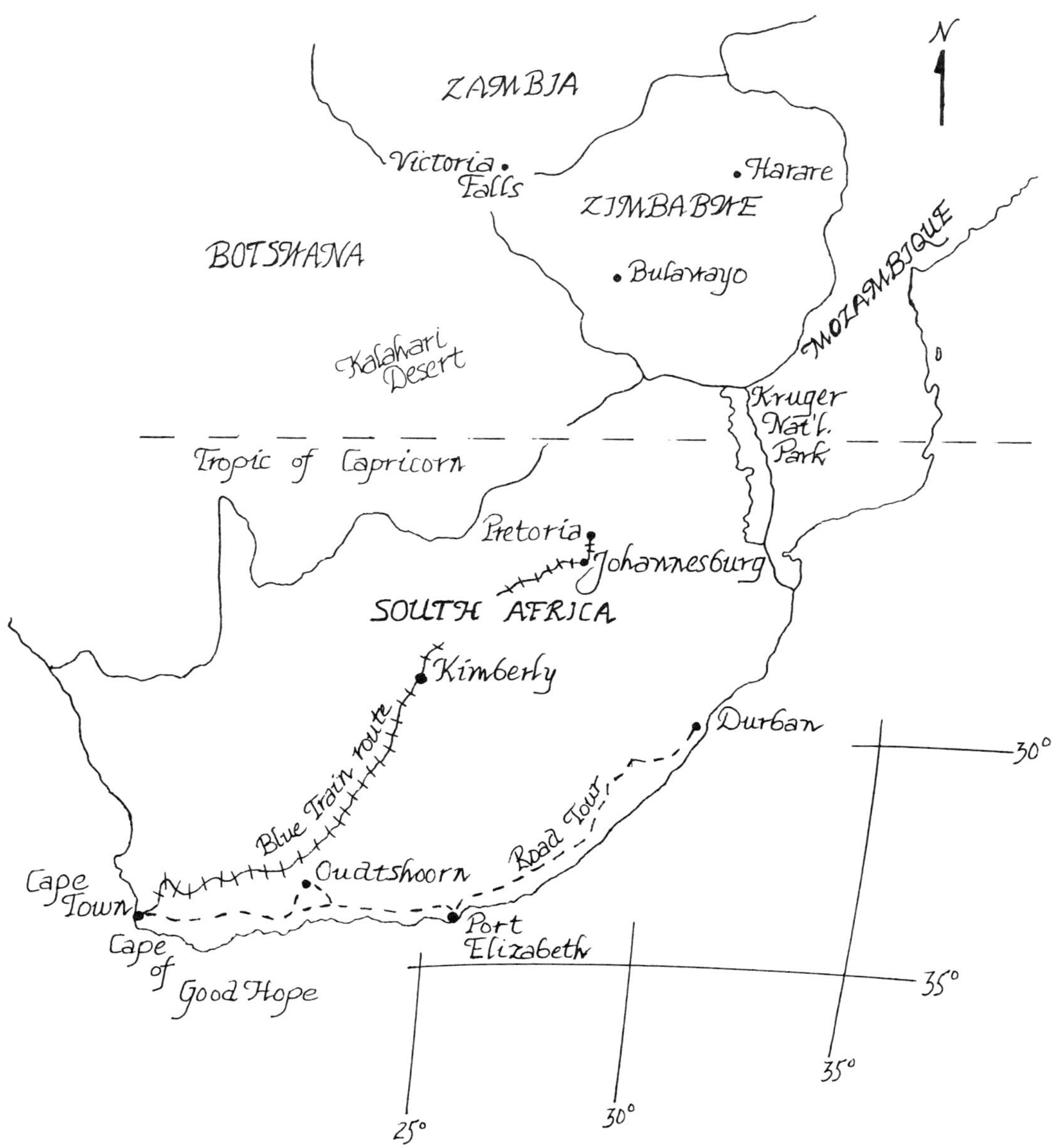

or her luggage." The luggage had been unloaded from the hold into a nearby building where, traveling around on the turntable, it awaited our inspection and tabbing before we reboarded the plane. At this time another head count was taken.

There were groans of relief, when, after another interval, the announcement was made: "Flight attendants, please prepare for immediate departure." Even after this came another half-hour of taxiing and the inevitable wait on the runway before the wheels tucked under and, at long last, South African Airways Flight 502 was sky-borne.

The plane was a combo with the cargo department on the second level. Its seats reclined way back for sleeping.

Dry white wine was distributed to celebrate takeoff. It tasted like apple juice but was good. This was to be dinner flight but most passengers had long ago lost their appetites. The food, held over much too long, was, of course, as unappetizing looking as it was inedible, and most trays were returned untouched.

A bomb threat and attendant unpleasantries can happen on any airline, but there was no excuse for the cabin crew to be surly and take out their frustrations on the innocent farepayers, as they did on this one. American newspapers had come down heavily on the evils of apartheid during the preceding week and leading columnists, along with the rest of the media, with customary know-it-all attitudes toward other countries' problems, had advocated the U.S. take punitive action against South Africa. So, not for a moment, did we take the bomb threat lightly.

I knew there were no easy solutions to the excruciating problems pressuring South Africa, but I hoped for some unbiased cloud-lifting (away from Jesse Jackson oratory) by probing, if possible, the knowledgeable guides who make their living there, people in homes we might visit, and other South Africans who might be on the same tour routes we were. My big hope was to sit in on a session of Parliament, which I'd been told was permissible. Unfortunately, when we arrived in Capetown, Parliament had adjourned for two months.

It was a long night-into-day aboard the aircraft, a seventeen-hour flight with only a forty-minute touchdown for refueling at Sal, one of the Cape Verde islands off the coast of western Africa. There are salt flats here where nothing but a sizeable inactive volcano looms in the distance and small squat white houses and a few larger, neatly fenced ones, dot the barren landscape facing the runway. Here, a small number of Portuguese eke out a living.

Back aboard, a handsome young Afrikaaner sat on the jump seat behind us practicing his violin — mute. A Julliard student, he was returning home to Capetown to perform at a concert. We wished he would open up and put us to sleep with sweet music. He fingered his instrument tenderly, and we watched him fill vials of water to place inside the case to keep the violin from drying out.

The main improvement was a complete change of cabin personnel at Sal. The new crew were genial and considerate. We heard a scurry in the kitchen and, expecting bacon and eggs at least, were offered coffee or tea and cookies. Because of the extra hours on the ground, the food put on in New York had to be stretched. This was all we were offered, other than orange juice, until brunch was served five hours later. If anyone could identify this food when it was presented, they deserved a medal. It too, was returned almost untouched.

On arriving at Jan Smutz Airport in Johannesburg shortly before midnight (there is a six-hour time difference from New York), we met Hal Rice, our young and vivacious tour leader who had, of course, been apprised of the reason for our delay. He had the great good sense to make the introductions brief and suggest we put our heads back against the comfortable seats of the darkened bus for the hour ride to Pretoria. We followed his suggestion and rested until we arrived at the Hotel Burgerspark where we were treated to a true welcome and led to lounge chairs and refreshment. We toasted our arrival with champagne mixed with orange juice while awaiting our room keys. Once in our room, Eme and I ordered hot soup, and then succumbed to blissful sleep.

But not for long. We were on the city tour next morning at 8:30. A line from one of Diana Ross' songs asks, "Do you know where you're going?" I'd have had to say, "Not really," but I agree with Daniel Boorstin who wrote in *The Discoverers*, "The most promising words ever written on the maps of human knowledge are '*terra incognita*' — unknown territory." It is this promise ahead of Eme and me that always sparks our enthusiasm. Having followed the Nile — both the Blue and the White — from sources to outlet, and traveled most other parts of this continent from the Sahara to Egypt, through Ethiopia, the Sudan and all of East Africa, this discovery was to add a new dimension to the trekking of our favorite continent.

Historians had given me the following background of this least African but most highly developed of all African countries: the Republic of South Africa. Though it accounts for only five percent of Africa's total population and three percent of its surface area, it contributes one-quarter of the continent's gross national product and forty percent of its industrial output. The total literacy rate is eighty-nine percent, and there is one doctor for every 2,000 people. South Africa's mineral wealth is legendary — it provides more than seventy percent of the Free World's gold and has over seventy-five percent of the world's known chrome, platinum and other minerals. Other African countries are dependent on basic food imports from here and it has growing trade links worldwide.

How did the Republic come into existence? A small fleet of three Dutch ships came to South Africa in 1652. To avoid trouble between these Dutch settlers and the native Hottentots, a means of physical separation, was the first step in South Africa toward apartheid. The Dutch had been warned to avoid trouble with the natives and to set up a small fort. Their primary purpose, originally, was to establish a station midway between Europe and the East where vessels could stop for fresh food and water.

This was to be the function of the Dutch East India Company. Instead, a permanent agricultural settlement evolved with labor performed by servile natives under a privileged landowner class.

Boers were South Africans of Dutch extraction. When the British later moved into the territory, wars broke out between them for land and conquest.

Boer is the old word; today, Afrikaaner means white; African means black.

The Union of South Africa united only the whites. Status became equated with pigmentation. Objectives were for white supremacy.

It's difficult, of course, to write history without any distortion. In theory, apartheid claims to be something other than political domination and economic exploitation. It argues that races of the world are best segregated. Its apologists have been many — both black and white. The double standard prevailed both on the farms and in the cities. After more than 300 years, apartheid is an unsolved problem.

Social patterns are, to some extent, like those of the Old South in America. But apartheid is not as despicable as our treatment and near annihilation of the American Indians and the entire aboriginal population. The United States is still ousting some of them from their lands because it wants the territory for MX missile sites or for other purposes.

It was only a few years ago that the opprobrious word apartheid was coined by the National Party of South Africa which has since desperately tried to rid itself of this albatross around its neck. It isn't the government, but its opponents who refuse to let the word die. Today it is only shorthand for oppression of blacks by whites.

Harry Oppenheimer, chairman of DeBeers and South Africa's most experienced and respected business statesman, in a major address to the Foreign Policy Association in New York, October, 1984, told of the folly of disinvestment. "Foreign investors," he said, "can do much more practical good by encouraging the firms in which they invest to eliminate racial discrimination and take positive steps to opening opportunities for black advancement, than by disposing of their South African investments in the hope this will force a change of policy in the South African government. The closing of the General Motors assembly plant, alone, here would deprive 9,000 blacks of jobs. Violent means never bring about the same conclusions as peaceful means and usually lead to tyranny instead of freedom and justice."

He went on to say, "Although I have spent a lifetime (he was seventy-six at the time) fighting against policies of racial discrimination in South Africa, I certainly would not willingly accept a political settlement which involved any serious risk of South Africa's developing into a Marxist-oriented one-party state. The new Constitution just adopted that now takes into the government both Indians and the Coloured, as well as Whites, must be accepted as a beginning, but only a beginning, toward sharing power with people of all the races in the country, including the blacks."

I'm sure Mr. Oppenheimer agreed with Horace Greeley who, in regard to slavery in our country, long ago said, "I am the inferior of any man whose rights I trample under foot."

Pretoria seemed the proper place for me to indulge in explaining this country's history and government, because this city is the administrative capital of the four South African provinces: the Transvaal in the north, the Orange Free State and Natal in the center, and Cape Province in the south. Capetown is the legislative capital and seat of Parliament, and Bloemfontein is the judicial capital. P. W. Botha, prime minister of the republic, claims the first order of business is freedom and peace.

Pretoria is a delight. Spring starts here in September, our local, knowledgeable guide, Bernadine Grant, told us, and in October it was in full stride. The petria bush, a ruby wine shade, lit the landscape of this fertile valley and the city streets were lined with jacaranda, not quite at the peak of their bloom, enveloping the city in a whispery haze of mauve.

I had been thinking what an attractive city it was, how clean, invigorating (at 5,000 feet altitude), unlittered and colorful. But Bernadine, in her neat British parlance, told us it was all very "dicey" because of the incredible three-and-a-half-year drought which had been so hard on the economy, some farmers had declared it an emergency. There was strict water rationing. Only those who had wells (called potholes) could irrigate and their lawns and flora were standouts.

Despite the dryness the giant protea, which is the national flower, was very prevalent. The protea tree, too, was a kaleidoscope of colored blossoms varying in shape from dainty to massive. Paradoxically, botanists named it after Proteus, the god who didn't want to change shape.

The population of Pretoria is 750,000, half of whom are white.

Next morning we went to see the Voortrekker monument built on a hilltop to commemorate the great journey of the Dutch pioneers known as Voortrekkers. They struggled from coastal lands to unclaimed interior areas to satisfy their land hunger and avoid British rule which legislated they stay in one place. Obstacles were horrendous, but culminated in the victory over the Zulus in the Battle of Blood River in 1838. The city was named for the hero of that battle, Andries Pretorius when it was founded in 1855. The monument, encircled by shrubs and flowers, is a granite altar with twenty-seven marble frieze panels depicting the hazardous trek. From this summit we had a marvelous view across the city.

As we passed the mint where Krugerands are made, Bernadine told us it is much costlier to purchase them here because they're minted to bring in foreign trade. The man for whom the gold coins were named, Paul Kruger, was a loyal patriot who contributed his wealth and talents to his country. He was an outstandingly great man, the head of the Transvaal government for seventeen years and four terms. His statue stands in a cluster of fine government buildings in Church Square. The Union Building, seat of the government, is architecturally impressive and overlooks formal terraced gardens. On the City Building two flags fly: the one on the left for South Africa, and the other for the Independent Republic.

In answer to questions en route, Bernadine said the military is multiracial with no differentiation in pay. Whites must spend at least two years in service after university; blacks come in on a voluntary basis. Malaria, once prevalent, was brought under control with eradication of the anopheles mosquito.

The heterogeneous society of this country includes the original Bushmen who have lived here since prehistoric times but were almost wiped out by smallpox. These tiny Stone Age people have been found scattered from the Cape to the equator and have left a visual record of their wanderings and their culture on the primitive rocks of caves. It is estimated they number 55,000 in the whole of South Africa, most of them living near the Kalahari Desert and the northern Cape.

In the residential sections of the city, tree orchids abound. Many jacarandas are interwound with bougainvillea. Bird of Paradise, we were startled to learn, is indigenous and has been exported elsewhere. The coral trees on Magnolia Avenue were a brilliant red. The price of a home here, on an acre of ground, is about 900,000 rands or $540,000 U.S.

We continued on to Cullinan to see the surface workings of the Premier Diamond Mine. "I'll go popping in here and get our tickets," said Bernadine. Diamonds were first discovered in India. In the eighteenth century they were found in Brazil, and in South Africa in 1860, by some children who played with the shiny pebbles. It was in this mine that the Cullinan, the world's largest diamond, was found in 1905. Weighing 3,106 carats, it was cut into smaller gems, most of the principal ones to be found in the British crown jewels. Also found here was the Eureka diamond (22 carats) and the Star of South Africa (80 carats). After that, the rush was on.

Cecil Rhodes came here from England in his teens to improve his health. Getting in on the diamond rush, he bought property from DeBeers Diamond Mines and later was able to buy claims in Kimberley for 5.5 million English pounds. He won a fortune in diamonds before he was twenty and as "Builder of the Empire", as he was known, was virtually dictator of South Africa, controlling both the diamond and gold mining interests before he was forty. "In Africa, think big," Rhodes said, and everything he did was magnanimous including the scholarships he later established.

The type of volcanic magma in which diamonds are found was first identified by an American geologist, Henry Cavill Lewis, at Kimberley in Cape Province. He therefore named it kimberlite. The oldest known deposits of kimberlite, 1700 million years old, are at Premier Mine. Since mining began at Premier in 1903, some two million carats of diamonds have been recovered for every ton of ore treated.

We watched the ore being hoisted from underground and screened to separate material of less than 125 milligrams. The ore is scrubbed to remove clay and then rescreened. In the crushing plant, ore is sifted out of the coarse crusher product and x-rayed to recover any large diamonds. Grease tables are used for final diamond recovery before sorting by hand. A significant plaque in front of the plant notes there has never been a fatal accident there. Given the preponderance of dangerous machinery, that is an enviable record.

As we were examining the various procedures wearing our vari-colored hard pith helmets, Bernadine told us that samples are given only on February 30th.

A short distance from the mines is the Cully Inn, where we lunched. Restored to its Victorian splendor, it's an inviting and pleasant old home. Because there was no decent restaurant in Cully, a general manager of Premier and his wife started this one. All waitresses are volunteers (mainly wives of mine employees), and all profits go to charity. Service was full of sunshine and smiles; the food was well seasoned and tasty.

In the afternoon we visited the Kruger House Museum, northwest of Pretoria, where Paul Kruger's private railway coach is displayed — furnished as he had it. Kruger occupied the house from 1884 until 1900. As state president of the South African Republic, he said in his Last Message: "Look in the past for all that is good and beautiful; take that for your ideal and build on it for your future." That, in essence, was his whole philosophy.

Returning to the hotel we could understand why Pretoria is known as the City of Roses as well as for its jacarandas (300 miles of them). There are no slums in the city and most of the population is young.

For dinner, Eme and I had the best hamburger we'd ever eaten. Especially appealing about this tour setup (and established in the original price) is the fact we may dine a la carte any place we choose, be it fancy or formal, humble or room service. If we go out on the town, we get a receipt and turn it in to our leader for immediate reimbursement, or if it's in our hotel, we just sign for it. It is a super idea.

We were joined by the last two members of our group who arrived from California by way of Rio — Tom and Mary Lindley. Mary and I, regretting our lack of exercise (she played tennis daily), did a few warmup laps around the airport while waiting for the plane to take us on the short flight to Durban, South Africa's principal port.

Checking in at the five-star Maharani Hotel, we had lunch before starting out in the bus with Hal Rice in charge. Hal was a marvelous organizer. At each airport or hotel or on returning to the bus, he had us check for our purses, glasses, cameras, passports, and sundries. He swore that on one tour the bus was en route to the airport when a timid voice said, "Hal, I forgot something at the hotel."

"What is it?" he inquired anxiously.

"My teeth," she said. "I left them in a glass!"

It took him three days to get them, he said.

Our local English guide told us about Durban. It's an industrial city and the most important harbor in Africa. With a population of one million, Durban is known as the Holiday City, although that is only one aspect of it. But, due to its subtropical climate and gold sand beaches edging the blue Indian Ocean, it is a most popular resort and year-round magnet for sun lovers, just as the Florida Gold Coast is. Many highrise hotels in all price ranges cater to this Leisureland. The famous Zulu rickshaws are near the harbor and the boys who wear elaborately decorated headgear, jump as they pull them.

It's a city full of color bustle. In 1497, Vasco de Gama discovered Natal, the smallest province and the one in which Durban is situated. Many English and Portuguese are here, our guide told us, as well as

400,000 Indian people who came in 1860 to cut sugarcane and fill women's jobs. Today the Indian women's fluttering saris blend with the tribal dresses of the Zulus and the bright assortment of summer clothes and beachwear seen in Durban.

Thirty-eight inches of rainfall a year keep the flora beautiful. Street flower-sellers bask in the midst of their giant mixed bouquets. The Botanic Garden is a wooded area in the heart of the business district which also has an amazing array of flowers. Flambouyants and orchids were abloom but the jacarandas, that last only a month in this climate, were gone. Orange creeper flooded the walks and bougainvillea draped the drives. Though vegetation in the residential area is beautiful, the architecture seems uninspired and often plain ugly.

Lawn bowling is a favorite pastime and yachting is very popular. Luxurious waterfront yacht clubs cater to the sailing set.

Both English and Afrikaan are taught in the schools. Private schools are expensive, but the government schools are practically free. All children wear uniforms. Four universities are open to all nationalities and races, but the University of Durban is mostly white. Professors are paid little and travel by bus; autos around the university belong to students.

Domestics are easily obtained. Zulu servants are efficient, moral and genial. Servants who "live in" are paid about $48 a month, but often they bring other members of the family to live with them and share the wealth.

Wide streets in the downtown area were built long ago to accommodate the ox wagons. We walked the streets at night without fear.

Stopping to shop at the Indian Market, we found a bazaar filled with Oriental and African spices, foods, brassware, ivory, and all types of souvenirs. The stench from raw fish and carcasses was not too appetizing, but the displays were interesting.

Shopping for our four grandchildren was always fun. For our five-year-old Ohio grandson, another J. Emerson Wolfe, we found a passel of carved animals to add to his collection. For ten and twelve year old Tim and Chris Porter, in Texas, there were miniature carved swords. For Stacy, a high school senior in Ohio, it was usually jewelry. And then there were the inevitable, easy-to-carry T-shirts, for all.

At the hotel we enjoyed freshly caught broiled fish (brehm) for dinner, then visited Raffles, the disco on the top floor. No touching takes place in native dancing. First the girls dance alone, then the boys choose partners from among them.

Starting out one morning, in our roomy and comfortable Mercedes bus, we spotted a red bishop bird and a large hornbill with red on its head and yellow on its bill, sitting in a papaya tree. As we passed the imposing Durban Country Club our guide told us ten people must vouch for anyone seeking membership. Bottlebrush trees highlighted the fairways.

The Ungeni River has two large dams that furnish water for Durban and along their banks pumpkin-shade proteas were in profusion. In the Japanese Gardens were many of the cheeky big black mynah birds that were very tame. Monkeys skittered along the road to Glen Ashley. Tea and sugarcane thrive in rich crops. Two million tons of sugar are exported annually. The rats that infest the cane fields are eaten by some black natives.

The mambas and other snakes are real pests. Our guide said that, peculiarly, there are more deaths from nonpoisonous than poisonous snakes because the black man is so fearful of snakes, he frequently dies of shock. Waving in the light wind were the prayer flags hung in the gardens of Indians.

A two-bedroom apartment near the beach costs about $300 a month. Prices are lower in Durban than in Capetown or Pretoria.

In the town of Kloof properties were cheaper still. The atmosphere is rural with spacious grounds around the homes. Gary Player often tees off at the country club. The park-like scenery is checkered with glades and shady woods. An acre of land with swimming pool costs about 130,000 rand or $78,000, we were told.

We stopped for lunch at a Rob Roy Hotel that had as appealing a variety of flowers outside as the wonderful smorgasbord of food inside. The valley below the restaurant is shaped like a bowl and was filled with yellow poinsettias growing wild. The temperature was 92 and the air-conditioned bus was a relief.

Farther into this picturesque, fairyland setting, we would be visiting Zululand, in the Valley of One Thousand Hills. In preparation for meeting these people and going into their homes, our guide gave us background material embellished with several extra-curricular stories. One story concerned some Japanese men. The guides had been assembled and told that high-ranking Japanese men would be touring the country, that they spoke little English, and that things must be described to them slowly and carefully, guarding at all times that nothing offensive be said.

Our guide was picked to escort them. She told the men they were going into Zululand and told of some of their practices. She said the women, for beauty, plastered their hair with ochre and dung. "Dung?" queried one man, "What is that?"

The bus driver watched her squirm as she raised the microphone to her lips. She cleared her throat and said, "You eat, then it goes through your digestive system and then . . . out."

"Out?" asked one man.

"Do you know the word manure?" she asked. When they said they didn't, she pointed out the window at some cattle. "They eat grass and. . ."

"Oh!" cried one enlightened man, "You mean cow sheet!"

Our guide had also been warned not to make mention of the Zulu women's large bare breasts, but one man, after gazing a long time at the topless women exclaimed, "Incredible!"

Zulu means "message from heaven" and the Zulus are known as the pride of South Africa and a most important part of the population. Some five million comprise 286 tribes and have their own language. They are handsome, intelligent and good natured. They can be found in all fields — industry, commerce, the professions, shipping, education, mining, agriculture, theatre and the arts — and greatly contribute to the country's prosperity. Zulus pay taxes only if they have well-paying jobs. There is a good relationship between them and the whites.

Northern Natal is Zululand. The Zulu national hero was the fierce warrior, Shaka, who gave them great pride in their race. He was the king of their vast empire when the Portuguese arrived. As a result of conquest and intermarriage, Zulus are a mixture of most of the Nguni clans of Natal. They find it difficult to reconcile their beliefs with whites and while they may adopt Western ways when working in the city, they revert to tribal customs back home. They keep tight control over drugs, but alcohol is a big problem.

All work connected with cattle is done by men. Their wealth is reckoned in animals, which are used not only for food and for buying wives, but also in rituals.

The practice of polygamy is on its way out. Women have always played a secondary role and wives are still purchased with livestock or cash. Young women are now migrating to cities, however, to vie with men for the jobs. They have become the backbone of nursing throughout South Africa.

Zulu beadsellers do a roaring trade on Durban's beach-front. Beads of varied colors were, at one time, a means of communication, a symbol of status and wealth. Yves St. Laurent Salon has become interested in the language and expressed interest in their wild assortment of necklaces, bangles, huge earrings, neck fringes and love girdles, so the craze is on for wearing them, by boys as well as girls.

A Zulu village is called a kraal. The traditional beehive huts have no chimneys, hence no evil spirits can get in. On their lands are lovely seringa trees with purple and white flowers and whole farms of azaleas. We saw one hut under construction and noted how the watt sticks are bent into the needed shapes.

I was entranced in one of the beehives we entered; we could take our choice, all belonged to a chieftain. It was cool, but dark inside, and when my eyes became accustomed to it I saw a tiny infant sleeping on the mud floor, its face poking out of a blanket. I used my flash camera quickly! The hut was high in scent, but clean in appearance. With garments, gear, and plants raised for beer-making hung on the walls, it was "neatened up". There were mats only — no furniture other than benches.

A very affectionate people, they touch frequently. The more modern ones believe in birth control but do it covertly. They divorce, but if this happens the cattle must be returned.

We watched the tribal dances being performed by the unmarried Zulu girls. They go bare-breasted, whereas married women wear covering. The dancing was uninhibited; the costumes imaginative. The small children danced with great intensity and were a riot. Having been told they love sweets, we brought some and their big eyes and wide smiles thanked us profusely.

Back at the hotel we drank Bellinghams, an excellent South African pre-dinner wine.

At 6:30, next morning we were off on a short flight to Port Elizabeth, and from there, heading west, had a bus trip of about 140 miles over the celebrated Garden Route to the seaside resort of the Beacon Island Hotel.

Previously we'd had delightful local guides, but our male courier, Ed, was not up to their quality. With a heavy English accent and poor enunciation he was hard to understand, but most patient with our questions.

Port Elizabeth, on the Indian Ocean, is a windy, highly industrialized city and may be the cleanest in South Africa, although we hadn't yet found a dirty one. All vehicles in South Africa are assembled here. The city was settled in 1820 by the British, and is the busiest port in the country. Diaz landed here in 1498 and made his acquaintance with the Hottentots.

Victorian architecture was much in evidence: old houses circa 1800, the usual village church, and a statue to Queen Victoria in the square. Lawns were strewn with flowers galore; ground orchids clustered along the highway, seemingly afloat under the billowing clouds. The two national parks here are true nature preserves.

We started down the southern coast of the Cape province, a region of bays, beaches, cliffs, inlets, small towns and villages, rocky capes and pounding surf. We passed long stretches of sheep ranches where Australian Merinos are raised. The road became most spectacular between Mossel Bay and the Storms River mouth where it curves between sea and mountains and shows up coral reefs and lagoons. The mountains in some areas are more like hillocks on one side with scrub vegetation on the other — than a complete change to cattle farms and orchards. The red soil we saw has to be heavily fertilized.

First the mountains became half pine clad, then fully so. Pines are not indigenous here. The mountains are the folded type, not volcanic. Miles of flowering Australian eucalyptus trees came into view.

Jeffreesbaal has the most perfect waves in the world. Under good conditions one can travel 800 yards. Many sharks could be seen in the high surf. Along the upper banks, bitterbush, wild mustard, white heather, anemones, and brilliant orange poppies completed the scene. One especially fragrant tree is the vigilia with the dainty purple flowers and a lilac scent.

Among the millions of flowers on this route, the indigenous ones include the proteas, geraniums, glads and bird of paradise.

At a seaside restaurant, we tried the delicious fresh kingklip fish for lunch. Wide windows brought the outside in; the mountains looked like a giant green roller-coaster. Two whales romped in the ocean and out back, large black rock rabbits hopped through the thickets. Many snakes, we were warned, such as coppers and puff adders, nest in the rocks of the 700-foot gorge.

On our way again, the forests we saw were home to the indigenous and much-prized stinkwood — really a misnomer for aromatic — tree. Lumber from it sells for $6,000 a cubic yard. Later we examined gorgeous furniture made from it.

At last we arrived at the Beacon Island Hotel in Plettenberg Bay, where the white whales were coming in to breed. These mother whales must have a midwife to assist them or lose the baby, since they must be able to come to the surface for air.

Each hotel seemed better than the one before, if that's possible. This one had the type of gracious elegance that made for a unique resort. At night, we went with Tom and Mary Lindley and June and Hank Walker to the Captain's Table for a tasty lobster dinner. The beacon, visible from the dining room, is of honey-colored stone and is a replacement for an ancient one that was wooden.

Next morning's weather was a change: the clouds were grumpy as we left for the Cango Caves. The drizzle had a chill to it and buttoned-up jackets felt good.

Cango means "the waters between the hills", and these waters have carved out magnificent limestone caves in the Swartberg Mountains. A music and light display featured illuminated sections and corridors filled with exquisite formations of fluted draperies and sequined curtains, pools with calcite roses, organ pipes, and waterfalls. The stairs were steep and winding.

Leaving the caves, we drove along through Georgetown, the valley showing off peach and almond groves surrounded and protected by mountains. Large lush vegetable gardens here rest on eleven feet of topsoil.

Ed told us about the workers. One wage earner in a family pays a small tax; all else is subsidized. Blacks pay an interest rate of 1.25 percent on homes; whites pay twenty percent.

Ed, who emigrated to South Africa after the revolution in Rhodesia, told us of one of his embarrassing moments. As guide to a group of women, he was reminding them of what they should have in hand as they got into the bus one morning. "Do you have your binoculars, passports and cameras and have you taken the pill?" he asked. Dead silence led him to believe he hadn't phrased that quite right. He was referring to the malaria pill South African visitors are required to take for eight weeks after arriving.

Our next stop was at Oudtshoorn, which is synonymous with ostrich, and is the city of the ostrich farms. Even before arriving we could see the big bold stalkers to the left and right of the road. The pretty black male sits on the eggs during the night, and the female sits on them from 9 a.m. on. Between times they feed. In this well-regulated and thriving industry 100,000 ostriches are farmed, and there are 50,000 more in the wild. The ostrich feather industry is also a large one.

Along this section of the coast we also saw angora goats with long curly hair and horns. These are the cashmere type that look like a cross between a sheep and a goat. Goats are fed here for export. Near the grazing fields, tobacco farms greened the landscape.

The laborers in this area are paid about eight rand or 48 cents a day, working from 7:30 a.m. until 4:00 p.m. But whether or not they work, they are entitled to social security to cover education, sickness and old age.

Some houses were like gorgeous palaces in Georgian and Victorian styles and date from around 1900. Hottentots lived in nearby caves until 400 years ago. These are dry caves with very lacy, delicate formations inside. There is an army training base for white men and women in the vicinity.

It has been found that blacks can, but coloreds can't, cope with alcohol. Eighty percent are alcoholics and theirs is the highest birth rate.

Coloreds are people of mixed blood — black with Indian, Malaysian, or white. If you legally declare yourself colored, Ed said, you get many government goodies, such as free heart transplants, for which whites pay $20,000.

Oudtshoorn is a town of 45,000 people. The climate is both moist and sunny, favoring the prolificacy of flowers. Water canals on the streets are for irrigation of crops and gardens. The school system is strict: misbehaving children are caned.

Probably the best ostriches in the world are found at the farm we visited. Feathers are an ostrich's source of ego, but they are stripped of them every nine months. The birds are temperamental but, placed with cattle, they are protective and will kill an intruder. Male ostriches turn black when they are eighteen months old. An adult ostrich, with the hoist of one leg, can disembowel a human. They can run forty-eight miles an hour, and grow to a height of seven feet. Up to 5,000 tons of feathers are exported to the Far East, primarily to Hong Kong and Taiwan. The ostriches are incubated for forty-two days, 800 to 1,000 at a time. Chicks are kept with foster parents until they are three months old. We passed from cage to cage, first seeing two-day old chicks, then three-month old ones, and so on.

Ostriches, in the wild, are completely uncontrollable but have a better rate of survival than those in captivity.

The birds are never cannibalistic. Although the ostrich is speedy, it is unable to keep up this speed for more than a half-hour, after which it drops with exhaustion. Poachers chase the birds to death to get the feathers and hides to sell.

When two birds are selected to breed, the male makes the nest and they will stay together for fifteen years or until one dies. A female will take a new mate at such time but the male never does. There is no inbreeding and the bloodline has been pure since 1850.

An ostrich has no sense of smell. It has one stomach with two compartments, one with a bunch of stones for grinding food. Its digestion is so complete that offal has no nourishment in it and can't be used as fertilizer. The ostrich lives as long as forty-five years, with a heartbeat that is faster than ours: 98 to 102.

Oudtshoorn was picked for ostrich raising because of the favorable climate. There is little rainfall which would make the chicks susceptible to pneumonia or respiratory ailments.

The ranch was fascinating with all helpers eager to give information and show off their prize birds. From a grandstand we watched helpers ride the ostriches around a ring. Our indomitable Hal Rice took a whirl on one, but lasted only about forty seconds. I got aboard one in a stockade, stroked its feathers, and dismounted.

We had lunch, and what an ostrich feast it was. First there was scrambled "egg" for the eighteen of us — all from one-quarter of an ostrich egg so rich that it must be diluted with water or milk. Then we had ostrich burgers which were delicious, and ostrich steaks which I didn't like quite as well. With this we were served lots of vegetables, potatoes and fruit.

We moseyed through the gift shop and fingered the soft leather billfolds and purses made from these gangly, swift-running but flightless birds, and admired the eggshells made into necklaces, bracelets and earrings.

After lunch we drove to the airport at Oudtshoorn for our flight to Capetown. En route we were struck by the beauty of the stinkwood trees, pink and smooth of bark, that grow to a height of sixty feet. The yellowwood tree grows to ninety feet. And wonder of wonders, there was snow on the mountains! An almost unheard of thing in October, our guide said.

Anna Marie, a real jewel, was our local guide in Capetown. The population of 900,000, she told us, is a cosmopolitan mix. There is a Malay Quarter, and a tiny fragment of the Stone Age Bushmen are included in South Africa's second largest city. A mosque for Moslems lies just off the main street.

The affectionate term for Capetown is "Mother City" . It is the second oldest in South Africa and the country's legislative capital. Started as a way station for the ships of the Dutch East India Company in 1652, it has grown into a great modern complex with Table Mountain, Camel Back, and Signal Hill as its dramatic background setting. The Atlantic stretches as far as the eye can see, and for sheer beauty, especially in an urban setting, the city is one of the dreamiest spots on earth. Perhaps its most striking feature is the great contrast in scenery and people.

The city proper is enchanting, full of old world charm: cobbled streets, oak-umbrellaed lanes and gabled Cape Dutch architecture, with both thatched and flat roofs. Green vineyards border the outskirts and ground orchids, unique to the Cape, cerise the banks.

King of the floral kingdom is the gorgeous protea, a symphony of velvety petals around satiny, silver stamens in exquisite rose, tawny gold and silver colors. Misty rain pampers the pungent vegetation.

This is the city where Christian Barnard did the first heart transplant in 1967, and where Barnard's hospital complex has become a distinguished research center and working clinic.

We took the cable car to the top of Table Mountain, a seven-minute ride on a brisk and windy day, to get a first-hand view of Devil's Peak,

Camel Back and Signal Hill, and record them on film. The record may have been a South African first since newfallen snow capping the mountain was so rare at that time of year. Numerous climbers have lost their lives attempting to climb this mountain. Seen from below, as its name suggests, Table Mountain is flat on top with a cloud cloth draping its sides and the setting is a feast. From it one has a superlative view of the immaculate city. On the other side of Table Bay is the province's one atomic power station.

The Castle of Good Hope, shaped as a five-pointed star and historically the most important building in South Africa, is fascinating. Built in 1666 as a fortress, then made into the headquarters of the Dutch East India Company, and later used to house the early governors of Cape province, it is now the site of military and maritime museums and a national monument. We were especially intrigued with the courtyard of Belgium brick at the entrance and the high ceilings and heavy beams inside. The acoustics in the conference room were remarkable. A wild fig tree stands in the yard which is full of margueritas or daisy bushes.

Continuing on to the Old Town House Market Square, which dates back to 1775, we dallied over the art collection of South African painters, and then went through the Koopman's de Wet House to admire the mellow woods in Dutch colonial antiques, dating from the eighteenth century. In the square, towheaded tots were feeding pigeons, and their pavement games, played during lunch hours, drew many onlookers. At the open flower market some of the characters bartering their wares were as flamboyant as their merchandise.

On the main streets of town are new hotels with outside elevators that give superb views of the environs, and escalators that take pedestrians to the underground malls. Some streets are for walking only, closed to all vehicle traffic. Readers Digest Corporation has a large office building on Strand Street. In one of the squares is a statue to Bartholomeu Diaz who first rounded the Cape of Good Hope in 1488.

With time to idle and recharge our batteries, we wandered around the attractive hotel, took a dip in its pool, combed the shopping streets and took a nature walk before indulging again in a blue-chip lobster dinner.

We left early for a day's excursion to Cape Point and Constantia. This exciting marine drive makes a circuit of the Cape peninsula. It is a rocky coastline along the waters where surfing is ideal in both the Atlantic and Indian Oceans. Swimmers and beach combers were busily feeding seagulls while lookouts were constantly maintained for sharks, both from fishing boats and from land.

Along here they've had television only since 1976, and for no more than six hours a day. Some programs are in English and some in Afrikaaner. Beautiful homes zigzag the mountains and, as Anna Marie said, "They fetch a big price." Many garages built on the house roofs.

Behind Table Mountain, along the peninsula, is a line of peaks known as the Twelve Apostles. Across the coastline beaches thousands of cormorants were diving for fish. Again, as Anna Marie said, "People come here to take up the sun." Quantities of seaweed are collected for fertilizer and medicinal purposes. Both Australian eucalyptus and acacias, imported long ago, keep the sandy soil at bay.

A small rock-capped mountain in the distance is Mount Rhodes (named after Cecil). It looks like a crown on a decorated cake. The bay is nestled against the mountain which has a saddle in its middle. There is contour planting on the hillsides, and near the stark homes of the colored people. Beyond are the holiday chalets in a horseshoe bay. Here you can rent helicopters to look for schools of whales that travel in groups of twenty-two.

On this national drive, built between 1915 and 1922, the Cape vegetation is the smallest but richest of the six floral kingdoms of the world. It's a radiant sight: diminutive flowers interwound with massive, heavy-scented ones over this undulating land. For so small a region the profusion is extraordinarily varied — 25,000 species. Of the 330 varieties of protea, only about ninety have flowers. Too, there is a mosaic of maize fields, vineyards, banana orchards and aloe groves. Cape-nesting weaver-birds try on a variety of trees for size; bee-eaters breed in colonies on steep banks of the sea. The setting is reminiscent of the Carmel coastline of California. With the wind blowing away the haziness, it made visibility perfect.

We came, then to a place that has haunted me since childhood. Perhaps the name itself intrigued me and gave me the nagging desire — as the early explorers had — to round it. Bartholomeu Diaz called this the Cape of Good Hope. His was the hope of finding a good route to India and the spices. Sir Frances Drake said it was "the fairest cape in the circumference of the earth." And here I was, at last, on this stark rock peninsula jutting into the ocean with magnificent cliffs descending into the crashing blue sea. Here I was, where the cold Atlantic meets the warm Indian Ocean, and where danger lies in the reefs beneath the water. The cape is forty degrees south of the equator. Heavy currents make it the most hazardous point to go around. Here, the cormorants nest in sheer rock and waterbuck frequent the streams. Seals are all over the place. The warmer Indian Ocean carries much more plankton, but the fishing is richer in the cold Atlantic.

The whole coastline, where a railroad parallels the sea, is 1,800 miles long. The nature reserve maintained here is owned by the government and specializes in indigenous species.

In Little Kalk Bay holiday cottages were being built close together. Nearby boiled many waterfalls. A number of golf courses and playing fields were in evidence, and since it was on the warm side, forests were springing up.

Lunch time came at Constantia, a wine-producing area, where we ate at the historic seventeenth century Alpen Hotel, a national monument. Used in the early days by officials of the Dutch East India Company, it stands in one corner of a great forecourt and is built in Georgian style. Much of its priceless furniture remains and blends well with the gracious setting. It has been said that no other house, through the years, has played host to so many notable people.

After lunch we visited some of the town's famous wine cellars and went through Groot Constantia, a farmhouse built in 1691, now a museum filled with rare antiques.

The Botanical Gardens, started in 1913, are a part of Cecil Rhodes' estate outside Capetown. The property was his gift to the country with the stipulation that no houses be built on it. It is filled with cork oaks, silver leaf trees, wild almonds and various indigenous trees. Native flowers and heaths spill cornucopias of color.

Leaving there, we drove past the University of Capetown and Groot Shuur, another hospital known for triumphs in the field of heart transplant surgery. The hospital is open to all races and has three kitchens: one each for Moslems, Christians, and Jews.

Stopping at a semi-precious gem center, we watched stones being cut, polished, and shaped, then we examined many, and purchased some necklaces in the showroom.

For some time I had been luxuriating in the expectancy of the next day's journey — a ride on the Blue Train. Coming from a railroad family, trains have captivated me all my life. My father was fifty-two years with the Chicago, Burlington and Quincy, as freight agent near Chicago. Among my happiest moments in the age of steam were listening for the mournful whistles of the trains, seeing the flagman waving his lantern down the long tongues of track, feeling the rumble and shudder over the tentacles of bridges, smelling the coal smoke and almost tasting the fire. I loved the swaying platforms between coaches, the chug, hiss and rumble of those giant behemoths, the clink of the coupling of coaches, the race of scenery, and even the grime cindering the open windows. Those childhood days I traveled on passes in every direction — indebted for romance to the bulky black monsters. In later youth, in the

Victoria Falls, Zimbabwe.

Baby ostriches.

Ostriches at Oudtshoorn.

Zulus dancing in Zululand, Pretoria, South Africa.

Zulu beehive huts in Zululand.

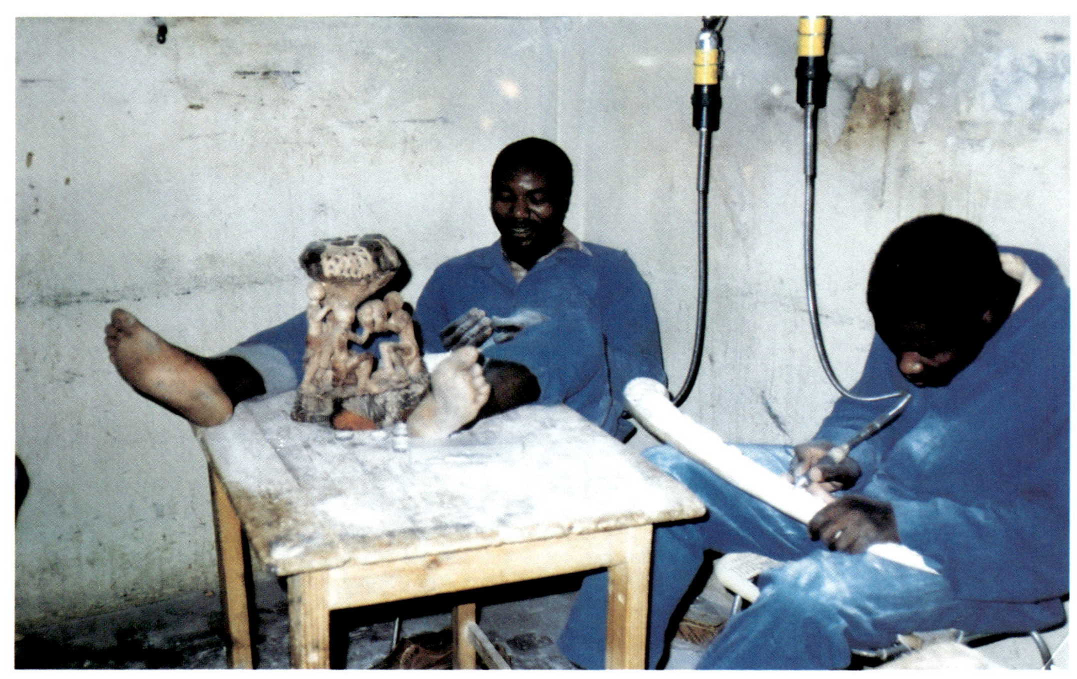

Ivory carving in Harare, Zimbabwe.

Protea plants in South Africa.

Jacaranda season in Pretoria, South Africa.

A baobab tree of Harare, Zimbabwe.

Elementary school children on a trip to the Art Museum, Johannesburg, South Africa.

Author holding stalk of burley tobacco.

Tobacco auction, Harare, Zimbabwe.

The Blue Train, Johannesburg to Capetown.

days of the streamliners, I free-loaded on the various Zephyrs, riding the Denver and Feather Canyon route west, well knowing I was hooked forever.

For many years our American rails have lagged behind foreign ones, and it seems a pity to have to go abroad to get a better ride.

It was but a short distance from our hotel to the Capetown Railway Station where we boarded the legendary Blue Train, after admiring its handsome exterior of royal blue with cream-colored accents. The moment of boarding has come (fifteen minutes in advance of departure) — long enough to have the luggage placed in our compartments, long enough to have complimentary champagne delivered to each individual one, with a welcome given us by the train superintendent, and long enough to meet some of the other personnel. The Blue Train leaves on schedule! Not one minute before the 10:30 departure time nor one minute after, but on the exact second.

We found our name on our compartment door and there we sat, free as birds and comfortable as all get-out. No seat belts were needed here, and there was plenty of room to stretch and walk around. Our compartment was spacious enough for two beds, side by side when made up, two writing desks and lamps, a raised magazine rack, lights above the beds, pastoral oil paintings on the wall, footstools, well-equipped lavatories, and room to store at least six suitcases. Blue drapes and blue upholstery melded into the blue and white carpeting. A rack for drinks was at the end of each seat. Air conditioning, radio and recorded music could be had with a touch. The train was a gorgeous, long, thin five-star plus hotel on wheels offering facilities only found in rarefied lodgings. If, for example, you desire grilled trout and cocoa three hours before breakfast, it is made and delivered with a smile, and at no extra charge. Nothing is extra except drinks.

Each coach has an attendant who usually knocks on the door seconds after being summoned by the buzzer. He phones in your requirements and the speed of service is dazzling, despite no tipping, and this five star service continues nonstop for the twenty-five hours it takes from Capetown to Johannesburg.

For this fabled rail ride and world famous experience (albeit at a pretty penny), you sink into plush lounge-type facing seats with wide walk-room between and immediately have that laid-back feeling of never-never-land. The doors are designed so that no one can see in; the door and enormous picture window are equipped with shutters that raise by the touch of a button and are mounted between double glass.

The Blue Train glides along at about seventy kilometers an hour. A midday concert comes clear and crisp over the speakers. We adjusted the temperature control, opened our paperbacks, and intermittently kept track of the beautiful vineyards in fresh sunlight running up the steep slopes of the Drokenstein Mountains near Paarl, and the other visual delights en route.

Hal Rice had opted for all of us to have first sitting at meals so when lunch was announced over the loud speaker, Eme and I made our way to the dining car. There was no swaying and no platforms between coaches. It was like walking through a carpeted corridor.

The dining car seats forty-six. Its appointments in china, edge-to-edge silver and fluted and starched napery are spectacular, its service meticulous. Lunch was a challenge, both in number of courses and size of portions. It began with stuffed tomatoes, followed by cream soup, fried kingklip or curried fish, duckling with rice, assorted vegetables, a cold crisp salad, and ended in a flourish with baked Alaska, cheese and biscuits, and coffee or demi-tasse. Silver finger bowls added the finishing touch. And this was lunch, mind you!

M. Fernandez, the dining car manager, and D. A. Botha, the head chef, inquired as to our wishes and indulged us accordingly.

Apart from bread and cold meats, everything is put on the train fresh and raw, to be prepared by three chefs.

Back in our compartment we found a late copy of *The Star*, placed on board at a station stop during lunch. Also, we had the train's monthly magazine — a pretty sophisticated glossy — the *Blue Horizon*.

The legendary Blue Train started at the turn of the century as a deluxe train built for Rhodesia Railways, to travel between Capetown and Bulawayo and to Victoria Falls. It was officially named in 1946 and came to be regarded as the epitome of luxury train travel. Then, in 1972, two completely new trains were built in South Africa and no expense spared to provide unprecedented comfort. Everything in them is understated elegance. The route gives an ever-changing view of picturesque landscape. On the train are three-room suites as well as compartments offering showers and toilet facilities. Service is given top priority: Place your shoes outside your door for cleaning; reach for the slim-necked tap for ice water.

The train is virtually noiseless and vibration-free, even at top speed. Driven by Rolls Royce engines, it is controlled by bogies (swivel undercarriages at either end of the coaches); it is a miniature power station on wheels, capable of producing enough electricity to light an average small town. Side entrances to the coaches are power-operated and lock automatically when the train is in motion.

Scenery along the way takes in Worchester, one of the prettiest towns on the Cape; DeDoorns, full of thorn bushes that cover the valley;

Beaufort West, through a farm belt; Orange River — over long trestle; Kimberley where the "Big Hole" is; Boenhop, scene of the diamond rush; Klerksdorp, the gold and uranium mining center; Potchefstrom, an educational center; and also passes endless picket lines of blue gums and trails of wild flowers. In between are the wretched homes (some like igloos) of the blacks and the faintly better ones of the Coloureds.

Dinner had the same hearty overtones as lunch, only more so. I slept like the proverbial log with no need to count sheep although, had I needed them, they were probably roaming right outside the window.

Breakfast was something else again — a fantasia of food and service with style. All good things must come to an end, but not the memories.

Arriving in Johannesburg, we checked in at the Carleton Hotel which Hal Rice considered one of the top ten in the world. But it was early to bed, to be up at 5:30, to leave from Jan Smuts Airport for Skukusa. Eme and I were taking two days and two nights by ourselves to go to one of the most outstanding of all African sanctuaries — Kruger National Park, a place we had wanted to see for many years. The Carleton allowed us to store our big suitcase, and we took our small carry-on bags to check in at the Mala Mala Lodge in Kruger Park.

Only eight of us were on the small plane. One couple might have been movie extras. The woman wore spike heels and a black silk suit, and the man was in jacket and tie — in the 90-degree weather. There was a delightful couple from Chicago. He had business with Masonite Corporation in South Africa and this jaunt was part business and part pleasure. The others were a young doctor and his wife from Johannesburg whom we badgered with innumerable questions.

The plane was met by two good-looking young rangers with impeccable manners, who put us into two Landrovers for a bone-rattling ride over fourteen miles of God-awful terrain up to the doors of the camp. The game viewing along the way was exciting but we could hardly wait to be out on safari and in the thick of it.

Each ranger had charge of three huts, two to a hut. Our Ranger, "Charley" Gormal Jones was a real charmer.

The camp consisted of terra cotta buildings clustered amid awesome shade trees, green lawns and dun-colored landscape on the banks of the Sand River. All huts were spacious rondavels under thatch with a front bay window, "his" and "her" bathrooms (ours in apple green and fawn), air conditioning, two three-quarter beds, large closet, rattan furniture, attractive animal and bird pictures on the walls and impala throw rugs on the wooden floors. Freshly raked gravel paths led to the swimming pool, reception lodge, and the reed boma (dining center). Our door opened on a wide sweep of cascading bougainvillea in watercolor shades. Speckled butterflies and wild canaries were our constant companions.

It is said there's magic at Mala Mala. Family-owned, these 128,000 acres are part of the four million acres that comprise Kruger National Park.

Thousands of animals are in the park but only to be seen from closed cars at a distance. What draws visitors from all over the world to this hideaway of Mala Mala is an absence of commercialism in a unique blend found nowhere else. There is game viewing, in natural habitat, of over 200 species of large and small animals at almost close enough range for them to hear the cameras click.

That everything runs so smoothly at such a distance from town (sixty-five miles) is incredible. The reserve must have a staff knowledgeable for any emergency. Water is pumped from the Sand River and flows through the reserve to a purification plant. Wells have been dug deep into the riverbed so that even during a drought there will be a source of water. The electric system is backed up by a standby generator; electric and telephone wires are buried out of sight.

By the time Eme and I donned our safari outfits (a mixture of high spirits and Florida bush) it was lunch time. Charley escorted us to the boma, a warm inviting room alive with colorful decor and comfortable rattan. Serving gourmet meals so far from a supermarket takes expert planning. The food wasn't fancy, but superbly prepared and presented.

The next order of business, they told us after lunch, was a siesta because we would be on safari until nearly 9:00 p.m. The Landrovers were ready at three o'clock and so were we. Charley, who hailed from Mozambique, was our driver. The rangers, selected for looks, charisma and knowhow, stay at the reserve about two years.

The Landrover had room for four passengers. Eme and I sat in front and the doctor and his wife, Grant and Nita DeEll, sat in back. Behind us, on a raised seat, was the tracker and spotter, Joseph Timatole, a black man. We were off and the thrill was on — binoculars and cameras beside us. Nita spotted first the great loerie, a bird with a fantastically long tail. The DeElls were ornithologists as well as animal and nature lovers. He was getting away from sick people for a while and Eme and I picked his and Nita's brains on South African affairs, as much as we could.

We watched a number of iguanas slithering up a tree and Nita pointed out an African red-breasted roller and a hoopoe. We bumped at random over wild yellow carnations and white gardenias, a part of the vast bushveld. Then Charley spotted a bevy of water buffalo and we went hurtling over potholes and bumps and brush to get proper shots of them. They're mean critters and unpredictable. He insisted we not stand. The buffalo is ironlike with horizontally swung horns.

Rattling along at a pace, we literally "held everything" and felt lucky our teeth didn't jar loose. There were frequent stops for boys-to-the-left and girls-to-the-right.

All vehicles are linked by radio communication and one Landrover alerts another to the location of game. Professionalism and pleasure seemed to work together.

We passed an apple leaf tree that looked like our golden rain tree except its flowers were purple instead of yellow. Nita spotted an eagle in a moroela tree and I cringed as we crushed a brown snake beneath the wheels. Because of drought, the Sand River was more sand than river.

Ah! We were on the track of lions. Our posteriors were aware of it, too, as the Landrover leapt and we left our seats by twelve to fourteen inches at each bump. The branches trimmed bits of our hair in passing. But there they were! Five of them — a pride of lions: the parents and three cubs. Before the day was over we would see another pride and a single lion.

Over the radio, Charley learned an elephant had been sighted and we finally edged close to a six-ton granddaddy swaying alone, although elephants usually travel in matriarchal groups. There are no gazelles at Kruger, we learned.

My favorites, the giraffes, we were a long time in finding. Surprisingly, their affinity is closest to the deer and the species is confined to Africa. Those we finally came upon were reticulated adults, and the oxpecker or tickbird was running up and down their necks removing insects. The short stubby horns of the giraffe remind me of exclamation points. Charley said their favorite food is acacia thorn and their voice is like a light bell.

We passed droves of impala, any number of zebra, lots of wildebeests, a cheetah, a whole pool of playful hippos, white rhinos in various sections, wart hogs, and more buffalo.

Dusk was coming on. Fireflies were out and frogs began their cacophony. As we stopped for drinks Joseph jumped out first, brought out a sterno stove, lit it, put on a small skillet and popped something into it. What turned out was hot appetizers served on toothpicks. Charley opened the bar — ice included — in the back of the 'rover and took our orders. This, we decided, was plush bushlife — a cushy oasis, to be sure.

Night was the time to be chary of silence and shadow. So when our toasting was over, it was the time for spotlight maneuvers with Joseph holding the torch. As the 'rover cruised in the dark, we saw eyes glitter on all sides in the distance — carnivores on the hunt, an exhilarating experience.

Back in our huts by 9:00 p.m., we showered for dinner, which was a starlit affair in the boma, open to the sky with, at one side, a 1,000-year-old Transvaal tree dripping its greenery. The scene is etched in my memory. We sat at tables placed in a semi-circle around an open campfire. The long-lasting leadwood logs come from trees that live thousands of years and are one of the very few that elephants can't knock down. This setting sharply contrasted with the formality of the meal which ran the gamut of soup, fish, choice of entree, and dessert. Among the meats we were offered was impala steaks cooked in red wine, much less wild-tasting than venison.

It is doubtless that the combination of rusticity and sophisticated smooth-running attention to minute details, gives Mala Mala its distinctive character.

Next day, there were more of the same stimulating talks with the South Africans and others, more identification of trees, birds and animals, and then the lovely late dinner by starlight and firelight. We returned, the third morning after breakfast, to the Carleton in Johannesburg, still tingling from the adventure.

Checkout was early, to leave on a flight for Zimbabwe, formerly Rhodesia, and clear customs there to go to Victoria Falls.

The Victoria Falls Hotel was of typical colonial style, restored to its former old world grace (to the tune of $5 million, we were told), but still in need of further repairs. The open courtyard was the hub of activity and relaxation. A giant old teakwood tree spread its shade over a goodly portion of the lawn. One could amble among an embroidery of flowers, dine out-of-doors, and listen for hours to the six-piece marimba band — which we did.

From the hotel courtyard a significant railroad trestle and walking bridge across the Zambesi River could be seen in the distance. This was where the treaty was signed ending the hostilities between Zimbabwe and its neighbor, Zambia. A small part of the eastern end of Victoria Falls, called Knife Edge, lies in Zambia and this must be reached to get the full panorama of the Eastern Cataract.

On a Sundowner evening cruise, we boated leisurely on the Zambesi. The river rises in a mountain in central Africa, and flows onto a plateau on its 750-mile course to Zimbabwe. Our cruise was a prelude to some of the startling scenery ahead.

Velvet monkeys played along the banks of the river, water birds dove for fish, and an elephant plodded through the scrub as we watched. It was a balmy night with a fair breath of wind and the stars were perforating the skies as we headed back to land and dinner at the hotel.

Morning found us at Spencer's Creek Crocodile Ranch. Tatenda, our black guide, was a soft-spoken girl I would judge was "learning the ropes". When she stated unequivocally, "Victoria Falls is one of the Seven Wonders of the World," who were we to argue? In outdoor pools we inspected many crocs of various sizes and ages. They breed here and the incubation period is ninety days. A crocodile has sixty-six teeth and when one falls out, another takes its place. The reptile is born with the killer instinct and is cannibalistic. One of its main predators is the civet cat. At the ranch, when they reach the age of ten months, five percent are returned to the wild. Although subject to all human diseases, crocodiles can live a hundred years. An example we saw was Big Daddy, seventy-five years old and still breeding. One of the largest in captivity, he weighed in at 1,000 pounds, and was almost seventeen feet long. Crocodile diet is fresh raw meat — anything from frogs to cut-up elephant and buffalo. They even imported cheetah for variety in his food. The price of a six-foot crocodile is $250 to $300.

In the museum, we were shown skeletons and the developmental stages of these cold-blooded vertebrates was described. We inspected reptiles, in cages, which ranged from three-day-old hatchlings on up.

On the ranch stood a magnificent baobab tree with a girth of fifty-one feet. It's called the upside-down-tree because, when leafless, it looks as if its roots, instead of its branches, were pointing to the sky. Its glossy gray bark, smooth in texture, helps prevent water loss. Being the meeting place for rollers, sunbirds, hornbills and many others, it was festooned with nests of large and small birds. When I see one of these trees I think what Arthur Rackum, the painter, could have done with one this size in placing his elves, gnomes, and other minute creatures, in its crevices and hollows. The strangeness of this tree is that it contains a woody tissue but no hard wood. The bark is full of calcium and provides food for elephants as well as fiber for humans.

The bus had us back to the hotel in time to freshen up and have lunch before the afternoon's excitement. As we met Tatenda again we were eager to see one of the compelling wonders and natural treasures of this country, Victoria Falls.

Year round, the Zambesi River plunges headlong across a mile-wide front of black basalt and crashes 350 feet into a narrow gorge below. The spectacle is a glitter of snowy mist, an avalanche of sound. The Kololo people who lived here called it "Mosi-oa-tunya" — smoke that thunders. No wonder Dr. Livingston thought, "scenes so lovely must have been gazed upon by angels in their flight." David Livingston, the explorer-missionary, discovered the falls in 1855 and named them for his British queen.

Awesome and tumultuous as the waterfall is, its spray is gentle and kind. As the stream boils up and hurtles into the downpour, water races down into the narrow gorge and is lost to sight in the cliffs. A fine mist perpetually rises from the gorge and a rainbow, like ignited fireworks, hangs in the spray as the falls pitch down the precipitous rocks.

We stood, entranced, and then aimed our cameras into the top of the sunlit spew. There are five separate falls: Devil's Cataract, Main Falls, Rainbow Falls, Eastern Cataract, and Horseshoe Falls. Collectively they are twice as high as the Niagara Falls and one and a half times as long.

When we had absorbed the spectacle as a whole from above, we followed the Rain Forest trail below. There were lots of steps, some slippery, but the walk was utterly enchanting. To keep the beauty intact, stones forming the path were laid by hand, using indigenous rock. Waste bins are concealed in tree trunks. Along the Chain Walk leading into the gorge we came to Livingston's statue. On November 16, 1855, he traveled by dugout canoe downstream to the very northern edge of the precipice. From Devil's Cataract, Livingston's statue is visible above the falls. From below, we could see the vegetation was riotously lush despite the terrible four-year drought which had dried up a small portion of one end of the falls and laid bare its sheer, striated rock. At the lower level, bird and animal life were also profuse. The climb back was exhilarating, providing another indelible memory.

We said good-by to Tatenda at the hotel. Dinner included a reconnoitering of the day's vivid imprints. Sleep came easily and "tight" to be ready for the grand finale of the coming morning.

That was when eight of us at a time took the fifteen-minute "Flight of the Angels" plane to survey, from above and at close range, the whole panoramic scene. The pilot skimmed so low we could almost feel the spray.

In the afternoon we flew Air Zimbabwe to the capital, Harare, formerly Salisbury, and checked in at the Hotel Monomatapa. Although native dancing and a barbecue were offered, we luxuriated in room service for dinner, a touch of television and some reading. Mail from the states was in our box and that made us happy.

In Harare we had a most personable and knowledgeable leader, Marian Craig, to take us on the three-hour city tour and give us an update on Zimbabwe's recent history.

When Ian Smith was prime minister of Rhodesia, she told us, there were many struggles and much fighting between the majority blacks and small minority of whites who controlled the government. After years of negotiations, guerrilla leaders and white officials agreed to a new constitution drawn up in London. In the 1980 election, government by the 220,000 whites was passed to the 7.2 million blacks. This was the end of Rhodesia, the country created by financier Cecil Rhodes some ninety years ago to spread British civilization in Africa. Zimbabwe is a country of independence envisioned by the blacks. Though wounds are far from healed, blacks and whites are trying a new fellowship.

Like the old Rhodesia, Zimbabwe remains two nations — one rich and powerful for the whites who still control vast resources, and one poor and impotent, because of their inexperience and lack of know-how, for the blacks. Among the first things the incoming black president did was to rename the country Zimbabwe, after a once great leader of the Shona people. To the natives, the name means "houses of stone" or "venerated houses."

There were bans on some picture-taking in the city, especially around military installations, where machine guns were kept, or around the army academy.

We watched the scenery along the way as we listened to Marian, and it was breath-taking. Jacarandas had reached the peak of vivid perfection. The scrambled-egg trees (whipped yellow) were in full flower. The boulevards were a mosaic of color. The streets were wide and clean. Rhodes, who left his powerful imprint on Rhodesia both in spirit and wealth, insisted all roads must be wide enough to allow a team of sixteen oxen to make a U-turn. The many students who have enjoyed Rhodes scholarships must often think of the largess of his vision.

Harare has 119 suburbs and three-quarters of a million people. It sits at 5,051 feet above sea level. Industries are gold mining, fertilizer manufacturing, and glass and ivory carving. There is more coal than they know what to do with.

Marian credited the blacks with having a great sense of humor. As a guide, she is known to them as "Get a Move On," "Foot Fire," or "Hurry Up."

Tobacco, which does well in drought, is the main foreign-currency earner. Other major crops are tea, coffee, maize and cotton. Cattle raising is no longer a factor in the economy. In 1983, a million and a quarter cattle were lost to the drought.

Marian's husband was a tobacco grower, and we were invited to a tobacco auction. Tobacco, she told us, brought in $200 million to Harare in 1983. The main strains grown here are Virginia, Burley, and cigar-leaf tobaccos.

The auction was held in a tremendous warehouse with several aisles filled with hundreds of open bales of tobacco. There were fourteen buyers from all over the globe to take part in the world's fastest auction:

a sale is made in five to six seconds. The auctioneer uses the roof of his mouth not his throat. Buyers silently signal to consummate a sale. They walk forward down the aisles, facing the auctioneer, walking backward, almost at a jogger's gait.

Behind the auctioneer, a clerk records the price and buyer's name. He tears the paper in half, puts one piece on the bale and submits the other to the office. The floor changes three times a day. The huge bales are open for inspection to the prospects for auctioneering, then closed by hand and moved out of the building by mechanization. That morning, 10,524 bales were sold — 165 bales every fifteen minutes. They don't work afternoons.

Continuing our bus tour of the city, Marian told us more about conditions in Zimbabwe. The country imports nothing it can make or manufacture. Eighty percent of all goods are made there. Imported whiskey costs $27 a bottle with a nineteen percent tax added. Gasoline is $1.05 a litre. There were 370,000 whites there before the revolution; only 100,000 have remained.

In the Indian section of the city lace makers were showing their wares. The Indian population is 7,000 and they are one of the wealthiest groups.

Rats are a problem in all parts of the city and so are snakes. Seventeen of the snakes are poisonous, including the adders, banded cobras, and the most deadly of all — the mombas. Only a dead snake is a safe one.

On the streets, the lucky bean tree was aburst with puffy flowers and pods. They are used medicinally to cure thrombosis. The sausage tree also has large pods and the white powder in the seeds is used by people with eye ailments. So many trees in the city have been cut down that more people are killed by lightning, which now hits the houses instead. The cycad tree we saw is a holdover from the dinosaur age. It is thick and ferny with a crown of leathery leaves. The aloe trees, known as Job's tears, produce a bitter purgative drug. Tremendous old trees were to be felled on Kopje Hill to make way for new Parliament buildings. What a pity!

There are 570 species of birds in Zimbabwe: the Old World hornbills, orange bishop birds and black and white bee-eaters are among the most populous; purple heron and storks with saddle bills are some of the largest, and the black and white storks, like the bee-eaters, are multiracial, as Marian put it.

Among the strange creatures we saw en route was the aardvark, a burrowing mammal that lives largely on termites. We passed a number of termite hills. Termites, Marian told us, work their hills three times as much underground as above. Jackals, former inhabitants that carried rabies, were exterminated by a government program.

We stopped to visit an ivory factory and I've never seen so much ivory in one place. As we watched the flawless perfection of the hand carvers, and the infinite care the workers gave the various pieces, it was obvious they take great pride in their creations. Out in the shop, we couldn't resist purchasing an exquisite pagoda with intricately carved detail.

Our next visit was to the National Museum where Marian made the history of the ancient African peoples from the Bushmen on, come alive.

In three weeks time, she told us, Harare would be resplendent in color from hundreds of flame trees. The birds, as colorful as the flowers, seemed to buttonhole all comers. It is a beautiful city and I hope it can stay that way.

The morning went far too fast, and, before we knew it, we were at the airport awaiting the plane for Johannesburg. On arrival we headed for the hotel. The others were going on for a week in East Africa, but Eme and I were headed home. Hal Rice gave us a standing farewell in the bus and we, in turn, rose to say farewell and wish them a happy continuing trip. After changing clothes and packing, we had lunch at the hotel with Tom and Mary Lindley, exchanged addresses, and regretfully left, hoping to meet again.

Hal took us to the airport, in late afternoon, for the dreaded trip to New York on South African Airways. At our insistence, he tried to get us passage on any other line but when he came up with a cost of $1,200 apiece to change tickets, we opted for the seventeen hours of suffering.

The plane took off promptly at 7:30 p.m. — a big 747 with only seventy passengers aboard. And what a surprise! In overseas travel we can't recall a nicer trip. Starting with hot towels, spiffy menus for choices of very creditable food, and exceeding consideration, we were pampered to pieces.

To top it off, New York Customs didn't even sniff our luggage. We passed through in a breeze and put up at the Airport Hilton overnight to get over our jet lag. We took off for Miami the next day and stayed overnight at the International Airport to await the dawn arrival of our friends, the Sherwoods, coming in from their Brazilian trip. We had a number of hours to exchange highlights of our safaris before we had to go our separate ways.

It was evening when we left for Orlando. The limousine which met us there took us to Mount Dora and home, where a happy holiday always ends.